Headspin, Headshots & History: Growing up in Twin Cities Hip Hop

WRITTEN BY ZACH COMBS
EDITED BY JOSHUA HOLMGREN

A young English major from the U of M named Kelsey Shirriff put in the work to correct the grammar in this book before she left for a six-month trip to South America. While she was out of the country we had a computer glitch and we think we lost her edits. Right before we went to print we noticed something was wrong and Josh and Dalia did their best to re-edit the book themselves. They did their best, but if there are mistakes, it don't matter. I didn't write this book to be graded. We want to credit Kelsey for the work she put in to help us, but we don't want to embarrass her by crediting her as an editor with our mistakes (haha).

There are hundreds of pages in this book. You can count them if you want. It is simple mathematics. This book is two stories told simultaneously, that is why it has two titles. First, it is Headspin, Headshots, and History: a documentation of Twin Cities hip hop culture as much as I know to tell it. Second, it is Growing Up in Twin Cities Hip Hop: the story of my personal growth within that culture.

If you don't have time to read the whole thing and just want the point of it all, these characters, in my personal opinion, are the coolest thing to ever happen to hip hop. I'm on their dick.

CONTENTS

When I was 25, I had a girlfriend named Shannon. She was a good looking white chick from the Southside who always dated gangster dudes. Because of that, I never knew why she liked me, but she did. During the short time I was with her, my friend P.O.S. told me on two different occasions that I should treat her right, but I didn't. Thinking with my dick, I cheated on her and she left me.

One night around 2a.m. when I was hella heart broke, I reached out to P.O.S. for someone to talk to. He let me come over to spend the night and talk it out. His girlfriend DESSA was there too. I think they were in love then.

CHAPTER 1 : KILDETH '87

My name has gone hand in hand with the South Minneapolis' hip hop scene for years, something I am very proud of. I love South Minneapolis very much and I am very thankful for what I have gotten from living there, but I was not born in South Minneapolis. I was born in a small town called Bemidji, Minnesota. My mother was a South Minneapolis native who moved to Bemidji to work for her parents after college. She was a Gemini who was a high school and collegiate athlete. My father was originally from Dayton, Ohio (also home of Dave Chappelle) who got his hippy-on out in San Francisco in the 60's during the Haight-Ashbury era. He later fell back with his parents who had bought land up in Minnesota in the late 70's. He was a Virgo who was addicted to heroin and already had two kids by two different women that he didn't take care of when I came along.

Female Geminis are known to make odd decisions. That's the best explanation I can come up with for why my mother married my dad. I've blacked out most of my memories from my childhood in Bemidji, Minnesota. Most of them are of my dad beating my mother in the night, police coming to the house, my mom and I in battered women shelters...you know...the usual. I don't have much good to say about my pops, though he did hip me to an honest history of rock & roll.

He was real big on music and even a radio DJ himself for a short time when I was young. Around the time I was born, 1977, he was on a big punk kick. My house as a kid was full of BLONDIE and RAMONES posters. He was always playing "Rock and Roll High School" by the RAMONES, so much that the song is embedded in the basement of my mind. I think the first time pops ever talked about rap was when Debra Harry (BLONDIE) put out a rap in one of her songs. Looking back it could be compared to if GWEN STEFANI put out a single endorsing and exposing the pop world to a new kind of music. My father sat me down when I was young and explained to me how ELVIS PRESLEY, JERRY LEE LOUIS, and the ROLLING STONES had got their sound from MUDDY WATERS and other black blues artists. He also explained to me that rock & roll music was originally made by black people in America even though credit has been misplaced a lot of the time. Knowing this knowledge at an early age benefited me in my understanding of hip hop.

In September of 1987, my pops somehow convinced my mother into moving us down to Minneapolis. The first time I ever saw Minneapolis, my mom, driving east on highway 94, dropped me just off the Broadway exit in the heart of the Northside. If you're not from Minneapolis this means nothing to you but Broadway and 94 East is a long way from Bemidji, Minnesota (especially in 1987) and I don't mean in miles. I took a small walk with my older half-brother down Broadway to get my first glimpse of the city and to grab some lunch at Taco Bell. It was a few small steps for man, one big leap for 9 year-old Zach. There were people everywhere and traffic was intense. I had never been scared to cross a street before. Bemidji, MN in '87 was I would guess 74% white, 25% Native-American, 1% other, and 100% small town. Broadway on the Northside that summer day was 1000% African-American and inner city besides my brother and me. I was extremely culture shocked from a new place.

About two months later I was walking to my new home on 26th Street and 29th Avenue in South Minneapolis with this older headbanger kid Michael, who lived on my new block (the block my mom, grandma, and I lived on from when I was age 9-18). As we cut through the parking lot of the factory that was behind my mom's house, Michael pulled out a rectangle piece of lead from his pocket and I witnessed a small event that would be the foundation of the rest of my childhood and possibly, my life.

Michael wrote the word KILDETH on the back of a thin metal sign that numbered parking spots. KILDETH was his tag he explained to me. I was so unstreet smart I didn't even know graffiti was illegal. Being nine years old and real impressionable, I started tagging to imitate Michael. I also started studying all the tags I saw, biting letters and styles, reading the words on the walls, and figuring out that the 3 letters underneath most tags represented the crew that the writer ran with. In 1987-88 on my part of the Southside, there were writers like HEAVY and the K.I.L. (Kicking It Live) crew, IGGY and the skateboard crew M.S.P. (Minneapolis Skate Posse), Michael's crew, which I later became a part of, C.I.A. (Criminally Insane Artists), and L.B.S. (Latin Bomb Squad).

If you had the most tags up around town, combined with the freshest style, you had "The Crown" like you were king of graf in the city. The holder of The Crown and the main influence over South in the mid-80s was FORCE C.B.S. I never met FORCE but I've always thought he had to have moved here from another city. He had styles and tactics that couldn't have originated in the Twin Cities. He had throw ups all down Lake Street when no one else was doing throw ups, his tags were everywhere, everyone bit his letters, and nobody else threw up his crew which makes me think his crew was from one of the coasts or Chicago (later I found out there is a massive graffiti crew from the West Coast called C.B.S. but I don't know if it was the same crew FORCE claimed).

As I started making friends at my new school (which was still much of a culture shock to me), I met this kid, Adam. He tagged ASK and lived in Riverside, the neighborhood next to mine. We talked about tagging a bit and he asked me if I had ever seen the "Big Force." I didn't know what he meant. He was like, "Dude, it's right by your mom's house."

After school that day we went down the train tracks to 31st Ave and 25th St, about two and a half blocks from my ma's crib. There was a factory that ran parallel to the train tracks. The side of the factory that faced the train tracks was covered in tags; hundreds of tags that were all different colors, every color in the Crayola box. All the main tags I saw throughout the neighborhood were up on the wall, but when we turned the corner, the side of the factory that faced 31st Ave (a block away from where the Bomb Shelter was later located) displayed the most beautiful thing my 10 year-old eyes had ever seen. "FORCE" in giant colorful letters was written on the side of the factory. It was done in spray paint but it wasn't a tag. It was much larger and more of a piece of art than just a styled word. In retrospect, I can't really recall how good it actually was, but to Adam and me, it was incredible. We stared at it forever wondering how FORCE got the lines so straight using spray paint. Anytime we tried tagging in spray paint it was a drippy mess.

Weeks later, I came back to look at it again and found that the factory had painted over it along with all the other graffiti. My small world was devastated. It was gone forever.

I didn't understand why someone would take something so beautiful away from the world. I never wanted something that fresh lost again. So, for the next ten years I obsessively took pictures of all the Twin Cities' pieces that I could find. I hunted in the shadows of the city, under bridges, behind buildings, and all of the places that one could live a lifetime in the Cities and never know existed, working to collect the real art that Minneapolis and St. Paul had to offer. Looking back at it all, I was way better at documenting the pieces than I ever was at painting them myself (haha). Writing lots of little toy tags filled the rest of my grade school and junior high years, I used tagging as an escape from the drug and domestic abuse that filled my house.

Less than two years after Adam showed me the "Big Force", FORCE disappeared and the whole graffiti scene on our end of the Southside died down (I guess he kinda started and ended the trend). Now, Michael (KILDETH) had The Crown of Minneapolis. He had a heavy-metal comic book influenced style and for a few years was the only writer putting in work on the Southside. Michael got into the first beef I ever witnessed in graffiti.

The skateboard crew, M.S.P., had transformed into a group of Southside and Southeast kids called THC. They were on some basic sell weed, fuck chicks, do dirt, party, and graffiti on-the-side shit. Michael got into a tag slashing war with THC, but the THC kids weren't punks. Even though they were all about 2-3 years younger than Michael, they jumped him when they caught up to him. He didn't get beat up too bad but it's hard on the ego when you're 17-18 and you get beat up by a gang of kids who are 14-15.

I kinda lucked out because I was only 12 years old and even though I was KILDETH's little homie I was too young to beat up. THC kids would fuck with me a little when they saw me around the neighborhood but nothing too critical. They might have beat Michael up a few times but eventually the beef got squashed.

It was nothing real big but it was good that I figured out early that I could get my ass whooped for what I wrote on a wall. Slashing tags wasn't a game. Because most of the THC kids were seniors at South High when I was a freshman, I would have had a hectic time through high school if the beef between Michael and the THC kids had never been deaded. I would deal with them on many levels in the future (matter of fact I bought my first bag of shrooms from a THC cat...but that's some other shit).

In 1990/1991 two writers popped up on the scene that had a huge impact, RES ONE and EMER. EMER (also known as the rapper I SELF DEVINE) had come to Minnesota from Los Angeles, California and brought with him a whole new attack on the game: a real West Coast hip hop original style. RES freaked that Cheech Wizard meets Aztec Hieroglyphics style. As teenagers they linked up with KILDETH (Michael) and formed AKB (Artistically Kickin' Ballistics). The AKB crew started in a South High School art class and grew into the biggest crew ever out of Minnesota, and to this day, still kings our scene as well as having the most nationwide recognition. I recognize what FORCE and L.B.S did over South in the late 80's and I know there was a whole scene I never saw over North that I was later told about by writers like STAGE ONE. But I believe the Minnesota graffiti scene that has existed for the last 20 years (1991-2011) descended from these three writers: EMER, KILDETH, and RES ONE.

I looked up to RES ONE a lot when I was a young teenager. He was a few years older than me and looked out for me a few times with some tough love. RES ONE got me drunk (my first time), let me hold a gun (also my first time), brought me to a party (where we almost got beat up), and then had his little brother pick me up (in a stolen car) all in the same night.

It was RES ONE's little brother Gato that gave me my name. I was imitating KILDETH so hard I was tagging "KILDETH TWO" in junior high. Gato thought that was wack and told me I had to come with something new so my tag became "NEW". You will find that the tag or name you choose in hip hop will help define who you are.

Sadly, when I was 17, RES ONE pulled a gun on a Mall of America security guard and got locked up. He was later deported to Mexico and I never saw him again.

KILDETH spun off from AKB and formed his own crew, MAS (Mental Art Structure). I wasn't good enough to be down but because I was KILDETH's little homie they let me "tag-along" anyways. MAS almost competed with AKB between '93-'96 finding and rocking spots like the Wall of Fame in '93 (the Wall of Fame was located where the current West Bank Light Rail hub is now), the Strip over Southeast in '94, and the Bomb Shelter in '95 (off the train tracks behind Ann Sullivan k-8 school over in Southside) but MAS fell off hard after 1996. KILDETH by other names continues to make a living for himself selling his art.

A writer from Wisconsin who moved to Minneapolis for school named EWOK P3 (Piss Poor Productions) hit the Twin Cities around '93. EWOK was incredible. Overall, he might be the fan favorite amongst heads in the Twin Cities and/or viewed as the dopest artist. He later did a few popular CD covers for hip hop groups and started the graffiti crew HEAVY METAL. EWOK did beautiful pieces of art.

Another West Coast transplant, EROS, who later joined AKB, is the final name to add to, who I consider, the five most legendary graffiti writers from Minnesota: KILDETH, RES ONE, EMER, EWOK, and EROS who are featured first in the photo gallery.

I took all the graffiti photos at the end of this section
with a 35-millimeter camera when I was a teenager.

I've heard the graf scene in St. Paul didn't really exist until the mid-90s (that could or could not be true). From what I can remember, the first St. Paul writers I knew were SMUSH and TERM. That TERM fool had crazy tags up in '95, everywhere in both St. Paul and Minneapolis. This was the first writer who caused such a stir that St. Paul police tapped his phone and raided his house. It was broadcasted on the news. We might as well call the St. Paul graffiti laws the "Term Laws". Cuz after TERM the punishments for graf got way harsher.

I was the first person to ever piece on the Bomb Shelter that was the Mecca of our scene from '95-'99. The Bomb Shelter was two full blocks of factory walls that run parallel with the train tracks in Seward Neighborhood directly behind the Ann Sullivan public school building. Originally, the back of the main building was covered by trees and bushes so I could easily paint there day or night hidden from anyone walking down the train tracks. But in the spring of '95, the building, the city, or whoever, cut down about half an acre of trees exposing the wall and about six pieces/characters my crew and I had riding at the time. It sucked that our spot was blown but it was fresh we could actually see our pieces now. Behind the brush you couldn't see the whole thing and it was hard to take a good picture.

On a what-do-we-have-to-lose move, the writer PEPE and I stepped in the front door of the factory, the "Bomb Shelter", and met with the owner. We just asked his permission to paint the back outside wall legally trying to sell the pitch that it would be a positive place for young people to express themselves. Either because the owner was just cool or because he just figured we were gonna do it anyway, he legalized graffiti art on the wall. Though the following months/years did produce some fresh graf, the fights and other incidents that took place behind the factory were not positive for young people.

The best fight story I got from those days that's worth telling is when Wes Winship (the current owner of Burlesque Design and former editor of *Life Sucks Die* magazine) fought DILLON PARKER (the current owner and beat maker for Stophouse Music Group). It started on some dumb graffiti/high school shit, but I think it's a fun story.

DILLON had drawn a piece in this kid Fred's black book at school. During lunch, Wes flipped through Fred's book and for some off-the-wall reason jacked DILLON's piece, scribbled over DILLON's work, and put his own handwriting tags up over it. By the end of the day Fred showed DILLON the destroyed page. Even though DILLON's piece was in marker or pen in someone's black book and not on a wall, this was still a big deal to us. Those tiny tags were some fighting words. With me as an audience, DILLON waited outside of Wes' 5th hour class and confronted him with a couple pushes, shoves, and hard words after the bell rang. Wes seemed pretty shook and scared but, instead of running, proclaimed he didn't want to fight at school and challenged DILLON to fight him at 3pm outside the Bomb Shelter. They could settle everything there.

Even though I was cool with both of them, Wes was in a rival graffiti crew so I was totally on DILLON's side. I liked Wes but kind of took him for being a punk and thought he had just used the Bomb Shelter challenge to get out of the fight. Because I didn't expect him to show up, I didn't go to the Bomb Shelter after school, I just caught the bus home.

Since my grandma had cable television and a small studio at her house when I was in the 12th grade, kids would come over to my grandma's house after school to hang out. My homies, Anton and Quincy (Quincy who later became BC of the rap group STREET KINGS), were over at my house on that day doing nothing. From what I can recall, Quincy was watching MTV and Anton was filing his nails or some shit. I heard a knock on the door at about 2:45pm, and with mad excitement in his energy and a foot long metal weapon in his coat, my homie Tony busted in the house saying, "Come on y'all, the fights gonna pop in about 15 minutes." I was like, "Yeah right, Wes ain't gonna show up."

I wasn't convinced and Anton and Quincy seemed more concerned with watching videos than going to watch an after-school fight at the train tracks. But with a little convincing by Tony, the four of us found ourselves stomping down to the Bomb Shelter.

On the way we picked up my little brother Eli and my 27 year-old cousin Jeff. With a childhood flashback in his eyes, Jeff said, "After-school fight at the train tracks? Yeah, I'm there man."

When we got to the Bomb Shelter DILLON's little brother Evan was there waiting, pumped up, and woofing about how his older brother was gonna whoop some ass. I remember there were seven of us: Tony, Quincy, Anton, Eli, Jeff, Evan, and myself (actually we'll say 6 and a half since Eli was only 13 years old). No one else was there. I said to Tony, "I told you no one's showing up." But over the next 25 minutes or so, about 40-50 people came out of the woodwork, and none of whom were our homies. I recognized maybe 4 or 5 of them as members of Wes' graf crew but the others I had no idea. I just knew none of them were DILLON and none of them were our people. When Wes showed up it was real apparent that these were either his friends and/or friends of his friends.

The six-and-a-half of us stayed to ourselves and just eyed up the 40+ dudes we were faced up against. Even though most of them looked pretty soft, there were almost 50 of them and they had one giant, light-skinned cat who looked to be in his mid-20s with muscles bursting out of his coat. The next 20 minutes went by pretty slow and awkward. Every once and a while, one of them would break the silence and ask where DILLON was. I would just shrug my shoulders but DILLON's little brother Evan stayed vocal. "My brother's coming, he just had to get off work," Evan yelled.

We totally assumed they were all here to jump DILLON. The seven of us were gonna have to either get jumped with him or take out 5+ guys each. If DILLON didn't show up we could probably walk away clean but that would be the worst possible scenario. If DILLON didn't show, our crew would look like bitches. I couldn't bear to stomach the thought of getting punked by these dudes in our own neighborhood. I was almost 18 and went to a lot of parties and spots around here.

These dudes weren't from the Southside, I would've recognized them if they were. My guess was that they were either suburb cats, St. Paul cats, or from way deep Southwest. They were mostly oddball looking white kids ages 17-25. They looked more clean-cut than us but not jocks or preppy kids. Tony kept his metal rod concealed but I had to guess that at least a few of them had weapons also.

The vibe got pretty weird right after my watch passed 3:45pm. DILLON was a no-show and the crowd started to get restless. If people left, Wes and his friends would walk away winners and our crew would take an L. But, as if it was scripted for suspense, DILLON popped his head up on the train tracks about a block east of us where 36th Ave crossed the train tracks.

As DILLON took the slow walk towards the crowd, he later told me, he saw the mob of people and said to himself, "Dope, all the homies came out." But the closer he got the less people he recognized. He only popped down there out of general principle. He didn't really think Wes would show either. With the drama of a good after-school special, a 50+ person circle formed around DILLON and Wes.

Even though we were still out-numbered, the seven of us were pumped when DILLON appeared and all the fear we might have had about being out-numbered disintegrated. Wes started by trying to stop the violence by stating the three ways he saw to defuse the situation. Being way less mature than Wes was at the time; I instigated a brawl by yelling out, "I only see one!"

With that being said the fight was on. Almost immediately DILLON got on top of Wes and when it seemed like the fight was over before it started, EWOK, who was in Wes's graf crew at the time, jumped in and ripped DILLON off Wes with 40+ dudes behind him. For a microsecond, I thought it was gonna crack. It didn't matter how many of them there were. The seven of us jumped in the same. But before the Spartans went to battle with Persia, Anton, who was a 16 year-old black kid from the West Bank, who always claimed to be in some sort of gang, threw up some gang signs and yelled "Crip" a couple times and the 50+ kids we were fighting jumped about two feet back. I don't even know if Anton was really in a gang. If he was or wasn't it didn't matter. These weird kids didn't know and were intimidated enough by 16 year-old Anton's claim to let the fight continue one-on-one between DILLON and Wes.

In round two, it took DILLON maybe three minutes to handle Wes. Even though he was taken down, to this day I am somewhat impressed by how much Wes held his own. We circled the fight like young boys do, yelling and egging it on. After Wes gave up I grabbed DILLON, put my arm around him, and the eight of us fled the scene in total triumph quickly so we wouldn't give them a chance to organize and jump us. Before we were 50 yards away EWOK ran up on us, called DILLON's name, and asked him if it was over. DILLON said okay and we left. But, in the year or so that followed, it was never over with them dudes. Our crew fought their crew again and again. I guess these two packs of wolves just couldn't co-exist writing on the same walls in the same city.

After the fight we stomped over to Matthew's Park, which was 4 or 5 blocks away on the other side of my mom's house. Pumped up and bragging to kids at the park about the fight, an older twenty-something year-old dude named Ramaa, who worked at the park and always tried to use hip hop to influence us in a positive way, overheard us woofing about the fight and asked me for the details. After I told him he said, "So, there was like 50 of y'all and nobody pulled out a gun? And the fight was just handled one-on-one?" I nodded my head. "Only B-boys can do that," he responded. Ramaa was trying to apply hip hop and take a negative situation and turn it into a lesson (looking back, why not).

Years later, when the beef seemed behind us, I ended up playing basketball every Saturday with EWOK and even shared some office space with Wes. They weren't such bad dudes after all. We were just young; fighting for what seemed important at the time.

When I was younger, I sometimes tried to define graf. Was I a writer or an artist? I got caught up in the culture of it and talked a lot of shit I probably couldn't have backed up on the wall or in the physical. I was a young dumb inner city kid who couldn't spell the words I was trying to write on walls. My crew and I used to get real caught up in dumb shit...then we discovered girls.

I never have thought of graffiti as purely hip hop like many people try to claim it is. Many writers in the world are B-boys and their hip hop influence is present in their artwork, but I came up with hella writers who were on some punk rock/heavy metal/homeless shit and could give a fuck about hip hop. A lot of businesses will sell the theory that graffiti is one of the four elements of hip hop but if you look at the history under a microscope, graffiti has been around a lot longer than hip hop and is totally its' own thing. I think you can say hip hop is graffiti but you can't say graffiti is hip hop. Anyway, you can make your own opinion on that.

I made the graffiti section the first chapter because many rappers, DJ's, breakers, party throwers, and other characters that will start to appear in this book, myself included, found their start in hip hop through graffiti. As if as kids we noticed inner city hieroglyphics everywhere we went. Invisible to most people, they stuck out to us like arrows pointing us towards who we really were.

Yo, respect to the writers that were around in my day that I didn't focus on in this story: RUNE, PEPE, WAR, MEST, MESH, POCER, CHEN, KREV, CON, NIMB, EROS, ALTER, ASK, ABYSS, EYEAM, SAR, APK, STD, SHINE, EGON, SAB, META, SHAPER, VIZ, and rest in peace to SNORK and THNX XYZ.

Plus, shouts to DESEASE and GIFT who still live like its '96 while most kids are writing like it's 2027.

The original graf photos that I took at the end of this chapter were confiscated in a police raid. Special thanks to Philly McCullough who paid for the negatives to be remade for this book.

AKB CREW

TOY KILLING AND KINGING THE TWIN CITIES
AND BEYOND FOR OVER 20 YEARS.

MAS CREW
THIS IS THE CREW I WAS IN

MAS was the second most relevant crew in the Twin Cities in the 90's behind AKB. MAS had some real creative and unique styles between all the members. MESH, also known as the rapper MESH from KANSER, was very underrated in his era. The bottom four pieces *(left)* were done by MESH. The white and black "MEST" piece *(left)* in the top right corner was done by DILLON PARKER who later went on to own STOPHOUSE MUSIC GROUP. I painted the yellow piece that says "NEW" *(left)*, and I also did the "graduating tiger" in the South High mural featured in the APK section.

ATD CREW
THE 3RD DOPEST GRAF CREW FROM THE 90'S

They were our arch enemies. My homies and I were constantly beefing and fighting these dudes and none of us were really hard. The writer EMB from this crew was the biggest shit talker I've ever met. He used to call me to talk shit all day. But that being years behind us, looking at these pictures reminded me ATD was dope and they got up a lot and put in a lot of work.

APK CREW
PROBABLY THE 4TH DOPEST CREW FROM THE 90'S

I used to hang with these kids so much I was basically in this crew. They were some real nice kids and very talented unique artists. I was such a dumb shit talking kid back then, I wish these kids had rubbed off on me more. They never talked shit, they were purely in it for the art.

EWOK
THE DOPEST GRAF ARTIST TO EVER BE A PART OF OUR SCENE

"Mid-day freestyle out the frame spelled correctly" (above) is a direct dis at me
back when Ewok and I were beefing over something dumb in the summer of '95.

EROS

HIS ARTWORK SPEAKS FOR ITSELF.
CLEAN, SHARP LETTERS.

KILDETH

KILDETH WAS MY TEACHER AND MY BIGGEST INFLUENCE.

Kildeth was like my brother from another mother. He is the
longest running, most legendary Southside writer ever, staying
up in the city for almost 25 years straight.

EMER

ALSO KNOWN AS THE RAPPER I SELF DEVINE.
A CHILD AND PRODUCT OF HIP HOP.

If EMER would not have moved here from California in high school there is a chance
Minnesota would not have a hip hop/graffiti scene. I can't say that's a for sure fact, but
it's very possible, and he should be remembered and respected accordingly.

RES ONE

MIGHT LOOK OLD SCHOOL ACCORDING TO TODAY'S STANDARDS, BUT IN THE EARLY 90'S RES WAS KING.

MEK by DAYLIGHT. Later he became the most famous breakdancer ever out of Minnesota.

JEST by SLUG.

CHAPTER 2 PART 1: SAVED BY THE BELL

The first time I saw a rap battle I was in the 8th grade. I wanted to run a 4-on-4 full-court basketball game in gym class but we only had seven players. The kid who would have ran as the 8th was in the corner writing in a notebook. Three or four times I was like, "Yo, Chris you trying to run?" He'd respond like, "Yeah, just give me a second. I gotta finish this before next hour." Basketball, being the most important thing to me in the Milky Way Galaxy at that time, should not have been overshadowed by some homework. With precious period time being wasted, I stepped over to Chris to get an explanation of why he was holding up my 8th grade all-star display of basketball skill. Chris told me he was writing a rap to battle this kid, Tamar Williams, in shop class next hour.

In shop class about 45 minutes later, I watched Chris read his rap against Tamar in front of a 7-10 person audience. It was an okay battle rap from what I can remember. Since the earth rotated around basketball and comic books back then, I didn't have a clue that MC battles would become a huge part of my life.

In the following fall I started as a freshman at Minneapolis South High School. I think I lucked out in a way because I pretty much found myself that year. I've learned mad shit since then and would like to think I've grown into a well-rounded adult. But, I found my overall flavor and basic beliefs that year. I'll take responsibility for everything I have done in life after 9th grade, mistakes as well as achievements.

Through life I would say you start to find yourself and who you are somewhere between 13-25. I've found most people who still have no idea who they are after 25 subconsciously just enjoy not knowing. High school, college, travel, work, relationships, hobbies, mistakes, lessons, goals, dreams, death, love...you know, all that stuff crammed into life. Metaphorically, I feel my experience with all these things were seen from the same road since age 14.

In the inner city South MPLS (Minneapolis) journey of finding yourself, lots of kids fall into a sub-culture. A label defined by fashion, music, political views, etc. If you look at it from the wrong angle kids can look like followers in sub-cultures; but, from a positive angle, they're just searching for what they identify with and finding other people who identify with the same things.

My freshmen year at South High, '92-'93, there was a multiple choice test of subcultures I could get down with:

A.   **JOCK:** Which implied playing sports, keeping a C grade point average, getting hazed by upper classmen, drinking cheap beer, wearing your jersey and being a hallway hero (hopefully smashing some cheerleaders). I love sports, but high school sports are all politics...or maybe I just couldn't make the team. I don't know.

B.   **ALTERNATEEN:** South High was packed full of hair dye Disneyland kids, lead by Kurt Cobain and the grunge movement. I did dig the music, especially PEARL JAM. I would get with these type of kids from time to time but I always thought most of them were just going through a cute little faze.

C.   **PUNKROCK:** I got down in one or two dirty Uptown basement drunken mosh pits in my day. But before the GREEN DAY explosion, punk rock parties never had very many girls in attendance.

D.   **HIPPY KIDS:** Well, I'm open-minded; I mean the girl who took my virginity didn't shave her legs. I like the vibe, energy, and drug selection, so I got a little hippy in me. But, growing up Southside, I needed something a little more based in reality. However...as I've gotten older, I've kinda been like, fuck reality.

E.   **GANGBANGER:** Well, first off...I wasn't tough enough. And second of all...I wasn't tough enough.

F.   **SKATER:** I'll watch that shit all day on ESPN but a 5th grade 6-inch skate ramp injury ended my career before it even got started.

G.   **RAVER:** It took me until the year 2002 to be able to get with the music and by that time the party was over. But I did get a chance to drop my first tab of acid at a two-day outdoor rave I rapped at. That was fun.

H.   **HONOR ROLL KID:** I don't think this is an actual sub-culture, but you know those kids at graduation that get their names read off with all types of honors, ribbons, metals, and valedictorian scholarships and as they recognize the kids for about ten minutes you sit there in your cap and gown and think, "I've been here for four years and I've never even seen any of these kids before." And you never see them again because NASA ships them straight from high school graduation to some top secret government space station. I wish I had been invited to their parties.

I. HEADBANGERS: Being a white welfare baby I would have just rolled with them but 80's hair band heavy metal music had just died (rest in peace).

J. B-BOY: Most of the kids that I wrote graffiti with vibed off East Coast hip hop like DAS EFFEX, KRS ONE and NATIVE TONGUES or West Coast hip hop that wasn't gangster rap (if you believe there's a difference) like THE PHARCYDE, HOUSE OF PAIN, and HIEROGLYPHICS. So I took in a lot of that sound just by circumstance. I started to be around and see kids who tried to freestyle and write raps but they were all in the puberty stages of it. An older kid from my graffiti crew told me the writer EMER (I SELF DEVINE) had a local rap group, THE MICRANOTS, that played around town and that I should check them out. That was the first time I had ever heard of an organized local rap group. I wondered what local rap sounded like. I thought that the name MICRANOTS sounded real tight. I never knew if the name came from the comic book *The Micronauts* or if it was a play off the word "microphone".

That summer I tried to catch a couple of their shows but working with a mom who had me on a midnight curfew, I never actually saw them perform. I went to shows on 27th and East Lake and the next summer I went to shows at the old Franklin Theatre on Franklin and 12th. Those shows were more like parties and they were some of the first parties I ever went to. In retrospect, it's kinda like I never left those parties.

I was mainly drawn to those parties because graffiti writers drew the flyers. Besides that I didn't know much about hip hop. At those parties, I saw live DJs for the first time. I used to wonder what they were listening to when they had the headphones to their ear trying to cue up the next record. The DJs spun dancehall and hip hop while people danced, smoked herb, and/or just hung out. Rappers would form circles in the hallway and freestyle to each other. Lots of kids I went to school with or knew from around the Southside would be at those parties. I have an intense memory of one hot summer night at the Franklin Theater.

The DJ dropped LADY OF RAGES first single, "Afro Puffs". When the chorus hit, 300+ black teenagers started throwing up gang signs in the air at each other yelling their sets out. I only noticed they were all black because, besides my black friend Derek, me and my two friends were the only white kids there. I didn't keep up with gang culture too much but I knew enough to recognize they all weren't throwing up the same gang. In a dark rectangle room with music blasting and sets being yelled louder than the speakers, my three homies and I played the wall intimidated and curious if this place was about to blow up...but it didn't. I guess the kids were just partying. My homies and I never got fucked with at these parties. We would just play the wall, scope the scene, and mind our business.

When I hit 10th grade, there was a 9th grader at South named Charles Lockhart. Charles later became known as UPSET THE LOCKSMITH. Word around school was Charles had real ill flows. The first time I heard Charles rap was at a MICRANOTS show on 27th and Lake. Being inexperienced, my homies and me showed up right at door time, paid $5 which killed our pockets, and sat stupidly in the corner as the first ones in the spot. We got to see the MICRANOTS sound check, which was kinda cool, but then we sat around for what felt like 6 or 7 days before anything at the show started.

The night eventually got started with an MC battle; the prize was the brand new DAS EFFEX CD, *Sewer Side*. Charles, at age 14, was one of the MCs.

Charles ended up in the finals against a rapper named OMAR. OMAR was a heavy-set black dude, about 19-20 years old, who just happened to be the best battle rapper in Minnesota at the time. There was only two rounds in the contest and OMAR tore apart the first dude, GOLDY, something terrible. He was flipping some "I'll fuck your mom and whoop your ass!" battle raps which went over well with the crowd because GOLDY was an adult, kinda looked nervous and was in a perfect position to be punked. Then OMAR went up against Charles.

Charles rapped first and just kicked a good freestyle that wasn't really aimed at OMAR and OMAR returned with the same tactic he used against GOLDY. Because Charles was only 14 years old, OMAR's "fuck your mom" style didn't go over as well. The crowd of about 60 heads didn't think it was as cute watching big OMAR try to punk a 14 year-old. I heard the DJs voice come out the speakers, "Yo, lets give the little dude another chance." The voices around me in the crowd agreed. Charles spoke in the mic, "Give me a beat and not none of that KRISS KROSS shit either." (KRISS KROSS was the corny little kid rap group out at the time). A beat dropped and Charles attacked OMAR on the mic with a real smooth flow with some simple to understand punch lines in the middle.

"I'm 14 I got the age / grab the microphone and kick your fat ass off the stage."

When OMAR came back with hard lyrics again, it didn't work and Charles won the battle. I learned then and there that crowds don't like when you get hard with someone who is obviously a lot smaller than you. I also learned that a battle could be won with one line. Battle rapping is much more entertainment than it is sport. Watching OMAR and Charles battle that night was what first triggered my understanding of battle rapping.

My high school had been built like a prison, riot proof with no windows. The second floor was a balcony that circled the lunchroom below. Between periods we hung out around a statue that was built in the lunchroom (well, they called it a statue. It was more like an abstract black metal blur of a Rubik's Cube). The "statue" had a 3-foot square fence around it that we would sit on as hundreds of kids moved like ants around us and I would watch freestyle cyphers pop by the statue.

Dan Jenkins, later known as PROSICE LOGIC, a 12th grader who rode my school bus and was the biggest rap fan on the planet earth, would usually kick the beat box. Charles would start flowing and a small crowd would gather. Dan's partner, Rasheed, who always played it real humble but then would snap something viscous, would jump in followed by X-KON (who looked like he was 26 with a full beard in the 11th grade) busting the big word/East Coast freestyles. The only white kid who had the skill and political status to bust and not get laughed at was SKATCH MC (he was a THC kid). He ironically looked kinda like VANILLA ICE or ZACK MORRIS from *Saved by the Bell* but with a way better fade. SKATCH had rhythm...real good rhythm. When other white kids, including myself, tried to rap we could never ride the beat right. It would just sound lame. But when SKATCH rhymed he would hit the beat perfect. Even if the rap was simple (kinda like LARGE PROFESSOR but a little smoother).

"I get fly / check one, two see I'm the type a guy." - SKATCH MC

The more into it SKATCH got, the redder his face was. Scoping the scene, I peeped that not only did you have to have skills but also you had to earn a spot. I learned a lot from watching SKATCH and how he held himself. He was real cool and he only rapped when there was an audience asking for it.

I sat in the cut almost all of my sophomore year writing raps at home and only rapping in front of kids I wrote graffiti with. I knew the school only had room for one white rapper and that SKATCH wouldn't be at South next year. I couldn't wait for him to leave or it would have looked like I started rapping in the 11th grade. I had to come-out-the-closet with my raps right before the year ended in front of everybody.

SKATCH was a pretty cool dude. He lived in the neighborhood next to mine. I drank a 40 at his house before so I didn't think he would front on me as long as I didn't challenge his position. I played basketball at the park with Dan Jenkins and some of the other black rappers so as long as I came tight I wouldn't get dissed. If I got dissed in 10th grade I would never recover.

When I finally dropped flow by the statue, I got set up perfect. About five heads were trying to have a cypher but it wasn't really sparking. So, Rasheed looked at me on the outside trying to listen and said, "What about you...I know you gotta have some flows." He implied that because I was always hanging around the cyphers. I stepped up in front of Dan, Rasheed, and two other listeners and kicked the 12 best bars I had. I hit 'em all on beat (barely) and ended with my hottest line:

> *"I send MCs to the back o' tha cabooze /they try and step to*
> *me but they ain't got enough juice."* ...Then the school bell rang.

The four-person audience oooh'ed my flow like, "OH SHIT," gave me dap, and then we bounced to class. HISTORY.......... well only to me but ... you know.

I couldn't freestyle at all so I had to go home after school/work and write a new rap, memorize it, and be fully-prepared if I had to rap in school the next day. I also had battle rap lines prepared for every kid I knew that rapped in my high school just in case I got challenged.

That summer I hung out with this cat from my graf crew MISHA a lot. He was kind of a goofy white kid from Southeast MPLS about three years older than me. But he could freestyle like nobody's business. We rolled around all summer in his mom's bucket while he smoked herb and freestyled over the radio. Rappers that want to freestyle all the time are starving for someone to pay attention, so MISHA must have loved having me around. I was a pretty attentive one-person audience and I learned a little about rapping from MISHA. He had a SOULS OF MISCHIEF quick wordy rap, and he knew how to drop funny lines in his freestyle. I'm not sure if you can teach someone how to freestyle but steel sharpens steel. Whatever you do in life, if you put yourself around other people who do it well, you have a better chance of excelling at it.

At the start of my 11th grade year, MISHA brought me over to a house in Midway St. Paul to meet these two dudes he was rapping with. This is the first time I met MUSAB (Who then called himself BEYOND). MUSAB is one of the most intelligent cats I've ever met. I could tell he was hella sharp right away. MUSAB had grown up on the Southside like me and stomped a lot of the same areas. Him and his cousin ran a dope house as teenagers, but just recently his cousin had been murdered at the house on a night MUSAB had slept at his mom's. I believe to escape that life MUSAB had started focusing on rap and Islam.

UNICUS, a Haitian kid who was a senior when I was a freshman at South, was the other rapper. UNICUS was a kid with real good energy, real open-minded, and just a cool dude to be around. He was easy to bring to parties, girls liked him, people liked him, and he loved hip hop. Their group was called LABYRINTH and I tagged along with them for almost the next year.

UNICUS and his brother moved in with MUSAB at the house over in Midway and we had some good times over there. MUSAB had a fake ID that didn't even look like him but they took it at the liquor store down the street. We used to drink hella Boone's Farm, a cheap wine that basically tastes like Kool-Aid, get fucked up, play cards, rap, and go to parties where everyone was older than I was. Those were some alright days, but I had this overwhelming feeling we needed to hustle harder. Rapping to each other drunk all night or even freestyling in front of a few other people at a party wasn't enough for me. At the time I didn't have any idea what moves to make, but I knew we were wasting time. Back then there wasn't really a scene to become a part of...later on we would help build it though.

They had a 23 year-old guy from Colorado producing them. The first time they brought me through the studio I expected a big fancy room like the studios on TV with mic booths behind glass and giant mixing boards. Instead I got ANT's basement/laundry room. I chilled in the back on an old couch and was seen more than heard. Ten feet in front of me the fellas took turns recording their verses while ten feet to my left ANT's wife finished the laundry. The basement lab was full of dusty records stashed in milk crates. ANT smoked squares and ran the session from a shelf that held a four track, a keyboard, an old turn table, and a few mic compressors or something (you know...something the mic ran through that had blinking lights and had a few knobs on it). Overall, ANT's basement was the coolest place in the world. I wanted to be there as much as possible... maybe move in and sleep next to the dryer.

ANT's beats back then were basic. Not super good but almost perfect for us to learn how to record. As we grew as rappers, he grew faster as a producer. Every new batch of beats was better than the one before and he was learning how to make better overall songs.

For the first year I knew ANT I thought he was Mexican. He had a long black ponytail and a slightly tanner complexion. I came to find he was 3⁄4 white and 1⁄4 black and had grown up around Mexican kids in Colorado where he used to make beats and DJ clubs and parties as a teen. In his late teens he got himself in a little legal trouble so he bounced to Minnesota to start over, met a girl, and married her. She kinda encouraged him to get back into music.

He went to a local record shop and put up a hand written poster with his phone number attached to the bottom that said, *"You got rhymes, I got beats."*

In ANT's own words he said, "UNICUS was the only dude dumb enough to take the note seriously and call me" (haha). UNICUS seeing that note and making that phone call changed Minnesota rap forever.

Watching LABYRINTH learn how to make songs kept my attention. They would lay down verses, choruses, and overdubs. I watched ANT try and teach them what he knew as he learned new things, and at the same time I watched as MUSAB came into his own and excelled past the others. He came to the lab more prepared, learned how to write songs and count his bars, wrote good hooks, and eventually could knock out a verse in the first couple of takes, the technical things that make up a good MC. UNICUS and MISHA struggled with these things so ANT put more focus on MUSAB. As for the non-technical side of emceein', MUSAB had figured out who he was at the time. He knew what he wanted to say; therefore, his lyrics were more real, interesting, entertaining, and relatable.

MISHA, UNICUS and myself were still focused on battle lyrics. Since we weren't quite sure what we wanted to say, when we would try to write deeper lyrics they would come out sounding confused. On top of that, MUSAB had more life experience by the age of 19/20 than UNICUS, MISHA and myself, so he had more to rap about. I don't think these things are taken into consideration when people often judge rappers. It's not until you've had friends pass away, had your heart broke, had a baby, had friends go to jail, or have gone to jail yourself that your lyrics become interesting. Some rappers can pull off writing in character or viewing things around them that happen and put it into song but most (myself included) have to experience the events to be able to make even a somewhat believable song.

ANT thought I was hella weak, once he told me I sounded like a little 10 year-old white girl on the mic. I shouldn't have had much of a future recording in ANT's lab, but he got stuck in a jam and had to move his family out of his house on short notice. I just happened to be home that day and had nothing going on when he called. After I helped him move I think he felt guilted into making me beats. He produced me and my boy Itoro aka FATCATS' first couple tracks so we could perform at our high school talent show (which was my first show). Nowadays (2011), there are some super cool recording programs that junior high and high school kids can get involved in around the metro area to start making and producing their own music at an early age. But, in 1995, Itoro and I having recorded songs on our original beats with real scratches was the shit! Anyone else we knew who might have recorded rap our age back then was on some old karaoke/ SNOOP DOGG instrumentals. Meeting ANT in high school gave me a head start on the game. That might have made up for my lack of natural talent...and when I say "might" I mean it did make up for me sounding like a 10 year-old white girl.

CHAPTER 2 PART 2 :
MIC CHECK SHOWCASES

In the 10th grade, about 70-80 percent of the time I was thinking about either rap music or graffiti when I should have been focusing on schoolwork. I didn't even get to thinking about girls until the 11th grade (or maybe they didn't start thinking about me 'til then, I don't know). I would spend a good part of my high school day chopping it up with Rasheed and PROSICE LOGIC talking about who was better, RAKIM or 2PAC, and other irrelevant to real life rap shit. Once in screen-printing class they told me they heard a rapper who was down with SCARFACE claim he was from St. Paul. I don't know if it was in a SCARFACE video, on a SCARFACE song, or on his album but the quote was:

"Stay up in St. Paul /clocking G's down in Texas." - DMG

In the following few months, I heard DMG's name come up a lot but it was always with a question mark. Nobody I knew knew anything about him besides that quote. But a rapper on a nationwide song claiming St. Paul was a big deal to our dumb lives.

At 16, since I wasn't clocking G's, I was clocking in at White Castle on East Lake were I got a myself a job making hamburgers. They only paid me $4.30 an hour and made me wear these lame tight square pants...but I got free food. I would kill like 20+ little cheeseburgers in one sitting, no joke. On weekends they would have me on until like 4am (I don't know if that was legal or not being I was only 16, but whatever). I learned early what the drunk after-bar crowd looks like.

About an hour and a half after the bars closed one weekend, three young black dudes in their young 20's slid through to grab some sliders. They had laminates around their necks, the kind you get when you play a concert. I peep that the laminates say DMG so I ask one of the dudes what it meant. "Oh, that's DMG, that's him right here," one of them said pointing at one of the other dudes.

DMG looks at me and asks if I like rap and if I had ever heard of him before. I say I know who he is but I'm more into rap like THE PHARCYDE and THE ALKOHOLIKS.

DMG says, "THE PHARCYDE's alright but THE ALKOHOLIKS ain't shit." I laughed and made him his food.

I tried to tell some of my boys I met DMG working at White Castle but I don't think they believed me.

When I was older, DJ VERB X told me he had produced DMG's demo in the recording class at St. Paul Central that he shopped, and that later it got picked up by SCARFACE and RAPALOT records. DMG didn't blow up too big but he should have a spot in our history for coming out when he did and representing Minnesota.

One random night when I was 17, my homie ASK (that was his tag) and I jumped on the eastbound Lake Street bus off Bloomington and Lake over Southside. Now this was back when the bus system wasn't high tech. The bus was only a quarter for kids under 18 and even if you didn't have a quarter you could just hand the bus driver an expired transfer you found in the trash can by the bus stop. Unless the bus was packed, we posted up in the back so we could put tags on the bus without the bus driver seeing us. With our average teenage South Minneapolis street smarts we could stereotype most of the other riders by the way they dressed: drunks, gang members, other taggers, etc.

Now this is a weird memory that sticks out in my mind, but that night we rode the bus with a dude who looked like he was from another planet. He was a short black dude, between 19-21 who was wearing a seashell necklace, a nose ring, a knitted beanie, brown pants, and a baggy sweater. To us he stuck out...he stuck out a lot. When he got off the bus, ASK looked at me and said, "Who was that?"

I thought the same thing but just shrugged my shoulders. Later that night we found out he really was from another planet. A planet pretty foreign to us, a planet called St. Paul. I can't recall the party/tag mission/drugs that went down between the eastbound bus ride and us getting to our guy MESH's house, but I do remember that MESH had cable.

Somewhere after 2am in the morning ASK, MISHA, MESH, and myself were couch surfing when we hit a performance by MC LYTE on cable access. MC LYTE had performed at a free outdoor block party downtown that summer and we had just stumbled onto the part of the show where she was opening up the mic, letting locals freestyle... it was pretty bad. But bad can be entertaining sometimes. To the side of the stage you could see a patch of young cats that were a little more animated than the rest of the crowd yelling to get on the mic. Finally LYTE let a couple of them jump on-stage. They went by SESS and KNOWLEDGE MC.

They each grabbed a mic, spit tight, and moved with a whole different confidence than anyone else who had been let up to freestyle. I kinda jumped up to pay more attention asking, "Who are these dudes?" "That's the ABSTRACT PACK," MISHA said.

"You ain't never heard of them before? They're pretty tight."

After the performance was over, the host of the cable access show got the ABSTRACT PACK together to continue the freestyle offstage. ASK was like, "Yo that's dude from the bus today." His name was RASTAR. He introduced himself in his freestyle and started dissing MC LYTE! We were all like, "Oh shit, that's dope."

"Tonight, MC LYTE wasn't quite representing." - RASTAR

Having the nuts to dis MC LYTE for not putting on a good show was impressive. Most wannabe rappers would ride the dick of anyone semi-famous on some fantasy that they would magically get them a record deal or some dumb shit.

My personal opinion: MC LYTE gets mad props she doesn't deserve. I saw her on the VH1 honors 2007 claim she was the best female MC of all time but I'm not sure she wrote half of her own lyrics. Check the Zach facts...go look it up yourself.

I'm not sure this is 100% fact, but I'm like 99% sure this is 100% fact: The first rappers to put out a full-length album on CD in the state of Minnesota were the NORTH-SIDE HUSTLERS CLICK, a gangster rap group from the Northside of Minneapolis. I believe the first B-boy/hip hop rapper to put out a full-length album was EXTREME. In 1994, he dropped an album on cassette called *E Da 5'9*.

EXTREME had a perfect voice, rode the beats perfect, and, most impressively, at only 5'9 could jump out the gym. I saw him on cable access in a local dunk contest judged by Isaiah "JR" Rider who played for the Timberwolves.

In the late 80's and early 90's, a crew called SCHOOL OF THOUGHT, who the ABSTRACT PACK came up under, held down St. Paul at the same time the MICRANOTS and their crew UVS (Universal Vibe Squad) held down Minneapolis before the MICRANOTS made a jump to Atlanta. I've been told this was a different era when you couldn't cross the river to do shows without getting booed. It's been said SCHOOL OF THOUGHT was the only group able to come to Minneapolis from St. Paul and get props.

MICRANOTS members I SELF DEVINE and DJ KOOL AKEEM, both originally from Cali, impacted Minnesota hip hop with new flavors brought from the West Coast. The third MICRANOTS member TRUTH MAZE is the cornerstone of all that is Minnesota hip hop. TRUTH was the youngest member of the IRM crew in the 80's and the veteran member of the MICRANOTS in the early 90's.

Before moving to Atlanta, the MICRANOTS released a maxi-single on cassette called *Hoods Pack the Jam* featuring a freestyle track, bonus track, remixes, and instrumentals of the single. I bought it before I realized that they had jacked over one of my graf pieces with the word MICRANOTS, took a picture of it, and then used it as the cover art. Though, I couldn't say shit since I was so weak at graffiti. Their thick MICRANOTS tag was better than my weak piece (added to the fact that if I did say shit, they would have probably beat me up). I consider the MICRANOTS and the UNIVERSAL VIBE SQUAD to be the Godfathers of Minnesota hip hop.

"Y'all should kiss the MICRANOTS pinky rings" - BROTHER ALI

So I've been told the IRM crew was the biggest rap group in the state in the 80's releasing 12-inches and doing big shows in downtown MPLS at First Ave Mainroom. I've also been told the best battle rapper and all-around rapper in the state before my time was KEL-C of the IRM crew. Going back before the IRM crew, I've been told that a DJ named TRAVATRON was the one who brought hip hop music to Minnesota from the East Coast. Their era was before my time and is not documented in this book, but, I pay them full respect. I would love to read a book about their story and recognize that my career was built on their backs. I am grateful for them and what they did.

What I consider to be the next era in Minnesota hip hop started in 1995 by the HEADSHOTS crew and the MIC CHECK SHOWCASE contest thrown by SIDDIQ SAYERS and the UNIVERSAL PARLIAMENTS OF HIP HOP. The contest was set like this: There would be ten local groups performing at each showcase. They would perform one original song and follow it up with a freestyle. The night would conclude with a national headliner. Between the fans of the headliner and friends of all ten groups combined there would be decent crowd at each contest. After three showcases, the winners of each showcase would compete at a fourth and final showcase.

At the first showcase, held over Northside at the Capri Theatre, BIZ MARKE was the guest DJ, and members of the Zulu Nation were guest speakers. I learned a lot about hip hop I didn't know that night from the Zulu Nation speakers. They talked about the birth of hip hop in New York City, the culture clash of punk rock's birth in New York at the same time, the positive things the Zulu Nation was trying to do for the community, and the viewpoint of a new world order being enforced by our government in the future eliminating paper money and instilling more control on the people.

"How you want it /the bullet or the microchip?" - BLACKTHOUGHT and GURU

The showcase was also the first time I saw the ABSTRACT PACK perform live. Almost as interesting as their performance was their support of other acts. In '95, Minnesota was still Haterville. It was and still is to a degree embedded in some peoples' minds to hate on local rappers while it's fully ok to slobber on the dick of any rapper from another state who gets a video on TV. While other rappers in the contest preformed, members of the PACK would go up front and bounce around while the rest of the audience stayed dead in their seats. I was one of up to five other white people and maybe one of ten kids under 18 there and just kept to myself. Still young, I was a little intimidated to be over Northside.

Even though it was a contest, the PACK basically headlined. They played last even after BIZ MARKE and had brought half the 100-person audience. They hit the stage from all angles with seven members. Some came from behind the stage while others jumped on-stage from the audience. They were the only group all night to connect with the crowd and get at least some people out of their seats by asking all the real B-boys and hip hop heads to come up front. GLORIOUS L, who sounded and kinda looked like OPHIO from SOULS OF MISCHIEF, grabbed the mic kinda playing the front man.

"Yo who out here is phat, I mean weighing in at least 350 mentally".

That was the introduction for their song, "Fuck Jenny," referring to Jenny Craig and the Weight Watchers diet. This is 1995 where the slang word "phat" was the term of the day. While all the other groups used popular beats for their freestyles, the PACK just came straight off a beatbox separating themselves even more from the other acts.

The seven ABSTRACT PACK members were:

GLORIOUS L: A real energetic performer and person who sometimes came off as the leader of the pack.

MSP: Short, heavy-set, cool looking cat with a real abstract flow.

KNOWLEDGE MC: Possibly the best freestyler I've ever seen in my life, and for sure was by that point, real charismatic on-stage.

RASTAR: Short, cocky, real original looking dude, maybe the best songwriter of the group. He had something that made you wanna watch him.

EKLIPZ: Sounded like a B-boy version of E-40. I think he might have been a couple years older than the others.

RDM: Cool ass dude, with a quick lip original rap.

SESS: Top to bottom always dressed in Adidas, SESS was the dopest out of all of 'em with full B-boy/hip hop skills. He had a little gangster in him too that made his flow the shit...SESS was fearless.

The PACK was hella fresh. I thought they were the coolest thing I had ever seen. I became a fan on the spot (I was on their dick haha). They represented St. Paul so hard in an era when most hip hop fans were ashamed to live in Minnesota.

KMOJ was the locally ran and operated urban radio station (I wrote "urban" radio station but I think that's just a politically correct way to write black radio station but it seems outta pocket for me to write black radio station). When I was 15, KMOJ was the only station where I could find hip hop. DJ DISCO T would spin on the weekends and, if I was at home, I would check it out. I was becoming an underground head and they mixed a little too much R&B and gangster rap for my taste at the time but it was better than nothing. KMOJ had been the light on the dial for local hip hop since before my time.

One Saturday night, around the time I was turning 16, I thought I tuned in to KMOJ on 89.9 FM but actually got KFAI on 91.3 FM. I was like, "Fresh, they're playing some cool shit: WU TANG, BLACK MOON, A TRIBE CALLED QUEST, etc." Between sets, the radio voice spoke and I realized it wasn't KMOJ humorously because the radio voice spoke as if a college kid was giving a report on hip hop while, on the other hand, KMOJ DJ's spoke with so much slang my grandma couldn't understand what I was listening to. The name of the person the voice belonged to was Chip. He was a white yuppie type dude who had got himself a show on community radio on Saturday nights. He called it STRICTLY BUTTER and played mostly East Coast and Underground hip hop from 11pm-1am.

The same radio dial mistake must have been made all over the metro area because within weeks everybody I knew was listening to STRICTLY BUTTER on Saturday nights; at parties, in cars, and especially if you were stuck at the crib on a Saturday night. Soon CHIP got live DJs like STAGE ONE to spin and help host. STRICTLY BUTTER became the spot to hear local MCs, freestyles, and an outlet to find out what was cracking with shows, underground parties, and hip hop in general in the Twin Cities.

The 2nd Mic Check Showcase was held at the Cedar Cultural Center on the West Bank in South Minneapolis. This was in the neighborhood next to mine, so a small handful of kids I knew from around the way were there (not really to check and support the local talent but because BLACK MOON and the BOOT CAMP CLIK headlined). I wanna describe this show with as much detail as I can remember because this show set a lot of things in motion.

I remember this show as being slightly dark and cold, dimly lit and I think me and my homies wore our winter jackets for most of the concert. Maybe I didn't feel that comfortable because I felt like the night dragged on with long breaks between the acts that were in the contest.

In this era of our scene the Islam religion was very intertwined in Minnesota hip hop. Not only traditional Muslims but the Nations of Gods and Earths, a spin off of the Nation of Islam founded in New York by Clarence 13X in 1964. Members of the Nation of Gods and Earths (referred to as Five Percenters) have always had a heavy presence in hip hop. It is the religious beliefs of artists such as WU TANG CLAN, RAKIM, BRAND NUBIAN and many others including the BOOT CAMP CLIK who headlined the 2nd Mic Check Showcase and, in turn, brought many Five Percenters out to attend.

Five Percenters and hip hop kids who were traditional Muslims would have small arguments or conflicts at times, and Five Percenters were also very intimidating to white kids who came to hip hip shows, both causing a light tension to be in the air.

I don't know much about the Nation of Gods and Earths religion but I have many black friends who practice the belief and found knowledge of self.

"I'm seeing brothers that I knew from back when / if they ain't five percent / then they selling drugs and clapping" – MUSAB/BEYOND

"The older god told me stay humble and grow" – ST PAUL SLIM

The Cedar Cultural Center was about half-full with a crowd of mostly hardcore hip hop heads from the inner city that night. It was the most white kids I had ever seen at a rap show before (maybe 40%). Some of the black rappers took shots at the white kids being in attendance in their raps. At the time, I didn't know how to interpret that.

As I slid through the crowd, I overheard stuff like, "See this group right here looks like a complete fad."... "Look at this dude with his wack afro."... "They're not even using their own beats." It was a tough crowd; groups would finish and get little to no applause.

This was the first time I saw MUJA MESSIAH perform. Five Percent Muslims like MUJA MESSIAH and his crew, THE GREEDY MARKS, got love from the other Five Percenters who made up a good and loud portion of the audience. They hit the stage with their chorus:

"How do we know that the mid will wreck / Cuz without the mid the east and west don't connect."

MUJA said before his beat dropped,

>*"Peace to the Gods and the Earths."*
>>...and the other Five Percenters in the crowd erupted.

I saw two cousins from St. Paul form a circle and dance that night for the first time. FELIPE pop locked and DAYLIGHT did gymnastic breakdance moves. DAYLIGHT, who I will mention later in the book, is the most legendary breakdancer ever to come out of Minnesota.

The ABSTRACT PACK had formed a larger crew called HEADSHOTS. I think I was coming out of the bathroom that night the first time I ever heard SLUG's voice on the mic:

>*"Yo I heard '95 is the year of the HEADSHOT."* - SLUG

The left side of the stage blew up with noise. The crowd had not been that loud all night. That caught my attention. Focusing over to the stage, I saw URBAN ATMOSPHERE (SLUGO and D-SPAWN). SLUGO, who looked mostly Caucasian with his face shadowed by a curved brim baseball cap beneath the hood of a beat up blue hoodie, got much more love from the left side of the stage then would have been expected.

A real vibey fun beat dropped and URBAN ATMOSPHERE dropped DEL THE FUNKY HOMOSAPIAN style flows with constant punch lines over it. Every time they dropped a punch line or said the word HEADSHOT the left side of the crowd would react.

>*"You can eat my dick with cheese and a pickle"* - SLUG

>*"You can dissect me but all you're gonna find is skills"* - D-SPAWN

SLUGO had a shaky voice with no breath control but he had charisma and hot lines. SPAWN played the plug-2 but was real solid with clever raps. Both looked to be in their mid-20s.

Many of the rappers on-stage that night came off either too nervous or overconfident. Both emcees from URBAN ATMOSPHERE looked a little nervous. But, they had an underlining confidence as if they were in on something that none of the other groups knew about. When they jumped into their freestyle, SLUGO took a shot back at the other local rappers who took shots at the white kids in the crowd:

>*"Talking all that white shit / I'll smack you with a vice grip."* - SLUGO

The crowd blew up louder than they had all night when SLUGO dropped that line. When I slid left I peeped that the left side of the crowd that was reacting to URBAN ATMOSPHERE was the ABSTRACT PACK and the other HEADSHOT members. It seemed as if SLUGO drew his confidence from GLORIOUS L, SESS and the others. Almost like it was strategic...like they were over-doing it to make URBAN ATMOSPHERE appear to be the shit. They were the shit though. They had that fun fresh feel that kept you engaged.

PHULL CIRCLE, a three rapper group who was also down with HEADSHOTS, won the 2nd Mic Check Showcase. They were technically the tightest and the most professional, plus they showed up with a secret weapon: a live band, CASINO ROYAL. It was drums, bass, keys and three tight emcees.

As winners of the 1st Mic Check Showcase, the ABSTRACT PACK were let on-stage to freestyle and SESS took shots at LL COOL J and all the rappers on the CRAIG MACK remix for "Flavor In Your Ear" whose video had just hit *Rap City* on BET. It was entertaining how fearless SESS was and how the HEADSHOTS crew from Minnesota had the confidence to proclaim they were tighter than rappers with record deals.

Groups that weren't Five Percenters or down with HEADSHOTS didn't get much respect. My homies LABYRINTH (MUSAB, UNICUS, and MISHA) played last, right before SMIF-N-WESSUN (part of the BOOT CAMP CLIK), and got no love. By that time the audience was so antsy for the BOOT CAMP CLIK, LABYRINTH could have been juggling flaming donkeys and the crowd would have yawned through it. CARNAGE also played that night without reaction.

As I've gotten older, I think the negative reactions of some of the black groups and audience members to the first signs of an enlarging white crowd at a rap show had an explanation behind it. Any other time in American history when African Americans invented a music or an art form, white people have eventually come along and made it into something else or "stole it". Looking back I can break down how this show affected the future of the scene.

When black rappers were on-stage and took shots at white kids calling white people "devils" or white women "dogs", no matter how it was meant, it obviously scared away white kids. Personally, as a white kid, it made me feel unwelcome and defensive at the same time. I definitely didn't clap for any group that took a shot at white kids no matter how tight they were. But when PHULL CIRCLE played with an all white band and SLUG hit the stage (being mostly white and backed by the ABSTRACT PACK who were all black and the most popular group in the Cities), that made white kids feel comfortable and accepted (I should also include any person of color that came to the show with a white friend, they might have felt similar).

The ABSTRACT PACK, PHULL CIRCLE, and D-SPAWN were all black men and were not catering to white kids in the crowd but left themselves open to a broader audience than say another black rapper who was equally as good at rapping but didn't seem interested in white fans. That would be a big reason the HEADSHOTS groups soon found more success than the other local rappers that performed that night.

In the following months after the 2nd Mic Check Showcase, I heard lots of people say things like, "Yo, the ABSTRACT PACK is tight." ...or... "PHULL CIRCLE's good."... even... "I would have rather seen the ABSTRACT PACK than BLACK MOON that night."

"Watching windmills and poppers /on the West Bank Boot Camp concert / we were in there /playing the rear /'95 first time I saw Atmosphere" - BIG ZACH (NEW MC)

To be fair and add humor to how far I dissected racial and other aspects of the 2nd Mic Check Showcase, I'm probably in my own world about most of it because the majority of people that came to the 2nd Mic Check Showcase probably only remember seeing BLACK MOON and the BOOT CAMP CLIK because that's all they came for.

In Chapter 18: Crayola Kids, I break down what I later thought about race and the Cedar Cultural Center show in '95.

The 3rd Mic Check Showcase was held in downtown MPLS at The Rogue (where the night club Element is now). The show was 16+ and was headlined by THE ALKOHOLIKS (who had just dropped their second CD and were somewhat popular at the time). I don't know who was the DJ at The Rouge that night but whoever it was tore it up. I stood next to a pillar in the middle of the dance floor and took in the energy when the DJ dropped classic hip hop records like WHODINI's "Friends" or "Rock the Bells" by LL COOL J. I was still a new jack, 17 and barely familiar with these records, but I dug the energy of the crowd.

As the DJ cut from record-to-record, their faces lit up as if he was droppin' the soundtrack of their lives. Even then I loved a good party and it was at that showcase that I learned how a DJ could control the energy of a crowd.

The 3rd Mic Check Showcase was won by BLACK HOLE, another HEADSHOT group that featured FELIPE (later of the NATIVE ONES or LOS NATIVOS). HEADSHOTS again dominated the showcase. They were everywhere in the crowd yelling, "HEADSHOTS! HEADSHOTS! HEADSHOTS!", making their presence known through the whole show.

I remember the ALKOHOLIKS set being wild, and after their first song, one of them looked out into the crowd and said, "I didn't even know there was this many niggas in Minnesota?" A couple songs later they announced that EAZY E had died that night from the H.I.V. virus. The crowd was asked for a moment of silence but somebody from the back yelled, "Fuck EAZY E!" to break the memorial. The crowd seemed a little restless; shouts of "Freestyle" kept coming from the audience challenging the LIKS to come off the head.

Finally, TASH (of THE ALKOHOLIKS) responded, "Freestyle, what does that even mean?" Then he pointed to two heads standing on-stage to his left and said, "Why don't y'all freestyle?" It just so happened that the two people he pointed out were GLORIOUS L of the ABSTRACT PACK and FELIPE of BLACK HOLE. They both jumped to the center of the stage, snatched the mics from the LIKS, and started ripping it off the head. They weren't shooting battle raps at the LIKS but kinda out doing 'em in there own way. It was pretty fresh. The ALKOHOLIKS crept off-stage and the show was over.

CHAPTER 3:
PHULL CIRCLE AND THE
SUMMER OF '95

The first show I ever did outside of high school was at Macalester College in St. Paul. UNICUS got it for me and we opened for LABYRINTH, PEEWEE DREAD, and URBAN ATMOSPHERE. My boy Itoro, who, at the time, rhymed under the name FAT-CAT, preformed with me. We only had two real songs plus a freestyle track from the beats ANT had given us. I dubbed the beats in the right order to a cheap cassette tape on my dad's old boombox (you know.... we're talking sound quality). Itoro told me to hop on the 21 bus westbound on Lake Street and get off on Snelling Ave in St. Paul. I had never bussed that far into St. Paul ever before.

Looking back I don't think we did that bad for our third show. We performed in the basement of a college rec room, got through both of our songs, and didn't fall off in the freestyle. The audience, that was mostly Macalester College students and a few St. Paul hip hop heads, even came up to the front of the stage. We weren't dope... but we were good for a couple of high school kids.

After we stepped off-stage, OMAR, the most badass battle rapper in the state, and his boy SONNY BLACK stepped on and basically punked the host/promoter of the show for the mics and started freestyling 'til they felt like stopping.

Before they started rhyming, OMAR called us wack, and I just went out like a bitch and sat in the back...wait, let me repeat that, "I" went out like a bitch. My boy Itoro was like, "Yo, yo Zach, they dissed us. Let's go battle these dudes." We used to battle in high school all the time so it wasn't like we didn't know how. But, I knew who OMAR was and I figured we'd be better off to take an L like this than go get served even worse. Itoro was tripping. I never backed down from a rap battle in high school or in my neighbor-hood so he didn't understand what was wrong with me. Itoro who, unlike me, was acting as if he had a pair of nuts in his pants, said he would rather us get served then be too scared to defend ourselves. While OMAR was freestyling, another rapper ECLIPSE (not EKLIPZ from the ABSTRACT PACK) got on the mic and dissed PHULL CIRCLE.

Even typing this part of the story makes me feel like a bitch again, I was young and scared, I guess. When I woke up the next morning I felt like a bitch ten times worse then the night before. That morning I started sharpening my freestyle blade and I promised myself I would never go out like that on the mic ever again, and I never did.... Not ever!!!

I went upstairs to sit in my puddle of bitchness. In response to this dude ECLIPSE dissing PHULL CIRCLE I watched the members of the PACK come in the door kinda hyped up. SESS, head to toe in a blue Adidas jump suit, came in saying, "The ABSTRACT PACK's in the house representing HEADSHOTS!"

The rest of the show was pretty fresh. I watched all the other HEADSHOT members lead by SESS in the front row hype up URBAN ATMOSPHERE by rapping along with their lyrics. SLUG was kinda making circles on the small stage while SPAWN stood in one spot and nodded his head like a bobble head with rhythm. The other HEAD-SHOTS rapping along with the lyrics made the other 50 people there feel like URBAN ATMOSPHERE was doing something important and that they should pay attention to. If everyone in the room is hip to something your not, you wanna play along.

LABYRINTH did good too. UNICUS, MUSAB, and MISHA looked cool on-stage though they lacked the confidence the HEADSHOT members allowed SLUG and SPAWN to have. After URBAN ATMOSPHERE was done the other HEADSHOTS either fell back, left, or went upstairs except GLORIOUS L. He played the pillar that was right in front of the stage and watched all of LABYRINTH's three songs.

I peeped GLORIOUS' steeze that night. He was cocky but supportive to the other groups also. Later, I found SLUG to be like that too. And, in time, I became the same way: a breed of rapper whose ego is not bigger than his/her curiosity. It's hard to explain but I believe it is a leadership quality. It's the ability to be supportive to a group you could tear apart if you chose to.

The next night there was an MC battle at the BEE LINE (which is now known as INTERMEDIA ARTS) in Uptown. Back then it was more of an abandoned building with graf pieces by AKB and EWOK all over the walls. That night I watched OMAR rip down a rapper or two. OMAR was mad confident. When the other contestants stood in a line, OMAR laid down on the floor to make the crowd laugh. I remember him killing rappers with hard lines like:

"I'm not your dog / the black man's God / I'll transform on that ass like Megatron"

Every time I saw OMAR battle he made the crowd ooh at least one good time per round. But he acted like he didn't care what anyone thought. He seemed like he didn't care about making fans, he just cared about ripping rappers to pieces.

The battle was mad sloppy, they had 4-minute rounds that were way too long and the bracket was out of order by the second round. To be fair, the heads that threw the battle (which might have been SIDDIQ SAYERS) didn't have a blueprint to go by. This was '95 before *8 Mile* or even Scribble Jam videos. It was from these battles that I learned how a battle tournament should be run: by fixing the loose ends.

SLUG battled at least three times that night and, in his first round, called out ECLIPSE.

"I'm down with EKLIPZ from the ABSTRACT PACK / not the ECLIPSE that dissed PHULL CIRCLE last night / I'll smack you with a flash light." - SLUG

SESS and the other HEADSHOTS who were in the crowd got amped up when that line dropped. That forced ECLIPSE to come out of the crowd and battle SLUG (SLUG served him). Since that battle was personal, to keep the energy of the audience under control, SIDDIQ took the microphone and told SLUG and ECLIPSE to shake hands and hug like real B-boys, which they did. SIDDIQ's statement had an effect on me. I've recycled those same words as needed when I hosted battles later in my life.

A teenage unique rapper named SHORTKUT, who was making a name for himself, also did well in the battle. SHORTKUT was dope. He kinda sounded like a black EMINEM back in '95.

During the battle I stood behind SONNY BLACK who was with OMAR when he dissed Itoro and me the night before. I think he was in a group with OMAR called the ILL NUGS. SONNY BLACK kinda resembled BUSTA RHYMES with shoulder length dreads.

SONNY BLACK, OMAR, and many of their crew were Five Percenters. When I was younger I feared the Nation of Gods and Earths because I did not understand them. But as I've grown up, I now believe that the God Bodies have always been the spiritual guardians of hip hop. Hip hop, almost a religion in itself, is accepting to all denominations. With that being said, the Nation of Gods and Earths, also known as the Five Percent Nation, have been the closest to watch over it from its beginnings.

Through the years at different shows I would overhear SONNY BLACK speak and he had an entertaining personality but always seemed to be dropping knowledge about things in the world as well. Besides the night at Macalester College I never had a bad run in with dude. But I did have a couple weird ones.

Once I wound up going to a party on shrooms in Uptown with him, DJ MASHOUT, and some of their crew who were all Five Percenters while the party was full of white skinhead dudes. I was on the porch when SONNY came out saying, "I'm tripping right now. I'm seeing bald white boys with tattoos that say discipline on the back of their necks." I remember thinking that was my cue to leave.

Another time on New Years Eve of 2003-2004 I saw him at a gas station when I was high as fuck on ecstasy. I had a girl in the car waiting for me to go smash buns but I was so high I thought it was more important for me to explain to SONNY BLACK some dumb shit I thought about hip hop at like 3 in the morning. I guess the reason I'm babbling stories about dude is because he was a big part of the hip hop scene back then.

Standing behind him that night at the BEE LINE MC Battle was fun. He was mad vocal, yelling shit when OMAR tore rappers up. When SLUG battled someone he knew, he was like, "Well, I know who's gonna win, I just don't know who to vote for," just to make his homies laugh.

During this time, 1995, I was still unknown around the city. But back at South High...I was the shit (at least in my own mind)! Since SKATCH was gone I was the only white rapper in school. It was basically my identity. About twice a month during lunch someone would start banging a beat out on the lunchroom table with their fist as the bass drum and a hairbrush as the rim shot. Itoro would start rapping, a small crowd would gather and my boy MINDSIGHT would come over and kick that BIG BOI/BONE THUGS flow. As the crowd got bigger you would have to rap louder so everyone could hear you. If you dropped a clever rap, half the lunchroom would ooh loud enough to bring the principal and his hall monitors out thinking there was a fight. When I would step to the center, kids would ooh just from me being white and all the alternateen white girls would go nuts...that shit was fresh. They would see me in the hallways and be like, "Zach, can you rap for us?" I would just act embarrassed and run away, but I liked the attention I got from girls for rapping. At the time that's who I was. I was the white rapper in school, MINDSIGHT was the best gangster rapper, there was a girl rapper, and a kid who kicked the best beatbox.

Charles Lockhart, who, by now, called himself UPSET, was still the best rapper in school and the only rapper to have any props outside of school. He pulled off one of the most legendary moves ever during my junior year. There was this crew called YOUNG LIFE at South. I could never tell if they were a rap group or a youth organization. There were like five cats in the group. They all dressed real East Coast but kinda kept to themselves and didn't really fuck with the rest of us too much. They would sorta act like they were better than the rest of us. We would hear rumors that one of them told so-and-so that Itoro was weak or that I had fake freestyles.

Well, at the end of lunch one day, UPSET stepped to the table YOUNG LIFE was eating at and spoke loud enough for people to hear. "I heard y'all YOUNG LIFE niggas are claiming you're the best rappers in school." They barely acknowledged UPSET's statement almost like they were too cool to answer. "I'm the best rapper in school and I can serve all y'all niggas if you don't believe me," he continued. That statement got a lot of attention and all of a sudden all eyes were on YOUNG LIFE. One of 'em just said something in the area of "yeah right" ...and it was on.

A beat came off the table and UPSET chopped through the first one who stepped up. By the time the second one stood up, a million people were surrounding the battle. UPSET chopped the second dude so hard, the third kid didn't even want it...he just took a pass. The fourth dude, Tyrone, stood up like the last of the Jedi. UPSET hit him hard but Tyrone who could rap a little bit hit back. Now the crowd was really into it. I was actually watching the battle from the balcony so I didn't hear what UPSET ended it with but I know the crowd echo reaction was like a sonic boom. It sounded like an explosion in the middle of the high school. Almost on cue, the bell rang and several staff members rushed over to break up the mob. Tyrone and UPSET shook hands, hugged, and that was hip hop. Upset stepped to a 4-man rap crew and chopped 'em up in front of the school just because they didn't recognize the fact he was the best rapper in school...man they don't make 'em like that anymore.

For some reason UPSET always liked me. While he was battling everybody else he was always telling me I was tight and that him and I were the only real hip hop heads at South. He told me his mom was Italian so he was half white and didn't look at me funny for being white and trying to rap. That shit meant a lot to me at the time because I would get sideways looks from some students and even a couple weird comments from teachers for trying to rap. At this point I was still treated like I was trying to act black most of the time.

In time I learned that UPSET's father, Charles Lockhart Sr., funded and managed TRUTH MAZE, KEL C and the IRM crew from the 80's, so UPSET had grown up around real hip hop his whole life.

There were two adults in my life that used hip hop to try and teach me something positive. One of them was Steve Wilson, a hall monitor at South High. Steve was probably about 25 when I was 17 and he had come up in the days of the MICRANOTS. He would set up hip hop classes in school that you could leave your 6th hour class to attend, and he was the first person to tell me I was a B-boy. Some people use the word B-boy to refer to kids who breakdance. In the Twin Cities at this time, B-boy referred to a kid that was into hip hop.

"It's plain to see you can't change me cuz I'm a B-boy for life." - SLUG
"I'm a B-boy and a D-boy I rap and I hustle." - MUJA MESSIAH
"Back in '89 I was a B-boy sparking." - RDM

The other adult who taught me a lot about hip hop was this dude Ramaa Hudnell who worked at Matthews Park two blocks from my house. He told me about graffiti and helped me throw my first rap show that was at the Matthews Center Park Building.

Both these dudes had a larger effect on my life than they probably ever thought. They were the only adults that treated me like I was doing something creative by rapping and doing graffiti. They also taught me guidelines and respect for hip hop.

The summer before my senior year in high school, I was chilling with this older kid from my graffiti crew, MESH. MESH had taking out a loan to get into music about a year prior and bought some studio equipment that he never learned how to use. I was like, "Yo, you should let me grab that equipment and give me like 6 months. I'll figure out how to use it and give it back to you."

MESH gave me one Tech 1200 turn-table, a 16 track Akai sampler with about 20 seconds of memory, a RadioShack mixer, and a four-track. By the end of the night, I had something working at least; I had sound running through an old guitar amp. Everything was plugged in backwards, but I had a start. I went over to ANT's crib and told him I had this equipment and he came over a couple days later to help me hook it up. Since I didn't know ANT that well at the time, he might have been scoping out my room to rob me. More likely he was thinking if I get this kid's studio up and running then he'll stop calling me bugging me for beats.

By the summer of '95, ANT was mostly just working with MUSAB who still called himself BEYOND then. MUSAB left LABYRINTH to do his solo thing and was drafted into HEADSHOTS that plugged THE ABSTRACT PACK, PHULL CIRCLE and URBAN ATMOSPHERE into ANT.

That summer, MINDSIGHT and me would sneak down to the Red Sea on Mondays to watch PHULL CIRCLE play with CASINO ROYAL. The Red Sea is a bar on the West Bank of Minneapolis. It was a 21+ bar, but since it was connected to an African restaurant we could sneak in the side entrance. I was 17 and MINDSIGHT was 16 so we would just sit quiet and play the wall. We weren't scared to be there but we weren't super comfortable. We didn't know anyone but I recognized bigger rappers from HEADSHOTS and OMAR. Kinda in a teenage way, we thought it was cool that we were there too.

Since PHULL CIRCLE played with a band they infiltrated the bar/music scene. They broke the barrier that got live hip hop accepted into the live music bar circuit. I think they won the Minnesota Music Award for "Best Rap Group" like three years in a row because they were the only group most of the people who voted had ever heard of.

LANCE, DRUGS, and GENE POOL of PHULL CIRCLE were three wild 20 year-old St. Paul street B-boys. They rapped about weed, guns, rap, St. Paul, chicks, life, and whatever. They did a lot of freestyling and improv music with CASINO ROYAL who were real talented musicians. LANCE told me back in '95 they were playing so many gigs, being the most available live rap act in the state, they weren't even working jobs pulling in about $300 a piece every week from bar shows while they still weren't even legal to drink.

PHULL CIRCLE Mondays at the Red Sea would be about a third to half-full. But, that was real good for a 21+ local rap show on a Monday back then. Some heads and some rock cats came out to check what was going on. It was cool and PHULL CIRCLE was fun to watch. They were high energy with good chemistry, always backing each other's vocals and staying in pocket with the band. I remember someone passing a spliff to them on-stage and DRUGS taking a pull and then he starting freestyling saying he was on probation and had a piss test next week and didn't know why he just hit the spliff. It seemed real and made me laugh.

At the end of their sets they would call other HEADSHOT members on-stage for a fat freestyle session. Places like the Red Sea were where I would watch and take in how members of PHULL CIRCLE and the ABSTRACT PACK held themselves. When they would walk into the room, they would give handshakes and hugs to all the other rappers and supporters. Looking at these dudes as a fan I wanted to hold myself with the same tact. They were so friendly to anyone who came to their shows and held themselves with this fresh confident B-boy energy. Man, I used to fiend for live hip hop like it was meth and I thought I was pretty cool sneaking into a bar when I was only 17.

In my world, Itoro had found a couple young kids from Matthews Park, MONK & BC (who years later became the STREET KINGS). They would all come through my gramma's house and try to record songs on my four-track studio. Itoro would steal 45s from his pops and we would make beats out of MARVIN GAYE and disco records. Combined with MESH, UNICUS, MINDSIGHT, and a few others, we called ourselves the CANCER TROOP (later spelled KANSER).

Back on the scene, The ABSTRACT PACK crowned themselves king when they won the 4th and final Mic Check Showcase. The final showcase featured the winners of the previous three Mic Check Showcases, THE ABSTRACT PACK, PHULL CIRCLE, and BLACK HOLE. This showcase was headlined by AG and COMMON SENSE. During COMMON's set, COMMON called KNOWLEDGE MC on-stage to freestyle with him.

CHAPTER 4 :
HEADSHOTS vs. CONCEPT

"SHOTS run the block!"

That was the phrase I used to hear HEADSHOTS crew say when they would freestyle on STRICTLY BUTTER. In 1995, unless you were blinded by hate, you had to admit they did run the block. Out of all the groups, they won all the Mic Check Showcases and were the tightest crew in Minnesota. Shots ran the block, but if you were really on the block...it was much more likely you would run into the CONCEPT crew. CONCEPT crew was a B-boy crew made up of MCs from all parts of the Twin Cities. They were everywhere, you couldn't escape these dudes. Picture a small gang of 16-23 year-old dudes that all dressed like the BOOT CAMP CLIK: baggy jeans, Timberland boots, bubble vests, big black bug-eye style headphones, skull caps, dreads, mini-fros, and backpacks running through the Twin Cities always rapping. Let me repeat that...ALWAYS RAPPING!!! If they weren't rapping they were either beatboxin', hollering at girls, going to parties, stealing shit, or whatever. I'd see CONCEPT kids on the bus, downtown, Mall of America, St. Paul, and everywhere else I went through the summer of '95 into '96, CONCEPT was always there. There were so many members and unofficial members I can't count them all off. The ones I knew the best were:

PROSICE LOGIC: Who I had gone to high school with.

VIBES: Who most people thought was the leader, he could imitate lots of different styles.

MASTERMIND: A very intelligent street kid from the Eastside of St. Paul who was in a group called the CUT that later became GUARDIANS OF BALANCE.

Q-DANGER: Pretty buff cat that must have had a couple kids early cuz I have memories of him freestyling at the Mall of America with two kids on his back.

SHORTKUT: A 5 foot something, mainy-ass kid known for drinking, doing drugs, fucking chicks, and always being in some sort of nonstop trouble.

ST PAUL SLIM: A militant hardcore rapper from St. Paul Central who was also in the CUT who later became GUARDIANS OF BALANCE.

DOUG MACKABEE: A young dread locked rapper who stayed out in Bloomington.

DJ FU MAN CHU: Another kid out of St. Paul Central. Never spoke much unless it was important. FELIPE and DAYLIGHT were his cousins.

CONCEPT in a raw way was what Twin Cities hip hop was in '95-'96. While HEADSHOT groups were winning the Mic Check Showcases, playing at bars, and getting on public access television and local radio, CONCEPT were cyphering in front of Pops Arcade on 5th and Hennepin Ave in Downtown Minneapolis or at the bus stop at the Mall of America getting small crowds on the street; basically street performing.

What separated CONCEPT from HEADSHOTS (besides a little organization) was HEADSHOTS was learning how to politic with fans. If a few KANSER TROOP members showed up at a HEADSHOTS show, a member of the ABSTRACT PACK would come over and shake all our hands like, "What's up KANSER, what's up with y'all?" If I was with a couple KANSER members downtown and some CONCEPT spotted us they would run up on us to battle or just test us and make us rap.

Proving myself in cyphers with CONCEPT members was like my training ground for becoming an MC because if you came weak they were quick to dis. I'm not sure but I think they all kinda ran under OMAR because I would see them with him a lot downtown. So it's possible OMAR had an influence on their development that helped make them as dope as they were.

I walked into South High on the first day of my senior year in September of 1995. That shit was a fresh feeling (going to school from preschool till now, if I didn't fuck up I would graduate on time and this was my last first day!). I got there kinda early before the buses arrived and the first students were getting their class schedules. In our generation, you could kinda spot a hip hop head. We must have all dressed alike or something. That morning I spotted this half black/half Puerto Rican kid sitting on a lunchroom table that still had the lunchroom chairs flipped upside down on it. I thought to myself, "This kid's a head."

When he saw me he gave me a head nod. He said, "Yo man, don't you rap?" I replied like, "Yeah, what's up?" He said that he had seen me perform at Macalester

College the previous spring. I told him I was NEW MC and he said, "I'm ANGEL, HEADSHOT breaker."

He had transferred to South from St. Paul Central, which I would later figure out was the hip hop high school of St. Paul as South was for Minneapolis. When I first met ANGEL, him and his homie Brian Dean were two sophomore B-boy breakdance kids that added more of a vibe to South my senior year. Not only would we have freestyle sessions in the lunch room, we would also bust out the boombox, push the tables back, and make space while half the school watched ANGEL and Brian Dean breakdance.

Now think back. This is 1995 in a Midwest Minnesota high school. Hip hop culture wasn't on MTV and VH1 like it is today. All-age rap concerts, especially all-age local rap concerts, didn't exist. We were bringing hip hop to kids who had never seen it before. It was a great time to be us.

That winter, BEYOND called me and told me to roll through Jitters Cafe/Bar. Jitters was located on 10th & Nicollet in downtown Minneapolis where the Target headquarters building is now. BEYOND said HEADSHOTS was gonna have an old school jam, spin records, freestyle, and have an open mic there. UNICUS, MESH, BC, and myself dipped down there to check it out.

The place was made up of two small rectangle rooms. One room was a cafe and the other was a bar. Because it was already packed with alcoholic/caffeine-freak regulars, there wasn't much room for hip hop, but they squeezed it in. HEADSHOTS was made up of:

THE ABSTRACT PACK
PHULL CIRCLE
BEYOND (MUSAB)
URBAN ATMOSPHERE
FELIPE (formally of BLACK HOLE and soon the NATIVE ONES aka LOS NATIVOS)
HEADSHOT BREAKERS (ANGEL, J-SUN, DAYLIGHT)
STRESS (aka SIDDIQ SAYERS who was more or less the
brains behind the sound systems and such)

The Jitters open mic was cool. About half the HEADSHOTS crew was there and they went in and out of freestyles, songs, and DJing. GLORIOUS L got into a battle with somebody who then tried physically to punk SLUG after GLO kinda roasted him a little. While some of the SHOTS defended SLUG and brought the fight outside, SESS let me and the other KANSER members on the mic, so we got to freestyle in front of a bunch of after-work drinkers who hated the rap music being played to begin with (haha, it was cool). Off that freestyle, UNICUS hooked it up so I got to freestyle on STRICTLY BUTTER that night. When I showed up to school on Monday, kids were bugging saying, "I heard you on the radio on Saturday night!"

The next time SHOTS threw down at Jitters, BEYOND called me and told me he had challenged VIBES from CONCEPT to battle him there so it would put a stamp on the fact that HEADSHOTS was doper than CONCEPT. My rumor spreading ass was all about this shit, I told a gang of my homies. "Yo! CONCEPT vs. HEADSHOTS this Saturday down at Jitters!! It's going down!" I said. I was kinda the news/gossip spreader back then. That's probably why BEYOND told me.

The night before Jitters, me and my homie DILLON PARKER had gone to a party at the Franklin Theater. Cats were flashing guns at the set so we dipped out to Lake Street and jumped on the eastbound 21. PROSICE LOGIC and another CONCEPT member were on the bus (like I said they were everywhere!!!). I tried to chop it up with PROSICE LOGIC who had been my homie for like three years but he just kinda acted shady towards us. I asked if they were gonna battle HEADSHOTS at Jitters the next night and they both got real funny on us. As soon as they got off the bus DILLON was like, "They were mad frontin', they knew exactly what you were talking about but they were acting like they didn't."

MESH, BC, MINDSIGHT, MISHA, SHIZ, ASK, and myself got down to Jitters the next night ready to see something pop off. The spot was maybe double packed with heads from the month before, lots of the locals, UPSET, DAYLIGHT, and OMAR who showed up in a samurai outfit with a real sword (straight up, I don't even know if that's legal to carry around with you). That dude was not playing. He was always ready to battle. The night went for maybe two hours and there was no sign of CONCEPT except SHORTKUT. He was kinda lurking around looking sneaky going outside and coming back in a bunch of times.

Finally, the right door to the Jitters bar, which usually stayed closed, opened and a gang of CONCEPT slid in and posted up on the right wall. The energy of the room immediately changed. I don't think anyone knew what was about to pop off. Two or three minutes went by and then the music stopped.

SLUG got on the mic and said, "Hey everybody, because there's so many under-age kids in here, Jitters is making us shut down the show early...but my guy BEYOND says he'll battle VIBES outside." For the next four seconds you heard a lot of voices and different commotion. Jitters bar and cafe exploded. Unified shouts on perfect beat "CONCEPT!" "HEADSHOTS!" "CONCEPT!" "HEADSHOTS!" (BC and I were yelling "KANSER!" but I don't think anybody heard us). All the other customers and staff that weren't in on what was poppin' must have been terrified like there was about to be a huge gang fight right in the middle of their cafe.

About 60 heads, all males and all black except SLUG, ASK, MESH, MISHA and myself, mobbed outside into the downtown night where thick snow illuminated the downtown streetlights around us. I could hear VIBES voice over everything saying, "Man, what's up? I don't even know this dude." We took it around the corner facing 11th St and waited on BEYOND who sparked the challenge but was the last one out. He had taken the time to throw on his leather jacket and grab his satchel bag that he carried over his right shoulder. The circle formed with VIBES and BEYOND in the center. "Yo we better hurry up. The cops ain't gonna let this many niggas chill on the corner for too long," a voice said over the crowd. PROSICE was forced in the middle to kick the beatbox and the battle began.

VIBES came with,
"I'll rip you outta your leather / I serve you in this snow or any other kinda weather."

BEYOND came back with,
"Mutha fucka you better kneel / cuz who's the
mutha fucka who's about to get a record deal."

BC and me stood on a bench and got a bird's eye view of everyone oohing at every line. The owner of the restaurant we were now standing in front of came out and said if we didn't cross the street he was calling the police. Some of the crowd left but most of the crowd went kitty-corner to Peavey Plaza.

Crossing the street I said what's up to PROSICE LOGIC. When he replied to me he called me NEW. A husky dread with a backpack overheard PROSICE, turned to me, and said, "You tag NEW?" "Yeah," I said. "Yo, your shit's wack...I be crossing your tag out whenever I see it." With my defenses up and thinking fast, I said, "What dog? I'll battle you right now." This dude didn't even call me out on no rap shit, but by responding like that made it look like I was just defending myself and it probably avoided a fight. Because OMAR overheard my "challenge", he announced that we would battle next and nobody ever argued with OMAR.

The dude who dissed me wasn't even a rapper; he was a DJ, DJ FU MAN CHU. He was down with CONCEPT but he was also FELIPE and DAYLIGHT from HEADSHOTS' cousin. After the VIBES/BEYOND battle wound down, OMAR was like, "Alright, these two dudes gotta battle." As the circle formed around us, all the KANSER members and a couple other friends stood behind me while a restless group of CONCEPT stood behind FU MAN. "It's one-on-one, no crews are jumping in, if anybody jumps in they gotta battle me," OMAR said gripping his samurai sword.

I ate FU MAN up real fast in like two verses. It was easy, he was a DJ and didn't really claim to be a rapper. On my last verse I spit,

"I represent the KANSER, K.A.N...(and, with MINDSIGHT
jumping in to finish the line and seal it)...S.E.R!"

That's how KANSER's name got on the scene. Everybody knew us after that. It's funny, looking back, OMAR, who dissed us less than a year earlier, in a way put us on. If it weren't for him we would have probably fought CONCEPT that night...who knows where that would have gone.

DJ MASHOUT, who came up under OMAR, made the OMAR rules:
Rule #1. You cannot get out-rapped in your own neighborhood by an outsider.
Rule #2. You cannot beat somebody up just because they out-rapped you.
Rule #3. If they're still talking shit after you serve 'em...then you can beat 'em up.
Sadly, OMAR caught a 30-year bid in the late 90's and his missing presence from the culture was felt.

CONCEPT faded down to about three members and did a few shows here and there in the following years. I don't have a fairy tail ending to write about their rap careers, but I wanna repeat what I said earlier about CONCEPT and include OMAR also... they were what hip hop was in '95. They were always down to battle.

In 2011, our scene is soft. If I went to a show today and called out a local rapper to a battle at his show, half the time, even if I won the battle, I would lose. All of their fans would think of me as an asshole and I would lose more sales than gain props. But, having a soft scene goes hand in hand with having a good scene where we work together to throw shows and cross promote. I've been around the country and played lots of towns that struggle to have underground hip hop. They're most often full of hater rappers who don't work together to build.

Going to other people's shows and disrupting them for no reason with booing is hella dumb. Challenging someone to a battle in the middle of their performance can be raw but it has to be the right situation. You have to have beef with them or the rapper has to be wack, weird, or claiming to be something he's not. You can't be in the audience watching a dude rap about their mom who just passed away and step on-stage and throw them off-stage (haha). That's stupid. For the most part it just fucks shit up. I'd much rather have a soft scene where you help weak acts develop.

"SHOTS to the HEAD /CONCEPT, everyone else" - EXTREME

CHAPTER 5 PART 1:
HIGH SCHOOL HISTORY

It was so legendary. I still remember the date, March 18th, 1996. The FUGEES, THE ROOTS, and GOODIE MOB played an all-age concert at First Avenue in downtown Minneapolis for only 8 bucks...ONLY 8 BUCKS! In 2011, you can't even get into a weak local show for 8 bucks. Overall, it was the coolest thing ever to happen.

My anger-issued dad had thrown me out of my gramma's house by then, so I had moved in with MESH. We had a house over South at 2523 14th Ave S (the birthplace of the Southside house party!). Me and a gang of friends left school early because the doors for the all-ages show opened at 4pm.

First, we went to my crib and met up with some homies from North High and we all mobbed 16 deep on the bus downtown. It probably looked like a scene from the movie, *Kids*: 16 multi-color kids ages 15-18 in baggy clothes, drinking liquor bottles out of our backpacks, and smelling like herb. The concert was the shit.

The FUGEES were the biggest group in the world to me along with most of the kids in my graduating class. I think their crossover into mainstream music popularized hip hop on a new level in '96. The millions of copies of their second album, *The Score*, which they sold might have been because of LAURYN HILL's cover of ROBERTA FLACK's "Killing Me Softly." With a little FUGEES hip hop twist it was a giant song in '96 and *The Score* was a giant record. Besides that song and the cover of BOB MARLEY's "No Woman, No Cry", *The Score* is an underground hip hop record. A good underground hip hop record that went pop and exposed millions of people to what, at the time, I considered "real" hip hop. This was right before or at the same time NOTORIOUS B.I.G. blew up and all the "ice/baller" rap started. Soon after, NAS released the single, "If I Ruled the World", with LAURYN HILL on the chorus, A TRIBE CALLED QUEST hit their sales peak with their fourth record, *Beats, Rhymes, and Life*, and BUSTA RHYMES had just gone solo and had a video, "Woo Ha", playing on rotation on MTV. All these things happening at the national level had an effect on spreading hip hop's popularity locally in Minnesota.

SIDDIQ SAYERS and the HEADSHOTS crew released a cassette tape that featured bootleg recordings of the FUGEES, The ROOTS and GOODIE MOB from the concert at First Avenue mixed in with ATMOSPHERE (who by now had dropped the "urban" and just went by ATMOSPHERE) and BEYOND songs that were recorded on ANT's four-track. They also released a tape with the same formula that featured a radio battle between CASUAL and SAFFIR that was recorded in Cali. To build the local support that exists today, HEADSHOTS had to kind of sneak their music in with The FUGEES and other popular groups in order for them to sell tapes and be accepted.

Following the FUGEES concert in '96, my roommate MESH had bought a keg to have an after-party at our house. Some people showed up...no, let me rephrase that... some dudes showed up. The first party thrown by MESH at 2523 14th Ave S was about 65 boys, 6 girls, and a keg of cheap shitty beer. One of the girls that showed up that night was named Vail, who was my age but from St. Paul and had attended St. Paul Central High School. She told me stories about the ABSTRACT PACK letting me know they had gone to Central except for SESS who attended Highland. I would later come to find that Central produced most of the dope rap artists from St. Paul, same as South did for Minneapolis. Vail called St. Paul "SHOTS PAUL", a phrase coined by GLORIOUS L that everyone used to use back in the day.

Side note: SESS and DJ DUZ IT from St. Paul popped up at this party. This was the first time I met DJ DUZ IT or any of the breed of St. Paul DJ's.

Vail started hanging out with my Minneapolis crew a lot. She was a super happy/loud half-white/half-Jamaican girl with real big hair. Most importantly, she had a car...she called it the hip hop Honda. We used to dip the shit outta that ride; shows, parties, road trips, whatever. She was always down to kick it and her car got such good gas mileage that it never needed to get filled.

Vail was the first person to bring me over to Northeast Minneapolis to the Mighty Fine Café where HEADSHOTS were trying to run the same type of free shows they had had at Jitters. SIDDIQ would bring a small P.A. and some turn tables and let SHOTS get open on the freestyle. Those nights weren't packed. It would be maybe 20 people in the audience, mostly friends of the PACK from St. Paul. Vail knew some people but I only knew BEYOND and ANGEL.

Watching the HEADSHOT BREAKERS that night was fun. DAYLIGHT and J-SUN did tricks I had never seen before. ANGEL didn't do the gymnast-type tricks they did, but he did have a real cool uprock and all his moves were smooth. HEADSHOT BREAKERS later became ROC FORCE which later became THE BATTLE CATS. The BATTLE CATS are the most legendary break crew ever out of Minnesota. By that time, KANSER TROOP was throwing our first shows at cafes like HEADSHOTS crew. Coffee shops were a lot more willing to experiment with live local rap music than clubs and bars were back then.

Learning how to throw your own shows is a trial and error process and the errors can be embarrassing. In the beginning, we had tons of sound fuck-ups, schedule fuck-ups, and performance fuck-ups. Once, MESH made a flyer for a coffee shop show and put the wrong address on it. To make matters worse at the same show, UNICUS didn't show up until the show was over. We were getting a way bigger rep for our parties back at 2523 14th Ave S than for our shows. Our raps and performances might not have been that tight, but the after-party was usually off the hook. Because me and half the crew were still in high school, MESH was old enough to buy liquor, and we had our own house, our parties became legendary.

Before I met SLUG, I met his little brother Nathan. He was a year older than me and went to Washburn, a high school a few miles deeper in the Southside than where I grew up. From what I knew of Nathan, I thought he was hella cool.

During my 12th grade year, I bumped into Nathan at a high school house party over in Seward neighborhood. It was late, dark, and kinda cold outside. The party was breaking up as 50 or so teenagers slowly scattered throughout a big backyard into the street.

A real buff Mexican kid I grew up with named Gato was also at this party. Gato was dealing with a lot pain at the time. His older brother, RES ONE, who he looked up to as a role model, had just been sent to prison. That hurt got laid on top of the pain from Gato's best friend, Montie, killing himself in the 8th grade. On top of both of these feelings, was the news that Gato's high school girlfriend was pregnant. I would guess all these events got mixed together on this particular night in forty ounces of malt liquor.

I don't know what was going through Gato's mind on this particular teenage night, but whatever it was, it triggered him to pull out a gun and attempt to rob everybody at the party. As he stood in the street arguing with a couple dudes who were trying to calm him down, Nathan said the word "peace" signaling that he was leaving the party.

For Gato's own reasons, the word "peace" set him off real bad so he aimed his anger at Nathan. Knowing Gato had a gun and that Gato might be just holding the wrong combination of pains inside of him, the image flashed in my mind of Gato shooting Nathan in the street. Nathan, not attempting to be tough, just held his ground and did not run. He just tried to explain that when he was saying "peace", he only was saying "goodbye".

Gato, with anger in his energy, shouted, "What did you say homes? Peace? I don't want Peace!" When Gato got within nine feet of Nathan, I stepped in front of Gato both to protect Nathan and to protect Gato from himself. "What the fuck are you doing Zach!? Get the fuck outta here!"

Gato and I had been friends since the 7th grade. I knew in my 18 year-old heart that Gato would not shoot me. But, he did pistol whip me in the street in front of the whole party. I stood my ground as I hoped that Nathan would get into the car behind me and leave safely.

Then, out of nowhere, a 19 year-old kid we knew attacked Nathan punching him in the face several times while saying, "Get in the car!" To this day I don't know if that kid was trying to act tough or help get Nathan out of the situation. Nathan ended up getting in the car and going home.

I cannot put the kid's name in my book because later on in his life he snitched on his three best friends and sent them to prison. I cannot pass judgment upon him because God has never put me in that situation and I pray that God never does. But, out of loyalty to the three men who were sent to prison I cannot put that kids name in my book. Those three men later on in their lives, out of loyalty for me, watched out for my little brother when he was sent to Stillwater prison.

Took a couple to the dome when knuckles were thrown / But nobody got shot and Nathan got home. - BIG ZACH (NEW MC)

The week before my high school graduation, I threw my first good show. It was an all-ages show at the RIVERSIDE CAFE on the corner of Cedar and Riverside on the West Bank. It was a hippy co-op cafe/vegetarian restaurant that had been on that corner for like 20 years. They had a built-in sound system, a stage, and were real open-minded. We charged $2 at the door and started at 6pm. Between all our friends and the help of a couple of South High rock bands, we packed the spot with over 100 people. In high school (in '96 especially), 100+ people at your show made you feel famous.

BEYOND, ANT, and SIDDIQ came, looked around for about 30 seconds, and light bulbs popped up above their heads. A few months later they called us up and asked if KANSER would open for them at the Mighty Fine Cafe. It was a simple formula. First, find a group that has a lot of friends. They don't have to be dope but it's best if they are okay or at least have some sort of potential. Second, book them while they're still new to the game. They'll bring all their friends if you can get them on a show that will run better with better sound and better flyers than the shows they're doing now. Third, get them lots of flyers..... lots and lots of flyers.

It's a fair trade. All the new group wants is to play a good show and all you want is for them to bring a million people who stick around and watch you play and pay to get in. I've used this same formula 1,000 times since RHYMESAYERS used it with us.

The original five RHYMESAYERS were D-SPAWN, ANT, SLUG, BEYOND and SIDDIQ. They were kind of a more organized spin-off of HEADSHOTS, and they really attempted to (and later did) do the impossible: Build one of the most successful independent hip hop record labels in the world while always staying true to the music or never "selling out", as they chose to define the term, and, at the same time, build debatably the biggest local hip hop scene in the country...in Minnesota...in the mid-90's. SIDDIQ told me once that the hip hop scene he had grown up around in the Twin Cities had died or disappeared prior to my time.

I think a lot of hip hop heads from SLUG and SIDDIQ's generation that had grown up as B-boys in Minneapolis tagging, breaking, rapping, and throwing parties grew out of hip hop or just went along with whatever trend was popular in rap (in their generation that would have been NWA and gang banging). Inner city Minneapolis was very Chicago influenced and sometimes was referred to as a big Chicago suburb. We're between the East and West Coasts and very impressionable. Put it like this: Minneapolis didn't have Bloods or Crips until the movie *Colors* came out in 1988, at least not to the degree that they exist now. When I was younger I saw kids in grade school who wore PUBLIC ENEMY shirts, FLAVA FLAV clocks, and African medallions around their necks join gangs as soon as NWA dropped. That was what you had to work with here, a base that the MICRANOTS had tried to build upon before leaving for Atlanta and what RHYME-SAYERS/HEADSHOTS/KANSER and others were trying to build upon.

There were advantages here in the Twin Cities also. We have a real good music scene compared to other smaller cities with supportive local radio stations and supportive press. The timing was right also being that there wasn't a lot of competition.

"Brent, Derek, Sean, Musab, Anthony / and the spark
they had inside to build the factory." - SLUG

EXTREME, CARNAGE, DJ EXCALIBUR, CONSENTR8, and others put out a CD compilation in the summer of '96 called *Smooth Compositions*. The album had its moments, and CARNAGE sold the shit out of them at the malls, the Valley Fair Amusement Park parking lot, and wherever else he could set-up shop. He was the first person I knew who used the formula of walking around with a CD Discman and letting people hear the CD off the headphones. I would guess they sold almost a thousand copies out-the-backpack.

Also that summer, RHYMESAYERS opened for LL COOL J to a packed all-age crowd as well as 21+ show that followed at First Ave and killed it! That show gave them a big buzz and probably locked them in as the first option for local openers at First Ave. Since then, this has always been the case.

The KANSER TROOP had split into two over some argument that seemed real at the time. Part of the crew became the VERBAL ASSASSINS while UNICUS, MESH, ITO-RO, and myself kept the name KANSER. All the other members fell off after high school. In September of '96, KANSER and the VERBAL ASSASSINS were booked to open for RHYMESAYERS at the Mighty Fine Cafe. This is a detail that seemed irrelevant at the time; but, in reflection, was a major event that effected RSE, KANSER and the rest of the Southside.

The first weekend of the '96-97 school year had hit and, since I still lived in Minneapolis, I went to a high school party down by the river. I was two months away from my 19th birthday. On the way out the door, MESH gave me a stack of flyers to the September Mighty Fine Café show. By the time I got to the river party the police were already breaking it up. Kids were everywhere scattering to their cars or cutting through yards. I quickly tried to hit as many kids with flyers as I could and handed three flyers to three girls sitting on a curb, Anna, Mora, and Jaina. I didn't do much interacting with these three cute popular girls who in high school didn't seem like girls that would come to a rap show but I gave it a shot and gave them flyers anyway. "So...are you gonna, like... rap there?" they said giggling. I totally misread the situation thinking they were making fun of me and just kept it moving and kept handing out flyers.

The Mighty Fine Show in September was cool, KANSER's friends definitely contributed to the crowd, adding maybe 60 people. The crowd was made up of RSE's (RHYMESAYERS ENTERTAINMENT) friends, KANSER's friends, and hip hop regulars like Brian Dean, ANGEL, UPSET, ect. BEYOND had a song called "The Factory" that we all liked and would bug out when he played it.

Brian and myself were standing on chairs singing along with the song when I saw the three girls from the river party walk in. I thought to myself, "Whoa, they showed up?" as they came around behind me. I kept an eye on them while they danced and checked the show out.

A couple weeks later I was cutting through the Electric Fetus, a record shop in South Minneapolis off Franklin where SLUG worked. SLUG hollered at me and asked if KANSER would open for them again at the Mighty Fine in October. I think SLUG was kinda trying to hustle me to promote harder. But it was cool...I was down. SLUG said, "You know if we never make it, I want people to say that we used to throw tight sets." In my young mind that's all I cared about too.

I almost feel a little emotional as I type this story. I was still 18 when we played those Mighty Fine shows. That was way before I started paying my rent off of rap music and before we sold product...before a lot of things. The Mighty Fine shows were also free to get in. All I cared about back then was hip hop.

"All I ever wanted was my name on flyers" - CHARLIE BROWN

On October 10th, 1996, Herbie Foster aka SESS from the ABSTRACT PACK was killed in a freeway car accident. I personally didn't know SESS very well. I was a fan of the PACK but I had no idea how much of a loved person Herbie was in St. Paul and how much influence he had on a whole generation of St. Paul hip hop kids.

Between KANSER's friends, RSE's buzz and all the Shots Paul/ABSTRACT PACK kids who came out for SESS's memorial, the Mighty Fine had over 200 people at the show in October '96. It was a big show for us. A lot of people saw us for the first time. That was also the last show KANSER played with Itoro aka FAT CAT who had started KANSER and was my first rhyme partner and best friend since the 6th grade.

After that show things started to change for me. The three girls I had given flyers to at the river party returned with a good amount of South kids to the October Mighty Fine show and it was the beginning of RSE, KANSER, and hip hop in general's popularity with upper class kids in Minneapolis, especially at South High and Southwest High.

A sophomore from Southwest High School named Adam Waits aka ADVIZER had also come to the Mighty Fine that day and seen live local hip hop for the first time. Later, he had told me that he had heard a HEADSHOTS song on Radio K (the University of Minnesota college station) and went in to the Electric Fetus to buy a tape where SLUG hipped him to the Mighty Fine. ADVIZER is the reason that lots of kids from Southwest MPLS started coming to RSE/KANSER shows. The right kid at the right time can blow everything to the next level.

In November of '96 the MICRANOTS came back from Atlanta and played at the Mighty Fine Café with ATMOSPHERE and BEYOND. I missed their performance (again) because the show fell on my 19th birthday and I was fucking my girlfriend at the time. Since it was my birthday she let me do some new shit so I got there late.

I feel like the MICRANOTS were the bridge between the hip hop scene from the 80's and the scene that HEADSHOTS/RSE built in the mid-90's that eventually grew into the giant beautiful scene we have in 2011. I SELF DEVINE later told me that it was at the Mighty Fine that he realized there had been a changing of the guard. As he looked around the café and saw many young white kids as the new growing fan base, he realized if he was going to survive and stay relevant, he was going to have to align himself with RSE. This at first was going to take a small swallowing of pride since I SELF DEVINE and his crew, UVS, had been teachers of the hip hop culture to some of these cats he was now going to have to align himself with. That alignment soon came with a super group project RSE released called the DYNOSPECTRUM featuring ANT, BEYOND, SLUG, GENE POOL and I SELF DEVINE. If that alignment is what has kept I SELF DEVINE relevant around our scene as an artist, leader, and teacher to all of us, then it was so important and cool that the MICRANOTS participated in the shows at the Mighty Fine. Those shows could be looked at as the birthplace of RHYMESAYERS ENTERTAINMENT.

CHAPTER 5 PART 2 :
HIGH SCHOOL HISTORY
(CONTINUED)

From ages 9-15, I lived with my mom in Seward neighborhood off East Lake. My mom was trying to raise four kids on welfare assisted only by random pop-ins by my drug addicted father who stopped by from time to time be beat her up. When I was 15, my moms threw me out so I went to live with my grandmother down the street. In my 12th grade year, after I turned 18, my father showed up one Sunday afternoon and threw me out of my grandmother's house. I think he threw me out before I left on my own, since I was over 18, just to prove he was in charge. So, I moved in with my older homie MESH from the KANSER TROOP and my old graffiti crew. As I've already stated, MESH and I lived in the Phillips neighborhood that we nicknamed "The Zone". My stomping grounds on the Southside as a kid weren't the hardest places in the world but they were tough enough and they gave me the street smarts I needed to get through life.

After I moved in with MESH, I would wake up, walk to school, sleep through my first period, finish out the day, go to one job, go to my second job, go home and get a few hours of sleep, wake up, and go back to school and sleep through first period. It was a little tough at the time but it was also a lot of fun and I made it through. No one could tell me that they were proud of me graduating high school to match how proud I was of myself. I know a lot of people move out for the first time and wind up back with their parents. I had to realize less than halfway through my senior year of high school, that I didn't have a safety net and that I was on my own from then on. In the summer after my high school graduation, while most kids from school held graduation open houses receiving money from their parents and parents' friends to live off of, I went to work full-time at a welding factory because I was late on rent.

In 1996, the Zone was hot that year and MPLS had it's highest murder rate ever. I was awakened one day that summer by someone getting shot in my backyard. Police marked bullet shells three feet from my bedroom window. I could tell a lot of crazy stories from that year.

Our crib stuck out from the vibe that surrounded it. All different color kids barbecuing and drinking 40's in the backyard and on the front porch bumping the PHARCYDE while all our neighbors were bumping 2PAC.

I've never been a real street dude, but I'm a Southside kid with an urban/inner city mentality. I've always tried to stay real open-minded though. I liked hanging out with different types of kids because I was curious to find out what they were on. After the Mighty Fine show we did with RSE in October of '96 and the shows we did into '97, lots of new kids entered my social life, most of them rich kids. Kids I had gone to school with just a year earlier, who had never spoke to me before, were inviting me parties. But, with me came a mob of East Lake and West Bank troublemakers. I was showing up three carloads deep to parties at rich kids' houses with a bunch of knuckleheads who stole anything they could fit in their backpacks. Plus, they would beat up anyone who tried to stop them.

My reputation was growing fast in two different directions. "Zach's a real cool dude but tell him not to bring his friends," was a common statement. I quickly got the rep for knowing where the party was at, even on weekdays, and on weekend nights my phone would ring off the hook to the point where I would just leave the party address on my machine and quit answering the phone. Those were some mainy times and they lasted forever.

I met all types of different kids back then, kids who grew up in different parts of the metro and lots of University of Minnesota students that had come from Wisconsin, North Dakota, South Dakota, and everywhere else. I "tried" to stop eating meat and started listening to more types of music and was being influenced by feminist girls who taught me how women have been oppressed while, in the same week, I would be hanging out with strippers. RSE, KANSER, and local hip hop's popularity in general was opening doors for me.

I really loved and appreciated all the new kids who would give me a pound after a show and tell me I did a good job even if we didn't, kids who would be real supportive by coming to shows and bringing their friends to come see us, and especially the kids who would get real excited and come to one of our parties screaming, "YO! YO! You're dude from KANSER! Yo, KANSER's mad sick! I saw you guys at that Riverside Café. You guys are SICK...Yo, where's the beer?" Those kids are what made my day and kept me moving.

By 1997 KANSER had made a few fans; most of which were upper class teenage white kids from South Minneapolis and a handful from St. Paul Central. It wasn't anything big, but being only 19, I was a little overwhelmed by it at first. My ego was a little boosted, and at the same time, I was a little creeped out. UNICUS, however, is one of the most down-to-earth and open-minded people I've ever met, so he handled popularity fine. Plus, being 21 and having a baby on the way, he probably had other things on his mind.

MESH took full advantage of it. At 21, he just started smashing hella girls.

Itoro, on the other hand, took the whole thing different. He was black and still a senior at South in '96-97. I remember one phone conversation we had around that time. He said, "I don't give a fuck about this local shit, they can keep that. None of my niggas give a fuck who HEADSHOTS are and now I got all these white kids coming up to me in the hallways asking me when my next show is. I ain't trying to rap for them. Fuck all that shit. Plus, we ain't getting paid...I gotta get this money." At the time I thought Itoro was being stupid but he was just choosing his own path. We got into this thing trying to get one thing and started getting something different that we didn't understand. Itoro started coming off to fans as an asshole.

South High school students had become the new most solid fan base for local hip hop and it all spawned from Brian Dean, ANGEL, myself, and mostly the three girls I gave flyers to that night at the river party. South High kids were coming carloads deep to shows and there were big articles written about RSE in the South High school paper. I think what bugged out Itoro so bad was that these were not the kids who came to KANSER shows just a year earlier. They weren't even into hip hop a year earlier which was fine, just real bizarre to us at the time.

I don't know how SLUG, BEYOND, and D-SPAWN personally handled a high school fan base. They were a little older than me so maybe they understood it more. Popularity can bring a lot of fresh advantages to your life, but it also brings with it gossip, jealousy, and hating. Around this time, SLUG told me once to recognize I was being watched. I already had started to understand that but he put it real well.

RSE had started to play at a lot of raves: underground techno dance parties that lasted all night and were usually filled with drugs...hella drugs. Ravers might have been a bigger sub-culture than hip hop at the time, at least in Minneapolis, but BEYOND and SLUG came to those kids like Jesus and converted many of them to slow down by like 50 beats per minute and become hip hop heads over night.

In January of '97, RSE released their first full-length CD, BEYOND's *Comparison*. BEYOND was my boy and I was hella proud of him. He was the most popular rapper in Minnesota in '96-97 and his CD was a good look inside who he was at the time.

A few months later, KANSER put out our first cassette, *Now*, with help from ANT. We dug through all the songs we had recorded in ANT's basement for the past three years and dusted off nine good ones and ANT made us a master copy on a good quality cassette. We bought 200 blank 30-minute tapes and dubbed them one-by-one. We made 20 for our next show at Riverside Café and sold them all.

Right before the show ended I told ANT we sold-out of tapes and he gave me the best advice I ever got in music. "Stay humble, especially in front of people," he said. I've never forgotten that and have told almost every artist I have ever worked with the same thing since. No matter how much you succeed in music and no matter how popular you become...stay humble, especially in front of people. It makes me laugh, looking back, that I had to be told to "stay humble" because I sold 20 tapes.

A 22 year-old computer worm with a screen name, "THE ILL WAFER", had a lot to do with spreading HEADSHOTS'/RSE's and KANSER's sound through the Internet. His real name was Shane. He used to trade SLUG songs from underground rappers from Cali and Canada for copies of HEADSHOTS 4-track recordings and spread 'em on the web. He moved to San Francisco, and in the summer of '97, I went to visit him.

Shane plugged me with this dude P-minus ATAK out there who sold underground hip hop at shows and on the Internet. I watched him sit in the lobby of a show and sell tapes like dope. He sold West Coast hip hop like HIEROGLYPHICS, LIVING LEGENDS, SACRED HOOP, etc. He bought six KANSER tapes from me and ordered more like a week later. I then plugged RSE up with ATAK, who had a lot to do with spreading ATMO-SPHERE to the West Coast for years until they had a falling out in 2000 over ATAK not wanting to sell BROTHER ALI tapes.

"Told 'em not to fuck with ATAK, he was hating so SLUG told him, bitch, send our tapes back." - BROTHER ALI

"I ATAK like P-minus" - THE GROUCH

In '97, I came home to a message from CRESCENT MOON, a younger homie who had been hanging around the scene that I kinda thought was a cool kid. He had been a freshman when I was a senior at South and was now a junior. The message said he had a rap show at a church on 50th and France Ave deep in the Southwest side of Minneapolis (also the richest part of Minneapolis). UNICUS, TRY'D, SLUG, my homie Jamal and I went to check it out.

I had never been that deep Southwest before. I didn't even think we were still in Minneapolis. The gig was basically a high school talent show. I saw Southwest groups like the BLACK PHAROHS and ADVIZER for the first time along with CRESCENT MOON. ADVIZER and CRESCENT MOON both had real bad breath control but real clever and well-written lyrics.

TRY'D's ass ended up getting jumped by some Southwest High School kids in the church, so the night ended badly with Jamal and I trying to get the kids to scrap with us. SLUG reprimanded us on the ride home. Sometimes I forgot that SLUG was an adult.

Around this time in '97 I showed up to a party with a few of my boys and the dude at the door was like, "We're full, we ain't letting nobody else in." We were like, "Come on dude, let us in...stop frontin'." He was a high school football/wrestler looking dude who looked at us like we were straight trouble. All of the sudden, the girl who was throwing the party saw me at the door and told the doorman we were cool.

As soon as I came in she talked my ear off about old times and how we used to be the only kids into hip hop at South, how all these other kids were just jumping on the band wagon, how good of friends she was with BEYOND, SLUG, and SIDDIQ, and how she had known me for so long but never realized how unique I was 'til recently. Unique... she kept using the word unique to compliment me. I always get suspect of a person who keeps trying to use weird words and force compliments on someone.

As she talked and talked all I thought to myself was..."I've never met this chick before. Why does she keep talking to me as if we know each other?" As she kept going I started to assume, "This chick is gonna let me fuck her for sure, matter of fact, I bet if I just whipped out my dick right now..." I was really surprised when she didn't throw the cat at me. She didn't want me to smash buns. She just wanted to tell people she was down with me.

This was my first experience with someone who wanted to be down but seemed to have some sort of an agenda. I don't have a slang word for people like this but they're not kids who just dig the music and wanna hang out. They feel you have some sort of status and you can help them achieve some sort of popularity. These people use flattery and compliments as a weapon. To her defense, she was real young and over the next two years or so she did a lot for RSE by promoting them. Unfortunately, I also saw her name drop them a lot and use her rumored friendship with them as means to talk shit about other girls and other rappers...it was weird.

My experience with her came to a head about two years later when I was trying to vomit up a sandwich and 80 ounces of Mickey's Malt Liquor. I was in the bathroom holding on to the sink for dear life when she knocked on the door and asked if she could come in and talk to me. She did most of the talking while I nodded my head and randomly spit up tomato chunks into the sink. She poured her heart out about how SIDDIQ didn't call her on her birthday, how she didn't relate to people her own age, how SLUG was her best friend but he didn't have time for her anymore, and how none of them were returning her phone calls. I don't catch everything as I'm puking, but from what I remember it was real sad. Because I am a little older than her, I tried my best to give her advice. I told her that they were adult men she was talking about and that I'm sure that they liked her and really appreciate her handing out flyers and stuff but, as a 17 year-old girl, maybe she misinterpreted her friendship with them. It either goes over her head or she shakes her head and says I'm wrong. Either way I start to get dizzy and pass out.

After that I tried to be responsible with any kid who ever tried to help KANSER out and hang around the crew. Even with the microscopic "local popularity", we had to be responsible. Since then KANSER has always just turned fans into friends. One day they think we're cool and the next we're kicking it with them and trying to holler at their female friends. Then we're just their homies passing out on their couch and they don't think we're that cool anymore. (haha)

There is nothing wrong with getting into new things but, back in the 90's, kids who were just getting into hip hop had this overwhelming urge to let you know how down they were with it. It would usually start by calling someone else fake. Then it would go into them telling someone which classic hip hop records they owned. It was silly.

All the gossip, dick riding, hating, and other negative things that surround hip hop only take away from it. I would be full-out lying if I denied ever participating in all of those negative aspects when I was younger but, with 30 years of life and a little bit of wisdom, I can now say it's just better to be positive. The best advice I can give about it all is this: just because you don't like someone's music doesn't mean that you have to tell everyone that you don't like it.

CHAPTER 6 :
SESS

SESS is often referred to as the dopest rapper ever out of Minnesota, and it's not just a cliché/polite statement because he passed away young. SESS was the shit. Instead of writing about it, I would tell any reader to buy, download, or somehow get a copy of *Headshots History*. It was released right after SESS' death and it will explain everything.

When I was 20 years old, over a year after SESS' death, I was working at a sandwich shop in Dinkytown. This knucklehead dude I worked with had signed up for an army recruiter to pick him up from work at 6pm. At about 5:20pm he started to get cold feet and asked if I would cover for him so he could take off early before the recruiter arrived. He was begging me to let him leave so I was like, "Yeah...whatever," and let him go. About three minutes after he left, this lady recruiter came to pick him up. I was alone in the store when she arrived and as soon as I told her that the dude had left early she started pulling Jedi minds tricks on me. She asked if I was interested in joining the army. I started laughing at her because as far as I was concerned the army was no place for me. But the next thing I knew she had scheduled herself to pick me up the next day at 6pm.

The entire next day I felt like a weak minded chump. How did she talk me into going downtown and taking the US army exam? The next day at work, I debated punking out and leaving early but something just told me to go through with it. As she was picking me up, during the ride downtown, the speech she gave me, and as I was taking the test I was thinking, "What the fuck am I doing?" I'm glad she didn't just bust out the sign up sheet right then, cuz the next thing I knew I would have been jumping out of an airplane or some shit.

She started to ask me questions about myself on the way home (probably to relate whatever I liked to the army and hypnotize me into signing up). I told her I was in a rap group, which was odd because back then I used to keep that to myself around adults. She asked me if I had ever heard of the ABSTRACT PACK. I said, "Oh for sure. I'm a pretty big fan of theirs." Then she told me SESS was her cousin and went on to say that she really regretted never seeing him perform before he died. She said she had even dropped him off at one of his concerts once and he begged her to come in and watch him but she said she would another time. She told me there were several members of her family that felt the same way.

When she pulled the car up outside of my apartment I told her to wait in the parking lot. "Just give me about 10 minutes and I'll be right back," I said. I ran into the crib and dug through about 12 unmarked VHS tapes. A little over 10 minutes later I ran out to her car, handed her a video tape, and told her I wasn't interested in joining the army but this tape had a live performance of SESS and GLORIOUS L doing two songs at the Whole Music Club a few years back and that she could have it. Energy moves in a way that make things happen for a reason.

"These niggas is good but these niggas ain't Sess"
- LANCE (GLOBAL) of PHULL CIRCLE

CHAPTER 7:
CRAZY ASS DJ FRANCISCO

My boy Jamison has a theory: never mix more than two drugs/substances in your body at one time. The first time I ever took three drugs at the same time was at a party over North at Heather Mackenzie's spot, 1515 Hillside. I had a buzz off the keg, ate shrooms, and smoked two blunts in an empty garage. I was straight Star Trek. Every second seemed like I was in a comic book panel. All of a sudden the DJ spun A Tribe Called Quest's new single, "1nce Again".

"You on point PHIFE / Yo once again TIP." - A TRIBE CALLED QUEST

I swear I could see the words of the song writing out in comic book text bubbles above my head. Next thing I knew someone tapped me on the shoulder and asked if I wanted to rap on the mic. I looked at the DJ and he said, "Oh, your dude from KANSER right?" After he handed me a microphone everything started blinking in and out...rapping...outside...sitting on hill...back seat of jeep...home...food...sleep. That DJ was RAY SKEE aka DJ FRANCISCO.

"Party over North / Who's spinning / RAY SKEE /
That's my man he's always grinning." - SLUG

DJ FRANCISCO is one of the mainiest dudes I've ever met on the hip hop scene. He's a Mexican dude maybe a year older than me and he was always partying, talking shit, getting in fights, getting high, being crazy, fucking with girls, just having fun.

Even though he was a mainy dude, DJ FRANCISCO was one of the hardest working DJs I ever met. There was a time where I bet he DJ'd six nights a week 'till 1 a.m. and then would go to work in the morning. Nowadays, every DJ I work with has a list of complaints. They complain about what kind of turn-tables they have to use, sharing equipment, and cry if they don't have the 2037 version of Vestax super mega mixer. DJ

FRANCISCO never complained about nothing. He would rock the party with whatever. If your parents were out of town and you were having a party, he would show up and pull a Tech 1200 out of the trunk, connect it with your parents' old record player, use a household stereo as a mixer, and would dig through your dad's old records to find music to rock the party. Next thing you'd know...the party was crackin' and everyone was dancing.

FRANCISCO was best known for his cracking club night, the BARBER SHOP, which he ran with fellow DJ's HENRY MOON and CORNELIUS (also known as the producer 84 CAPRICE). It was held in the Record Room at First Ave for a couple years.

The first time I finally saw the MICRANOTS live was at the First Ave Mainroom at ATMOSPHERE's CD release party for *Overcast* in the summer of '97. I don't think a local rap group had headlined the Mainroom at First Ave since the IRM CREW in '86 and none of us were old enough to remember that anyway. On the bill was EXTREME, ILLUSION, BEYOND, LOS NATIVOS, KANSER, ATMOSPHERE, and of course THE MICRANOTS who were back from Atlanta for a hot minute. That was the first time I ever played the main stage. There was only like 300 hundred people in the main room that can squeeze 1700, but it still felt like the top of the world being up there.

On top of I SELF DEVINE's monster stage presence, watching DJ KOOL AKEEM really DJ for a rap performance was new to me. This cat DJ MEDEK was backing up KANSER at the time but all we had him do was scratch over our DAT tape. KOOL AKEEM used records and backed I SELF DEVINE like JAM MASTER JAY backed RUN DMC.

The MICRANOTS went last even after ATMOSPHERE, and since the show was running behind, they started letting Sunday night dance party kids in. By the time the MICRANOTS were halfway into their set the crowd doubled...it was dope.

We used to play a lot of shows with the NATIVES ONES who later changed their name to LOS NATIVOS. Long time HEADSHOTS member FELIPE and rapper/producer BALAM rapped sets that were half English/half Spanish. What I dug most about LOS NATIVOS was that they would bring up more political and racial world issues than all the other local groups we would play with. They would point out little things that as a white kid I didn't notice, like how Taco Bell commercials were offensive to Mexicans. FELIPE was also a pretty good popper and a somewhat leader of the only breakdance crew in the state back then, ROC FORCE, who soon after changed their name to the BATTLE CATS.

EYEDEA got his start doing backup vocals for LOS NATIVOS when BALAM was late for a show. EYEDEA was a 14 year-old white kid who lived off West 7th St in Shots Paul. He was an original member of the BATTLE CATS back then and from what I can recall, a pretty good breaker.

To this day I've never seen a better freestyler at 14 years old than EYEDEA.

SESS had a giant influence on EYEDEA and you could hear it in his raps. At 14 he rapped with SESS' skill minus life experience, and without life experience what can you rap about?...........Battling.

The top ten weirdest dudes I've ever met came out of the St. Paul house music/ rave throwing team called FAMILY WORKS. They would later switch the name from FAM- ILY WORKS to MODE ONE when they would throw hip hop parties. MODE ONE St. Paul house parties were where DJs like ABILITIES, JUDO, and DUZ IT got their start. MODE ONE really put themselves on the hip hop map by throwing this giant DJ tournament on 27th and Lake (same spot I went to my first shows). As an organized DJ battle it might have sucked, but as a party it was off the meter with hundreds of kids that included lots of rave girls dancing, breaking, and partying.

Soon after MODE ONE asked us, KANSER, to play one of their shows which was at a different spot on East Lake, the JVC (Jungle Vibe Collective) space. The JVC space was a pretty plain square room warehouse but it was a fresh show and they paid us...for real...with real money...$60. Three years in the game and that was the most KANSER had ever been paid. I dipped out early on the ever-moving search for more fun so I missed the group that followed us. It was a high school rap band called HEIRUSPECS. But I did meet the MODE ONE member in charge of sound, SKYE ROSSI.

After a couple more bump-ins with SKYE we finally exchanged numbers, and click, we were a team. For the next six years we threw shows together. Overall, pretty good shows too. We put a lot of acts on and made a little history, but we never made any real money.

SKYE picked me up from work one day and drove me deep into St. Paul so I could see HEIRUSPECS for the first time. SKYE tried to switch lanes and we got smashed in the blind spot and wound up in a snow pile. Everybody from the show saw and came out to see if we were okay. It was a little embarrassing but more funny. After I diagnosed myself with not being dead we parked the car and went into the tiny cafe packed to the brim with about 50 St. Paul Central High School underclassmen. HEIRUSPECS was like a school band back then with bass, guitar, drums, and a horn section.

Lead by the bass player, Sean McPherson aka TWINKIE JIGGLES, HEIRUSPECS generated a lot of energy. The lead rapper, FELIX, was dressed in full black and white army fatigues, and with a braces smile, bottle top glasses, and a strong rapper voice announced, "Everybody give it up, a member of KANSER just entered the building." Only a couple of kids knew who I was but they all clapped cuz FELIX told them to.

Back then they had a second rapper, LEE, but he left the band after a little bit. Soon after that show, HEIRUSPECS put out a tape called *Live from the Studio* and at the release party we formed a new crew. We called ourselves INTERLOCK. SKYE ROSSI,

KANSER, BOOKA B, HEIRUSPECS, TWISTED LINGUISTICS & CMI (Case in Mistaken Identity) who later became ODD JOBS.

BOOKA B was a real cool laid back St. Paul cat who made beats for TWISTED LINGUISTICS and FELIX. BOOKA is crazy talented. His music can be so well orchestrated it's hard to rap over cuz it's so complicated to complement.

TWISTED LINGUISTICS was a group down with HEIRUSPECS. NOAH B and MU AH DIB were both my age (20). NOAH B was featured on HEIRUSPECS' tape.

CMI which ADVIZER & CRESCENT MOON were apart of, was already its own mob of 15-17 year-old rappers, DJs, and graffiti artists from St. Paul and Minneapolis. CMI were the first rap kids I knew whose parents had money and who came from functional families, for the most part. They were a fun bunch of beer drinking and drug doing hip hop heads. All those little fuckers were teenage girl magnets too. I can personally claim I slept with at least two girls in my life because they thought I was in CMI.

There was also TRY-D, an older white dude already in his mid-20's that was running around town like a teenager with CMI until they kicked him out. I don't think TRY-D was ever asked to join INTERLOCK, he just started claiming it and coming around. He had it pretty rough growing up on the West Bank, his dad wasn't in the picture and his mom and him didn't have much money. When he got into rhyming he became the white dude that tagged along with the CONCEPT crew in the mid-90's and got props on the street for freestyling. It took me a while to understand TRY-D. He was a loud mouth kid in an adult body. But as we all matured in time, I found him to be a good friend with a very good soul.

INTERLOCK started out pretty fun. FELIX tried to take the lead, getting meetings together and trying to build. UNICUS, MESH, and myself all of a sudden had a gang of new friends and we started rollin' with all these kids to new parties meeting new people. During this time in my life I started hanging more in St. Paul.

I was kicking it with DJ ABILITIES, FAMILY WORKS, and members of the BATTLE CATS like GROOVE and EYEDEA. All these kids were real funny style to me. Let me respell that...they were real FUNnystyle. They were fun to hang out with but a little weird or, better yet, they were just different. Different than the kids I grew up with. Most of them were sober and they were constantly sarcastic...constantly sarcastic...oh, and none of them could play basketball.

We hooped a few times. The majority of them knew they couldn't play but just tried to have fun. The sad case was DJ ABILITIES. Somebody must've lied to him when he was young and told him he could do anything that, by default, included basketball. I had built a friendship with ABILITIES. We used to go to lots of parties together. He was kind of an arrogant kid but I admired how focused he was on becoming a great DJ. Almost every time I'd call him and ask what he was doing he would say, "Practicing DJ'ing. I'm getting ready for the SCRIBBLE JAM battles." Even though the battles were still like five months away.

He was super competitive and would challenge me to play him one-on-one in basketball. I liked ABILITIES, so I would try and play about half-speed against him and just beat him quick to get it over with. Sadly, our friendship came to a head one day at Lyndhurst Park. He got to trash talking so I gave it to him bad. I was talking hella shit in front of the audience, CRESCENT MOON, ADVIZER, BIG JESS, and DJ TREY. ABILITIES didn't speak to me on the ride home or for the next six months. Our friendship never recovered. (haha)

The rap scene sarcasm got worse when the BATTLE CATS stretched out to a St. Paul suburb, Roseville. That got a handful of new and even more sarcastic members like my man Adam Garcia, a real ill popper in his day and the king of hip hop sarcasm. The BATTLE CATS even pulled a couple girl breakers out of Roseville, Sara and Bridget. They added the female element and were both crazy cute. Eventually I got to make out with both of them...which really has nothing to do with anything, just something I wanted to brag about randomly in this book.

I had a lot to do with connecting St. Paul hip hop kids to Minneapolis and so did ANGEL from the BATTLECATS. But Jessie Kelly, aka NAMELESS from CMI, was the main connection. Jessie was a mixed skateboard rap kid who loved to hang out and could get along with just about everybody. He told me some of his black friends called him a "daywalker", a vampire metaphor meaning he could walk amongst people of other colors (haha). He went to junior high in South Minneapolis with a lot of kids who wound up at South, he went to St. Paul Central for part of high school, and then transferred to Southwest High School. He was also friends with everybody and was a lot of people's links to each other, whether they ever knew it or not. Jessie Kelly had a lot to do with our scene's growth by breaking down the border between cities so we could start to work together.

CHAPTER 8 PART 1:
SOUNDSET WEDNESDAYS
AND HEADSPIN SUNDAYS

In '97-98, KNOWLEDGE MC of the ABSTRACT PACK put out a solo EP. I bought it and it was good, but it didn't have the same feel of when the PACK was all together. Around the same time, KARDEL, a rapper who was down with the PACK and from Shots Paul, also put out a CD. They both got a good amount of local radio play and spent some good money on local advertising; billboards, commercials on cable, and even previews that ran before movies in the theaters at Mall of America. I don't know how well spending big dollars worked out for these two cats but you can't blame them for trying.

Breaking into mainstream pop music as a rapper and hip hop culture are two different things, and personally, I don't know much about the first. I would guess KNOWLEDGE and KARDEL were trying to make enough noise around here to get noticed by a record label or someone that could help them from the outside.

The first dude (well, maybe second to CARNAGE) I saw hustle his CD on the street to a level that should be remembered was RICOCHET. He was the first dude I saw slinging burnt CDs. I would see him everywhere hustling CDs on the street, on the bus, Uptown, Downtown, St. Paul, Dinkytown, and Lake Street. About three times I saw his CD at someone's house in their collection and thought, "They must've ran into RICOCHET on the street." The music he sold was also all self produced. He might have been the first self produced solo rapper I knew, which is a whole other level of the hustle. RICOCHET had to have moved over 1,000 CDs that summer at $5 a pop, and at less than a dollar to make, RICOCHET put a little dough in his pocket that summer.

I've hustled CDs on the street before and it's some real shit. It's work and it's tiring. That's why RICHOCHET sticks out in my head. The fact that he would hustle that hard is impressive. You can only go so long doing it before it tires you out. That's why I tried to focus more on selling my music at shows.

BUDAH TYE and STAGE ONE from UVS were the only people that threw MC battles on a regular basis back then. I would make it a point to steer clear of BUDAH TYE because I hadn't figured out how our energies were to interact yet. That's why I never entered one of his emcee battles. He's an old school battle rapper who grew up in Sacramento and held himself with strong energy. He was known for punching kids who weren't black in the face if they dropped the N-bomb in front of him. I found that respectable.

I first discovered spoken word emceen' around '98. I caught TRUTH MAZE, the former MICRANOTS member, hosting an open mic in the back room of Jitters. I was blown away by the way TRUTH MAZE, PENSOUL, BRO SON, GENESIS, MICHAELA DAY, FRANK SENTWELI & EDU PO, and other poets on the scene by the way they would speak to the audience, by the topics they would speak on, and the deep emotion they would use. When they would speak about racial issues, political issues, and social issues, they opened my mind to a lot of things.

TRUTH MAZE was always incredible. He was probably about 31 with a strong beard and powerful dread locks. His strength and confidence in his words combined with his beatbox abilities was simultaneously moving and entertaining. When he was on the mic it felt like God was speaking through him. Even as a poet, TRUTH MAZE fully embodies being an emcee.

I later learned that TRUTH MAZE grew up on the Northside where his father was murdered when he was very young. He is a very spiritual person and the universe has put him through many-a-test to make him who he is. Lots of us younger ones looked up to TRUTH MAZE. What was also awesome about him was he loved to party. You could catch TRUTH MAZE well into his 30's dancing at a club, hosting a party in a dirty house basement, or taking shrooms and walking around town on a nice day.

Before INTERLOCK formed we had been playing shows with the same circle of groups for over a year: LOS NATIVOS, EXTREME, ILLUSION, PHULL CIRCLE, LITTLE BUDDY, KANSER, VERBAL ASSASSINS, ATMOSPHERE, EYEDEA & ABILITIES, BEYOND, BUDAH TYE & DJ STAGE ONE, and RAW VILLA. Most of the shows were at coffee shops, 7th Street Entry, or sometimes the Red Sea. Those days we were just okay, but on the bright side, kids were coming out to the shows and all the groups we played with pretty much got along. There wasn't much shit talking, probably because nobody had anything going on big enough for anyone to be jealous of.

On the flip side our crowds were becoming real stiff. There would be kids at the shows, but if you didn't know better you would think they weren't having any fun. They didn't dance and the shows felt more like performances than parties.

Ego aside, ATMOSPHERE and BEYOND were better than the rest of us. Nobody could match their all-around performance and presentation. I could also tell that ATMOSPHERE was becoming more popular than the rest of us, even BEYOND. If

ATMOSPHERE didn't headline, then a good amount of the crowd would leave after they played. I was chilling by the RSE product table in First Ave and I overheard someone ask SIDDIQ which album was selling better, BEYOND's or ATMOSPHERE's. SIDDIQ said ATMOSPHERE had a broader audience.

The first SOUNDSET was held in March of 1997 on 27th and Lake Street as an all-night hip hop rave. KANSER played it but I was out of town visiting a girlfriend in Oregon. UNICUS told me that they had to play at 5am in the morning, second to last, right before EYEDEA.

Then, in the beginning of the summer of '98, RSE threw SOUNDSET Wednesdays at First Ave. It was an all-ages hip hop night club style show and maybe the coolest thing RSE has ever done in my opinion. Everybody was at the SOUNDSET shows that summer...I mean EVERYBODY. I would guess at least 1,000 kids on average showed up every week; all types of kids too... lots of girls. There were crazy girls everywhere. RSE would have DJs and one group a night play but the real headliners were the BATTLE CATS. When the First Ave screen would raise exposing the big main stage and the BATTLE CATS would start dancing on-stage, the place would go nuts. The average kid in Minnesota had never seen live breakdancing in '98, or real hip hop for that matter.

SOUNDSET, combined with RSE playing raves, spread local hip hop to the suburbs of the Twin Cities where there were thousands of new kids ready to get down. I think the SOUNDSET shows only ran 5-6 weeks and were eventually shut down due to extreme violence. It could have been the culture clash of suburb kids and inner city kids or it could have just been more club kids coming out. With my own eyes I witnessed First Ave security try to hem up some dudes from my neighborhood. The bouncers were getting handled so bad by the dudes that First Ave just locked the doors and waited for the police to show up. I had been going to First Ave for years and knew their security had a reputation for muscling around young kids but this was the first time I saw First Ave security get fucked up.

At the end of that summer, HEADSPIN Sundays at Bon Appétit started. Bon Appétit was located in Dinkytown by the University of Minnesota campus. My friend, DJ SYRUM, had called me up and asked if I wanted to start throwing a weekly rap show with him at Bon Appétit. He would be the house DJ, I would be the host and do most of the booking, and our guy Detrik Fizer, who was a local graf writer, would draw the flyers and work the door.

We ran 2-5 acts a night from 9pm-midnight every Sunday. HEADSPIN was all-ages and we only charged 2-3 dollars at the door. HEADSPIN popped off something legendary. First off, INTERLOCK had the spot locked down. We were like the new

HEADSHOTS screaming out, "INTERLOCK!" anytime we had the chance like we were gang banging it. If you go to a spot to see a band and half the audience seems to be a part of something together with the band and the music, it makes you wanna know what's cracking and it makes the band seem hella popular. That's what INTERLOCK did for ourselves and almost every other group that played at HEADSPIN.

Outside Bon App, kids of all colors and from all neighborhoods would be on the sidewalk. Rappers would be freestyle cyphering, other people would be smoking herb, and others would just be chilling. Inside in the front room of Bon App was a restaurant and the Sunday special was 2 gyros for $5. The front room would be filled with graf writers showing each other pictures and drawing in each other's sketch books. The booths would have people eating or sitting around pitchers. There was a great social atmosphere.

The show was held in the backroom that had a wooden stage and a shitty sound system. The legal capacity for the whole building was only 79 people but we would squeeze 200+ in the backroom alone on a weekly basis. To make up for the crappy sound system, SKYE immediately became our volunteer soundman and saved us from disasters many-a-night.

Besides the music, the draw to HEADSPIN was that it was all-ages. Not only was it all-ages to get in, but HEADSPIN was also all-ages to drink. Bon Appétit had a beer & wine license, and since the owner was foreign and the place was too packed to regulate ages, minors were drinking all the time. I can remember seeing whole tables of high school kids drinking out of pitchers. The beer gave HEADSPIN that dirty-house-party-feel to it. But it wasn't just kids, we pulled in TRUTH MAZE and the old school heads too. Matter of fact, we pulled in everybody.

I won't give us too much personal credit, though we always did do a good job of flyering, booking, and running the night. But HEADSPIN struck at the right time and place. Dinkytown geographically is between the Southside, Northside, St. Paul, and Northeast and was easy to find right off a few major bus lines. Plus, we got to flyer the last two SOUNDSETs, and once those were over, the city wanted more.

We wanted to go beyond the same circle of acts so we put hella new groups on as well. SIDDIQ SAYERS once called me to tell me I was doing a good job over there and asked where I was finding all the new groups. I told him some people were finding me and dropping off demos at the restaurant and I was searching. I was going to high school talent shows, I was going to other sides of the city and attending every rap show I could looking for new acts. HEADSPIN was responsible for putting mad groups on and exposing groups from other parts of town to each other. UNKNOWN PROPHETS from Northeast, STEREO TYPE CLICK from Eastside St. Paul, BROTHER ALI, CLEVA, BUCK KAC, CMI (ODD JOBS), and many more did some of their first shows at Bon App.

CMI had six rappers and two DJs back then. Six out of the eight were still in high school, so they would bring out a gang of fresh kids. Technically they were young, but energy-wise they were real fresh. All the members would be all over the place and kind of reminded me of the ABSTRACT PACK in their day. HEIRUSPECS, RAW VILLA, KANSER, TWISTED LINGUISTICS, EYEDEA & ABILITIES, the BATTLE CATS, MUSAB, LOS NATIVOS, CONCEPT, DJ MEDEK, TRUTH MAZE, DJ ANDREW, OSP, EXTREME, PEE-WEE DREAD, DJ FRANCISCO, GENE POOL, LEROY SMOKES, OMAUR BLISS, SELF-ISH, CARNAGE, and anybody else you can think of from that time had a legendary set at HEADSPIN.

Lots of different people pitched in too. Every week we would have to call in a favor from somebody: borrowing mics, turn tables, needles, slip mats, DAT players, CD players, etc. DJ SYRUM, who was supposed to be in charge of the equipment, was going through his drug phase in his personal life. I would call this dude around 7:30pm on a Sunday and in a real tired voice he'd answer, "Oh fuck...is it Sunday again? Man Zach, I left my turn tables at the studio," or, "Oh dude, I don't know what time I'll be able to be down there tonight." Luckily, I had this kid who lived a block away from where I was staying at the time named Matt Cavis who had decks and never put up too much of a fight when I would ask him if I could borrow them at the last minute.

Like Los Angeles' underground had the GOODLIFE and Detroit's underground had the Hip Hop shop, and like I'm sure many other cities had their own center of hip hop of that era, we, in the Twin Cities, had HEADSPIN Sundays. What doesn't match up with the other scenes is that HEADSPIN only lasted 42 weeks. But, in less than a year, there was a lot of history made.

DJ EXCALIBUR, who was one of the best DJs in the city but hella hard to drag out the house, did a scratch routine set at HEADSPIN. He totally had about 120 kids' straight attention watching him scratch for almost 20 minutes. BUCK KAC (Greg Buck who hosts Rhymesayers radio) came on-stage when I was standing above EXCALIBUR and told me BIG L had just been killed in New York. He handed me a record of BIG L's newest 12 inch and told me to have the DJ play it. When X-CAL was done and the crowd was clapping I leaned over and told him the demo. I announced on the mic that BIG L had just been killed. Half the crowd was like, "Oh Shit." The other half didn't know who BIG L was. I told them he was a member of DITC, and was down with FAT JOE. Then, I asked if the crowd would be silent and listen to his record. The crowd listened to the first half of the record in a respectful silence. By halfway through the record *Size 'em Up*, the 120 person crowd was bouncing. When X-CAL cut the song everybody in the room put an L in the sky with their fingers and held them up. I hope BIG L saw that from heaven.

Open mics at HEADSPIN were well run. Eventually, EXTREME started helping me host and we always ran a tight ship. I believe TOKI WRIGHT touched the mic on the scene for the first time at HEADSPIN. One Sunday, when the last act finished about ten minutes early, I called rappers one-by-one up to get open in front of maybe 60 people: CRESCENT MOON, SLUG, and VIBES. After maybe the 5th emcee had busted I asked the crowd if there was any girls who wanted the mic.

To my right hand side of the stage a small group of people cleared out to shed light on a pretty white girl with long brown hair, she looked around 23-25. At first, her facial expression was stuck on scared but then it looked like she took a breath, and then stepped towards the stage. I turned to VIBES and asked if she could rap. "She does poetry," he replied. She took the mic and waved toward the DJ and me that she didn't need a beat. We cut the record and she kicked about 16-20 bars kind of half poem/half rap. After she was done all the girls in the crowd started screaming. SLUG quickly got in my ear and said, "Cut it Zach, you won't be able to top that." So I did and we ended the show on that note. That girl's name was DESDAMONA.

To expand on SLUG's statement about ending the show, SKYE and I learned how shows should be run back then. I realized that hip hop as a culture/art form was something I loved and held very sacred, but as a host/promoter/performer I learned that it's not about me or the raw MC who wants to freestyle on the mic all night long. To the average person, hip hop is entertainment. Going to a show for them is an escape from whatever they got going on in the real world. Once someone pays the cover to get in the door, you're working for them and you have to do your best to theatrically make the night fresh.

DJ FU MAN CHU vs. DJ KAY SALAAM was a good HEADSPIN highlight. They had a little beef going on so they came and settled it on the Bon App stage. The crowd gave it to KAY SALAAM but FU MAN had a good highlight getting a cell phone call in the middle of the battle and telling the person on the other end he was chopping some chump up. That battle won KAY SALAAM his props and he went on to move to New York and do some big things.

Later, I talked MU AH DIB into challenging TRUTH MAZE for the states beatbox crown. It wasn't anything personal, it was just for entertainment. All the INTERLOCK members kinda thought MU AH DIB had a chance because he could beatbox jungle music and we didn't think anyone else in the world could beatbox that fast. So we told MU AH DIB to save the jungle music for the end. FELIX hosted the battle and it went two rounds. MU AH DIB, the challenger, went first. Then, TRUTH MAZE EXPLODED with a new GANG STARR beat, The Real, and the crowd finished his line yelling out "HIP HOP!"

The second round came and MU AH slowly built up into a jungle beat, it was done well and the crowd definitely responded. Our dumb asses wondered if TRUTH could respond. We probably thought something ignorant like, "TRUTH is over 30, he don't know what jungle music is." Without flinching, with ten times the stage presence, and with double the volume MU AH DIB had, TRUTH MAZE smashed into this crazy chopped-up dancehall beat. BOOM, BOOM, BOOM, BOOM, and everybody fell out their seats...never doubt TRUTH MAZE.

During HEADSPIN's peak, TRUTH MAZE walked by me one night at the Red Sea and told me, "You know, you're not the first one to hold it down in Dinkytown." "What do you mean?" I asked. "The Varsity Theater on the next block was our spot back in the day." He proceeded to give me a brief break down about the Varsity telling me in the early 90's that's where the MICRANOTS, UVS, SCHOOL OF THOUGHT and FACULTY OF SPEECH came from.

CHAPTER 8 PART 2 : SOUNDSET WEDNESDAYS AND HEADSPIN SUNDAYS (CONTINUED)

When I was in junior high, kids were always talking about DJ DISCO T parties. The way I overheard it, he threw the biggest all-age hip hop parties in the state. I'm pretty sure he even threw a giant party at the Target Center. If you can pack the Target Center just as a local DJ, you must throw a good party. I wasn't hip on who DISCO T was back then. When I got older I heard him spin on KMOJ and I saw him on cable access shows but he was almost a myth to the super backpack underground circle I was a part of, at least until one Sunday night.

I was working the door at the Bon App HEADSPIN Sunday and a cat with glasses and dreads who looked to be in his late 20's or early 30's came through the front. As he headed towards the back I went to charge him but BIG MIKE, who was the Bon App bouncer, waved me off and let dude in with a head nod. I didn't sweat it, but I looked at MIKE for an explanation of who dude was and he was like, "Yo that's DISCO T." I was like, "No way! For real?"

I thought to myself, "That's fresh." We've made enough noise doing our little underground weekly that the most popular DJ in the state came to check out our shit. But DISCO T only walked into the back, looked around for about 20-30 seconds, turned around, and walked out. I was crushed. I thought he must have thought our shit was weak. HEADSPIN had just got a big article in *The City Pages*, a weekly alternative paper. He probably saw the article and came to check the hype but wasn't impressed.

In the middle of the show the following week, the back door of Bon App, which faced the parking lot, opened and DISCO T popped up again. This time with a record bag. He walked across the stage and chilled in the crowd until whatever group was performing finished. As soon as they were done he stepped on-stage and asked DJ MEDEK, who was the house DJ that night, if he could jump on the wheels. MEDEK nodded his head and signaled to me, "Is that DISCO T?" I signaled back that I thought so and to let him go.

DISCO T didn't scratch or do a bunch of fancy tricks; I don't even know if he blended songs. He just smashed-dropped records with perfect timing. When A TRIBE CALLED QUEST's "Award Tour" smashed-dropped into MOBB DEEP's "Shook Ones", a few girls up front started dancing and it was hard as hell to get a HEADSPIN crowd to dance.

DISCO T kept it moving playing quick splashes of songs record into record and the crowd reacted off the energy. EXTREME (who had joined INTERLOCK by now) grabbed the mic and told the crowd that the legendary DISCO T was on the ones and twos live at HEADSPIN. I wished I could time travel back to junior high and tell the girls in my first hour that DISCO T was spinning at one of my shows. He played for 15-20 minutes but in that time must have played 15-20 records. Then he packed up, gave us all a head nod, and left. To this day I don't know what he was thinking. Maybe he just felt like spinning some records that night or maybe he wanted to let us underground heads know he was still the king.

After SESS' death in October of '96, the six remaining members of the ABSTRACT PACK recorded a CD with Milwaukee producer, MR. BILL, *Bouts to Set it for the Record*. The PACK had broke left of HEADSHOTS, and a good portion of the CD was pointed at RSE. With the release of the CD, the PACK disintegrated down to three members who played live and pushed the CD - GLORIOUS L, RASTAR and EKLIPZ. The PACK caught their second wind at HEADSPIN. They played there four times, and hands down, the top three nights that ever happened were because of them. Everybody loved the PACK; black kids, white kids, Mexican kids, Asian kids, Native kids, St. Paul kids, and MPLS kids. They had the support of the older heads like TRUTH MAZE and his crew and also had the new generation of the CMI kids and had a single called "Yeah" that got regular radio play on KMOJ and Radio K. The second breath of the PACK made everybody feel welcome. Suburb kids were coming through, but the hood was still thick. It was the shit.

One of the best memories I have from all my time in hip hop was at the HEAD-SPIN holiday party in December of '98. I was in the back center of the crowd when the PACK performed "Yeah" to a more than packed house. Detrik had hung Christmas lights up all around the room and had drawn a big white banner that said HEADSPIN in fresh/simple to read graf letters that hung behind the PACK on-stage. They had the whole crowd yelling the chorus, "Yeah! Yeah! Yeah!" I looked around as the Christmas lights illuminated the room and it felt like people of all ages and colors were swinging off the ceiling and jumping off the walls. I felt so good to just be apart of it.

BROTHER ALI is the most successful act to come out of HEADSPIN. He did some of his first shows there and he hopped on the open mics whenever he could. He really got on and claimed a spot when he challenged CARNAGE to an MC battle in the top of 1999. I think he thought it out pretty well and it was a strong move.

CARNAGE had more props than ALI at the time and this was right before CARNAGE joined INTERLOCK, so he was the biggest name who wasn't associated with any crew. CARNAGE wasn't INTERLOCK, RSE, UVS, CONCEPT, RAW VILLA, or in the ABSTRACT PACK. If BROTHER ALI would have started conflict with anybody down with one of those crews it might have set off something bigger than ALI could have handled and he would have been outcasted.

Now, this is early '99. We're not talking about the same BROTHER ALI from RHYMESAYERS the world knows now in 2011. We're talking a 20 year-old albino kid who catches the bus down to HEADSPIN every week, most times by himself, who is just trying to find a place to fit in, get on the mic, and earn props. At this point, ALI had probably done less than ten shows in his life, and that would be counting high school talent shows.

ALI left me a message that he had some beef to settle and he wanted to settle it at HEADSPIN. I was all over it. We wrote on the flyer BROTHER ALI vs. CARNAGE like a boxing match. RSE had just done three battles at the 7th Street Entry in the same fashion (I'll talk about that in the next chapter). Those battles were real friendly between people like MUSAB and SLUG. At HEADSPIN, CARNAGE and BROTHER ALI had an actual score to settle. I don't know how the conflict started but it was real...not too serious, but real enough to sell.

The show was gonna be packed so it was easy to promote and hype up. Not only was the crowd huge, but the stage was full too with all the big names wanting to be close to the action. DJ SYRUM, the PACK, and many INTERLOCK members were posted on-stage surrounding ALI and CARNAGE. EXTREME was on-stage with a mic instigating the battle, making it out as if he was on CARNAGE's side and I was on ALI's side. It made it more entertaining so I went along with it. When the battle began ALI set it off.

"You get ran through like toilet paper in a Mexican joint."
"You just rhyme fast to cover up the fact that you ain't saying nothing."

He was also taking shots at CARNAGE's weight.
"That fat shell a gelatin your dwelling in" - BROTHER ALI

The crowd was going bananas off almost every ALI punch line. This battle went down as being mostly one sided with ALI coming out on top. To CARNAGE's credit, he did have some good lines but his style is so fast and complicated that most of the lines went over the crowd's head. I caught a couple of lines but it wasn't until the next day when I watched the video and could hit rewind that I understood what CARNAGE was actually saying.

*"I spit facts and rip raps / I'm about to use your mouth
for my magical dick disappearing act"* - CARNAGE

The battle went two or three rounds with ALI on top, but the crowd got rowdy when we tried to call it a night. They wanted more and the energy started getting hostile. DJ MASHOUT started booing from the front row trying to spark himself in the battle. EXTREME and I tried to calm down the crowd, and in a blink, signs of a fight popped to our left in the center of the packed audience. Two dudes cleared out to make space to throw fists but could barely get space between each other cuz people were so close. Squished like sardines in the back room of the BON, there was no room for error. Detrik, TRUTH MAZE, and myself dove into the crowd, broke the fight up, and got the more hostile one outside. With so little space and so many people surrounded by the adrenaline of an MC battle, if that fight had had two more seconds to pop off the outcome would have been terrible.

As I was out on the sidewalk trying to calm one of the kids down, I believe ALI stayed on-stage, talking to the crowd, and freestyling which helped settle the energy. That's how BROTHER ALI earned his props around here, fair-and-square by the rules of hip hop. And, if you've followed his career since, the rest is history.

9 p.m. is when we would start letting people in at HEADSPIN Sundays. There were always a few stragglers in early. We would get a little rush around 10pm and then put on the first group somewhere between 10:15-10:30. By 10:30 the place would be full. After midnight, Detrik and I would count up our money behind the counter or in the basement. Detrik, SYRUM, and myself would pull $30-$60 apiece each night which doesn't sound like much but it would keep my pockets straight through the week. We would pay DJs and acts $15-$25 a night, which today don't sound like shit but back then people loved us for it.

Nobody was getting paid for shows back then. When you give $20 to a rapper who has never been paid for a show before, he's happy with you. After the shows would be over, lots of us would head over to this Mexican restaurant, Little Tijuana's, that's open till 3 a.m. in South Minni. We would take up a whole section, or sometimes a whole side of the restaurant. I have warm memories from those nights at Little T's. Lots of INTER-LOCK members, DESDAMONA, GENESIS, MICHAELA DAY, Sara (from THE BATTLE CATS), Detrik, and all our friends/local rappers from back then. We would laugh, eat, and talk about life.

I was 20/21 years old and hosting the hottest night in the state. I had the power to help a lot of rappers/DJs who never made it further than HEADSPIN Sundays. Many times on Monday afternoons I would have a message on my answering machine from someone who had performed the night before thanking me for putting them on. That shit was way better than the $30-$60 I got from the show. Plus, that was when INTERLOCK was at it's peak and we held it down hard with new members EXTREME, CARNAGE, and ILLUSION. I felt like we had the dopest crew in the universe.

Sadly, HEADSPIN Sundays started showing me the ugly side of music too; the politics, the gossip, and how cut throat the game can be. This might sound out-the-sky but there was a deep lesson I learned from a sex story back then. In the days of HEAD-SPIN I met a lot a girls; so did all the other dudes who came every week. HEADSPIN on average was about 50% cuties in the crowd, and even though SKYE, Detrik, and myself were more focused on how the show ran, it was a good time to be us. At that time DJ DETOX of CMI had his own crib in the 12th grade in St. Paul off Dale and Selby with lots of drugs, high school girls, liquor, and rap music.

Once upon a time at a DETOX house party on a Saturday night/Sunday morning at 3 a.m., I sat sober waiting to get a ride home when a real hot 22 year-old girl followed by three other girls came over and asked how I was doing. I looked the girl dead in the eyes, and with balls that I didn't know I had, said, "Why don't you and your girls bring me upstairs and all have sex with me." She took two seconds to think, and with more confidence than I had, replied, "Only if you bring your homeboy, SKYE." Before we got down to business, and to make a good story short, SKYE ducked out and a couple of INTERLOCK and BATTLECAT dudes ducked in and we had a small two-hour orgy in the upstairs of DETOX's house. Since there was a party going on downstairs, it wasn't really a secret either.

The rumors that followed that night were larger than life. I learned then that the more popular you are, the more people are interested in your business. I also learned the hard way that you should keep your mouth shut when girls let you do really cool things like that...cuz they're more likely to happen again if you don't get caught yapping about it. But hey, I was only 21, it was a hard thing to keep to myself. All of us were young and just having fun. We didn't know how it would outcast the girls. The next night at HEADSPIN when I saw one of the girls, I said hi and told her I thought that party was fun. She said, "Yeah, that party was really fun."

About two weeks later at Little Tijuana's after HEADSPIN, UNICUS and myself were half-heatedly confronted by DESDAMONA and GENESIS (the two most righteous babes on the hip hop scene). They asked us what really happened and they tore into the girls pretty hard, calling them names, saying that those girls must not have had any respect for themselves. What GENESIS & DES didn't know was that one of the girls who participated was sitting with us at Little T's. She stayed quiet through the discussion but when she gave me a ride home she cried real bad in the car. All the girls from the orgy stopped coming to HEADSPIN. The way the girls' reputations were destroyed while our status doubled was totally fucked up. I have much respect for those girls who weren't afraid to experiment.

Towards the end of HEADSPIN, EKLIPZ called me to check on flyers and make sure everything was good for the ABSTRACT PACK's performance the coming Sunday. I told him everything was in line. He then told me that a writer from THE SOURCE magazine was coming down to HEADSPIN this week to check out the PACK. He told me he was serious and I was like, "Whoa!"

THE SOURCE, the biggest national hip hop magazine in the country was coming to our hip hop night. ATMOSPHERE and BEYOND had previously been featured in the independent section, and LITTLE BUDDY had been just recently mentioned. Now, they were gonna come check out the PACK at HEADSPIN. I only told three people cuz I didn't want it to get out of control; ANT, SKYE and Detrik. Unfortunately by the weeks end...it was out of control.

One of the performers on Sunday's bill was OMAUR BLISS, a good local hippy/poet rapper and a HEADSPIN regular. Through the week I started getting phone calls from groups who wanted me to cut OMAUR and let them play so THE SOURCE could see them. I was like, "Are you serious? Fuck no, OMAUR got his spot." Bon App was over half full by 9:20pm that week. GLORIOUS pointed out to me that people who never came to HEADSPIN were there. Long story short the PACK destroyed it, it was the biggest performance ever, I feel like Minnesota kids gave a lot of love to the PACK that night, maybe even over doing it, to make them appear bigger. They were our hometown heroes and we all wanted something big to happen for them. I spotted the writer for THE SOURCE come in during the PACK's performance, watch about half a song, and go back to the lobby.

Later that week I was in the studio recording a posse cut with CARNAGE and SLUG for ODD JOBS' first CD. When everybody left the room SLUG confronted me asking why I told people that THE SOURCE came to HEADSPIN to see the PACK play. I don't know what was behind his question. I did know whatever was behind it was ugly. SLUG, one of the coolest cats in the music scene, had helped get KANSER our first local press, but even he was susceptible to the dark side along with almost everybody else.

Maybe a month and a half later, THE SOURCE printed an article about Minneapolis hip hop. It talked about the ABSTRACT PACK, RHYMESAYERS, Bon Appétit and LITTLE BUDDY. The Source wrote that LITTLE BUDDY claimed he had locally sold 10,000 copies of his last CD single which...was probably exaggerated (haha) but you can't knock the hustle. In the end, the SOURCE article put an end to HEADSPIN.

During that week, I went to grab a juice from the corner store that was three businesses down from Bon Appétit. I grabbed what I needed and checked the magazine rack. I flipped through the latest issue of the SOURCE and bam; I saw three big pictures taken from HEADSPIN. It was the coolest thing I had ever seen. The lady behind the counter asked what I was reading so I showed her that this national magazine had done an article about our Sunday nights. She was already familiar with our Sundays and told me she had to schedule an extra person to work on Sundays because it had become so busy with the overflow from Bon Appétit. Later that week, the lady at the corner store took the magazine and showed it to the 70 year-old lady who owned most of the buildings on the block, including Bon Appétit.

On what would end up being our last Sunday, we held the after-party to the all-age SLIM SHADY concert that was held at First Ave earlier. We had a packed house, and instead of acts, I hosted an open mic that lasted about a half an hour and featured all the hottest MCs around. I called them up one at a time, announced who they were, and let 'em kill it...and they all killed it. NAES of RAW VILLA, EYEDEA, UNICUS, VIBES, CARNAGE, and SHAWN SKIE who also had the hottest line of the night. He turned to a guy on the side of the stage holding a camera and said, "Let the picture snap." Simultaneously, the flash of the camera lit up the stage and the crowd bugged. While I was on-stage the owner of the building, the 70 year-old white lady, came in and told Samir, the owner of Bon Appétit, that he had "to shut down and get all the niggers and spics out" or she "would take away Samir's lease."

I later watched the security video and it was disgusting. I was a 21 year-old white kid from South Minneapolis, and up to then, I had no real idea what racism was. My dumb ass thought racism was when black kids called me names on the basketball court to psyche me out of my game. I had little idea that people hated other people that much that they would go to that extreme to end or take away something from all of us. I was young and ignorant. *The City Pages* and *The Minnesota Daily* ran articles about what had happened. I was even interviewed by Channel 9 News (though it didn't air). The next Sunday, Bon Appétit closed at 7pm. CARNAGE and I stood outside and told about two hundred people throughout the night what had happened. CARNAGE said it was as sad as if one of his close homeboys had just died. The saddest thing was that since THE SOURCE article had just ran, many people were showing up for the first time. Cars packed full of people that we had never seen before yelled out the window, "Yo, where's Bon Appétit at?" Up until that point it was the saddest day of my life.

"The KANSER TROOP holds it down at Bon Appétit every Sunday." - Rap Pages

"Sundays at Bon Appétit are the hottest nights in Minnesota." - Blaze Magazine

*"It all began a few years back at Bon App / when me and SON
hooked up and started to rap."* - Big Jess (UNKNOWN PROPHETS)

*"I remember HEADSPIN at Bon App/ I used to get nervous when Zach
would grab the mic and ask the crowd where the MCs at."* - P.O.S.

*"Me and ARRON MONEY used to rock HEADSPIN /
been catching rec of the rep ever since."* - Brother Ali

"Headspin Sunday's all-age shows." - New MC (Big Zach)

"I remember SOUNDSET Wednesdays and Headspin at Bon App" - Mike Mictlan

"Bon Appétit / but it too got shut down because of racist views."
- A-Ron (PUREST FORM)

CHAPTER 9 : GOLDEN MIC

During the time when we were running HEADSPIN, a U of M student named DJ AARON MONEY from Wisconsin started the BEATBOX radio show on Radio K. It aired on Saturday afternoons from noon till 2pm and was the major radio outlet of our scene after STRICTLY BUTTER started playing jungle music.

The crew of dudes that I called the "Beatbox Crew" included BROTHER ALI, Nick the Stick, and DJ BK-ONE could be found in the studio every Saturday hanging out having a good time. This is where BROTHER ALI and BK-ONE met.

I didn't like BK-ONE and for the life of me I can't recall why? All I remember is I really didn't like him for what seemed like a long time. Then, one day years later I was talking to him outside of the Cabooze and I thought of him as a good dude and my friend.

Anyways, BK-ONE went on to DJ for BROTHER ALI and later put together and funded a popular compilation album called "Radio Do Canibal" that featured famous rappers such as SCARFACE, MYKA 9 and BLACK THOUGHT over music BENZILLA made by sampling albums BK-ONE had found in Brazil.

Also during the time of HEADSPIN, RSE held the GOLDEN MIC battles at First Avenue's 7th Street Entry. Once a month, two MCs would battle for the golden mic; a spray painted gold mic with a rope attached so it could be worn around the neck of the winner. The winner of the golden mic would return the next month to defend the title. The first month's battle for the golden mic was SLUG vs. MUSAB. Since MUSAB and SLUG were friends, the battle was pretty lighthearted. Because MUSAB and SLUG were the two most popular rappers in the state, there was a good all-age crowd that came to watch and the battle was entertaining and fun. SLUG won and returned the next month to defend the golden mic against BUDAH TYE.

BUDAH TYE, originally from California, is an old school gangster battle rapper from the UVS crew. He's a big dude and likes to hold himself in an intimidating fashion, especially in front of weak rappers.

Right before the battle between SLUG and BUDAH began, ILLUSION and EXTREME were standing next to BUDAH at the bar and asked him if he thought he could get SLUG. ILLUSION told me BUDAH looked at them with a blunt expression and said, "Man, I'm about to serve this kid." About eight minutes later BUDAH had chopped him.

SLUG came with a couple of lines at first saying BUDAH looked like an old bear and that he couldn't give away as many records as SLUG had sold, but as the battle went on BUDAH to my surprise got in SLUG's ass. Finally, after about the 4th round BUDAH said,

"You're only popular because you make white boys feel accepted."

Surprisingly, the crowd, which had to be at least 50% white males, exploded! It was a fresh line and was really on time. I've seen SLUG perform, host, talk, and just chill around town about a billion times and he always plays it cool and holds himself well. This was the only time I ever saw him look awkward. He didn't look that dumb losing the battle. SLUG looked dumb because he wouldn't get off-stage after he just got served. He kept talking on the mic trying to host the show after BUDAH beat him. I was standing by EXTREME and ILLUSION and I could overhear them like, "Damn SLUG, put the mic down." It was awkward (I'll explain more in Chapter 16 when a similar thing happened to me).

BUDAH TYE defended the Golden Mic against EYEDEA at the following challenge. FELIPE of LOS NATIVOS announced BUDAH TYE and big BUDAH stepped on-stage with the golden mic around his neck...it looked pretty dope.

With the 7th St Entry full and with hella BUDAH TYE's homies and RSE members on-stage, they went to war. BUDAH and EYEDEA went back and forth, round for round, blow for blow. As the battle went on, more of the crowd started to side with EYEDEA because BUDAH started to get rough using physical threats.

As I've seen reinforced time and time again, most crowds don't like when a rapper who is obviously harder keeps trying to punk a rapper that doesn't claim to be hard. EYEDEA was a little 16 year-old kid who rapped with a funny voice and punch lines while BUDAH TYE was like the hardest dude in the scene; it didn't balance out. The battle didn't end well with EYEDEA winning and BUDAH's people starting to get upset saying EYEDEA was coming with written raps.

Whether or not EYEDEA was "freestyling" is debatable. EYEDEA was definitely not reciting full pre-written verses; however, he probably did prepare himself for the battle against BUDAH. To be honest I've always done the same thing.

If I know I gotta battle someone on Saturday night I start thinking about it on Thursday or Friday by coming up with lines, caps, or just shit I should use against them.

I don't necessarily write lines down but I store them away in my head and throw them in the battle. But BUDAH TYE's from the old school. He probably didn't premeditate anything about EYEDEA. Matter of fact, he probably didn't put one ounce of thought into the battle until the show.

You can make your own decision about what freestyle battles should really be. Whatever they are, they gotta be entertaining and BUDAH TYE vs. EYEDEA was very entertaining. Even with a little drama, it was definitely worth $5 at the door.

Maybe it was because nobody wanted it with EYEDEA after that or maybe because RSE didn't want to deal with the drama, but that was the last of the Golden Mic battles.

EYEDEA later won SCRIBBLE JAM in Cincinnati, Ohio, the BLAZE BATTLE in Chicago, and then the finals of the BLAZE BATTLE in New York that was shown on HBO. I don't have to describe these battles cuz you can buy the DVDs or see them on YouTube.

EYEDEA was more than the best battle rapper in Minnesota. He was probably the best battle rapper in the world. Punch line after punch line, EYEDEA redefined the sport of tournament MC battles. I would guess that when SESS looked down from heaven he was proud of him.

SLUG, DJ ABILITIES and CRESCENT MOON also did well in SCRIBBLE JAM battles back then. DAYLIGHT and Bridget from THE BATTLE CATS were on the winning breakdance team the same year EYEDEA won as well. DAYLIGHT and ABILITIES have battled and performed all over the country and world really holding it down for the Twin Cities.

CHAPTER 10 :
THERE WAS A PHAT CREW
THAT CHILLED IN THE PAUL

A good amount of this book has been about the ABSTRACT PACK, when I was a kid they were my favorite local rap group, and in St. Paul everybody knew them. Sadly, there are probably less then 1,000 heads from Minnesota that remember the PACK as being legendary like I do. While other groups from their day and after have been able to tour America and other countries, sold thousands of CDs, made tons of fans, and generally, got the most out of hip hop that they could, the PACK, in comparison, have been forgotten. I wish I could re-write history instead of write history but this is what I believe happened.

Right before the death of SESS in 1996, the PACK had a major falling out with SIDDIQ SAYERS. What the falling out was over is not my business to say. What I will say is that the PACK, who had started the HEADSHOTS crew and helped put URBAN ATMOSPHERE and MUSAB on to more popularity in the city, did not become a part of RHYMESAYERS ENTERTAINMENT. After SESS passed away I think they tried to patch things up. RSE released a cassette called *Headshots History*. It featured songs from SESS, the PACK, and other HEADSHOTS' members.

However, soon after the cassette was released, RSE and the PACK, probably for what would seem like dumb reasons now, couldn't work it out. The PACK announced on the STRICTLY BUTTER radio show that they were leaving HEADSHOTS. Live on air, EKLIPZ said, "Yo, don't be coming up to me asking when such and such got a CD coming out. We are not a part of RSE or HEADSHOTS...SHOTS is dead. The PACK came into this alone and we'll go out alone."

In January of '97, RSE held the release party for MUSAB'S first CD, *Comparison*, at 7th Street Entry. A week later, THE PACK held their own show at 7th Street Entry. I was at both shows and they were evenly full of people. But as MUSAB and ATMOSPHERE grew in popularity, the PACK took the next year and a half to reassemble.

Then, in the spring of '98, GLORIOUS L of the ABSTRACT PACK took some small shots at RSE on tapes released by the STEREO TYPE CLICK and by us (KANSER).

*"CLICK OG, PACK OG, HEADSHOTS now
known as RHYMESAYERS OG." - GLORIOUS L*

*"And now you wanna try and dis I love it / When the
PACK made most of you motherfuckers public." - GLORIOUS L*

It was a big mistake for STEREO TYPE CLICK and KANSER (including myself) to let GLORIOUS do that. We should not have put ourselves in the middle.

To make matters more complicated, EYEDEA & ABILITIES, who had joined RSE, were also on STEREO TYPE CLICK's tape. In fact, EYEDEA was on the same song as GLORIOUS on our tape. I don't think they knew any better either. RSE was salty at all of us and ANT was real salty at me; we did later apologize.

SLUG acknowledged GLO's dis in a review of our tape in *The Pulse* magazine, a weekly local Twin Cities paper that SLUG wrote a weekly hip hop column for called *Permanent On Surfaces*. "I got that joke," SLUG wrote in response to the verse.

Soon after in the summer of '98, the PACK released their first and only CD, *Bouts to Set it for the Record*. It was a good CD, but much of the humor and personality that the PACK was known for was missing and replaced with anger towards RSE. It's like the energy of half the record was anger while the PACK weren't angry dudes. I think the beef kinda knocked them out of their square a little. The CD would have been doper if they would have just made one hard dis song and kept the rest of the record fresh with PACK flavor.

*"Whatever happened to our poem saying daughters / Somebody
poured chocolate in the water / Wishing to slaughter" - KNOWLEDGE MC*

"HEADSHOTS is a dead flock so please don't ask me." - RASTAR

*"Built up a small following / Brain octane from
all the high school girls hollering." - RASTAR*

Parts of the record were dope of course. All of them still had skills up the ass and they were still felt. They got a lot of local radio play and the buzz was back. But before things got started, the remaining six members of the pack split apart. RDM's wedding fell on the same day the CD was to be released which caused a major fall out. The remaining three, GLO, EKLIPZ, and RASTAR, didn't give up though and had a good year in '98-99 blowing up local spots like HEADSPIN and getting a lot of local and national press. They even did a handful of shows out of state.

Now everything I just wrote so far in this chapter I remember as fact, but most of what I'll finish with in this chapter is my own opinion.

The PACK was the third most popular rap act in Minnesota in '99 behind ATMO-SPHERE and MUSAB. So, their disses were not unheard, but RSE chose to ignore them for the most part.

"No response nigga, you should have kept it." - MUSAB

First, RSE hurt the PACK by not responding to them, making it appear as if the PACK were kicking at the feet of giants. Second, the PACK killed themselves by not really going for it. If they would have called RSE out to a freestyle battle we could have handled it at HEADSPIN and it would have been so fucking legendary!!! The PACK would have had the chance to really set it for the record. If they didn't want to do it organized, they should have got gangster about it and stepped to the 7th Street Entry and called RSE out at their own show. EYEDEA would not have gotten involved because he came up under SESS and GLO (the beef had nothing to do with him anyways) so RSE would have been without their best weapon. Plus, at least three of the PACK were real heavy freestyle battle rappers.

If GLORIOUS L, KNOWLEDGE MC, and RASTAR would have faced off against SLUG, MUSAB, and FELIPE, it would have been the dopest story told in this book. If I had to guess, the PACK would have won. SLUG would have been able to hold his own but, straight off the head, KNOWLEDGE would have gotten SLUG in front of a neutral audience and RSE knew it. That's why they didn't respond. They had more to lose. But... the PACK really didn't want it with RSE neither.

Beyond the rapper egos, most of them motherfuckers still loved each other. Deep, deep, deep down the PACK was hurt HEADSHOTS didn't work out. Once GLO gave me a big speech about how him and KNOWLEDGE could go stand back to back and eat up all the RSE cats. A matter of days later, SLUG called me and told me to tell the PACK if they really want it they can come get it. Days after that I saw GLO, EKLIPZ, and SLUG all run into each other downtown and start laughing and hug each other. Shit, KNOWLEDGE and MUSAB were cousins.

"If we can't do it together / We'll do it apart / Ain't no way we'll ever make it like it was in the start." - SLUG

After HEADSPIN ended in May of '99, RSE was left with basic control of Min-nesota. They got all the opening gigs for national artists at First Avenue which exposed them to thousands of rap fans who hadn't checked out the local vibe yet. On top of that, the local music press, which was made up of mostly white rock & roll coffee shop type cats, were all over SLUG's dick. Here was a rapper they finally could relate to, who spoke their language, and did not make them feel slightly threatened.

Papers like *The City Pages* and *The Pulse* wrote articles about RSE every week. Every time SLUG took a shit...they covered how long it took him. Plus, when other rappers would get write-ups they would either be compared to RSE or RSE would be name dropped so other rappers would be overshadowed even in their own articles.

That is how it appeared to many of us at the time but what SLUG later told me no one knew how hard he was working it. He said he was going out every night hanging at bars buying drinks and trying to make friends with local writers. Through working at The Electric Fetus record store, he watched how rock band members did it and he learned how to speak the language that the writers spoke, which no other rap kid spoke. I didn't speak it. My first interviews with *The City Pages* were tough. They would ask me questions about hip hop and I would answer them with slang and cuss-words. The interviewer would have a tough time understanding me. The ABSTRACT PACK did not speak the language either.

Ego aside, ATMOSPHERE and MUSAB were better than the rest of us (us being all the other local rappers). And, with ANT banging beats out the basement at a rapid fire rate, they made more songs and better songs faster than everyone else. They had the talent and they worked hard so they deserved to get more attention than the rest of us. The PACK had the best live show. Even down to three members, their high energy pure B-boy hip hop live performance was the best in the state in the opinion of hip hop heads. But, SLUG/ATMOSPHERE crossed over better to other crowds.

There is obviously something very special about SLUG that the whole world soon caught on to. The saddest thing about HEADSHOT's breaking up is that the ABSTRACT PACK was some of the first people to notice there was something special about SLUG and believe in him, which in turn, helped him believe in himself. The PACK was young, as dumb as the rest of us , and probably should have just waited their turn and everything would have worked out.

By about 2000-2001, the three remaining members of the PACK couldn't hold on anymore. I can only guess that they must have felt jealous in RSE's shadow, on top of how hard it must have been to make such a big comeback after the death of SESS, that they couldn't take living here anymore. RASTAR moved to Seattle and EKLIPZ and GLO moved to Los Angeles. Maybe they felt they could get something started out there like the MICRANOTS did in Atlanta. Or, maybe they just had to take a different step in their personal lives. In the end, they had to do what they had to do.

In retrospect, it's a shame that the PACK had more going for themselves here than they could be recognized for at the time. RSE was packing almost 1,000 kids into First Ave, but the PACK at this time could still draw maybe 250+ kids to a spot with the right promotion and their crowd was more diverse and more inner city. It might have been hard for the PACK to see the value of what they had.

Right before they left town, GLO played for me and SKYE what would have been the PACK's second record, *The Brail Method*, which just featured the remaining three. It was real dope. I only heard it once but the beats were better than the last CD and the song concepts were better. Sadly though, the real ABSTRACT PACK album was never made and will never be heard, because SESS passed away so there was never a full album made that featured all seven of them.

What I learned from the conflict between RSE and the ABSTRACT PACK was beyond rap. Anything that you try and do in life usually is a long road. Even though some drive by you in faster cars, in the end of your life the race is only against yourself. I guess the race between the PACK and RSE was so deeply personal that when RSE pulled ahead the PACK had to just let go.

"In my home town we got a silent battle / To see who can get up on the map first." – RASTAR

I think the end of the PACK hurt Minnesota. To put it as simple as I can, black kids/non-white kids rarely came to local shows in large numbers from about '99-'02, quite simply because the majority of popular local rappers and DJs were white. My beliefs may be getting old but the PACK represented what I considered real B-boy hip hop, and I'm truly thankful that I was exposed to them.

I was a HEADSHOTS fan. When I was a teenager they were the tightest crew around and their shows were real fun to go to. I've spent over two decades submersed in hip hop, and in that time, I've seen it change into a lot of different things. Some changes I find to be almost abominations of what it was. But when URBAN ATMOSPHERE, MUSAB, PHULL CIRCLE, FELIPE, the HEADSHOTS BREAKERS and the ABSTRACT PACK were all together, that's what I truly think hip hop was suppose to be. That's when it felt real. As a fan, I wish they had done it together.

"As SHOTS run the block with multi-record releases / I believe this / in my mind I've engraved it." – KNOWLEDGE MC

- MSP did a few shows through the years, always did a good job, and released some music on an indie St. Paul label, Gladiator Records.

- RDM took a while off but had a resurgence around 2002. I began to think his style had developed so far it was going over people's heads. Maybe you have to be a rapper to understand how dope he is.

- SESS has a younger cousin BDF. You can find him rhyming around town and on mix tapes. BDF even won a $1,000 MC battle hosted by TALIB KWELI in 2004.

- KNOWLEDGE became a Christian rapper and released *BOOK OF KNOWLEDGE* in 2006

"Pockets I'm depending on you son / To pull your family through / And I could give a damn what you got to do / You can get to jacking or even selling pearly yay / But you gotta get that loot today / I won't be here tomorrow and the rent was due yesterday"
- SESS

CHAPTER 11:
SHORTKUT THE IDIOTIC

The most unique person I ever met in my whole life was a little rapper dude named SHORTKUT. KUT was maybe a year younger or older than me. He was a short skinny black kid with a "DEL the FUNKY HOMOSAPIEN" piercing through his lip as well as an overall look to him.

KUT stuck out as a little character around town. Before I knew KUT I would see him rapping at battles and open mics. He opened for BLACK MOON at the 2nd Mic Check Showcase. He was down with the CONCEPT crew and most of the other 5%ers. My street smarts used to tell me to stay away from KUT. Something about him from a distance seemed sketchy. But I caught myself kicking it with dude just because we were at a lot of the same places at the same time.

KUT was mad talented. He rapped with the style of LIL WAYNE back in the 90's, wrote good songs, sang, and played the guitar. I used to tease him and say, "Shorty black sings the blues."

KUT had two kids and a baby's mom somewhere in like St. Louis or Kansas City. He was spiritual but struggled with his own demons, intaking any drug you put in front of him. I don't need to make a list cuz I mean ANY drug. He told me he was a Five Percenter but felt he got better results when he prayed to Jesus Christ. I think he struggled with beliefs even more than most of us do, but a few different times KUT was there for me to give me God's words when I needed it.

SHORTKUT was gay.... not gay like he fucked dudes (not that there would be anything wrong with it if he had) but gay like he used to paint his finger nails and wear purple scarves and lots of other weird shit. Not that that makes him gay. I mean, PRINCE is the hardest dude in Minnesota and he wears that shit. But KUT was...you know...gay.

On a hot summer night back in 1999, I was sprawled out in my bed in just my boxers. It was so hot in my room I wasn't even using a sheet. In the dream I was having, something started to tickle my nose. It tickled 'til I woke up and saw that my light was on and SHORTKUT was in my house and in my room...rubbing my nose. Now let me paint the picture again, I came home by myself and crashed out. Now I just woke up spread eagle in just my boxers and my gay friend is rubbing my nose. I know it sounds weird but when I asked what he was doing he said, "Shhhhhh," in a whisper. "Zach, I met this girl at a party a few blocks away. I didn't have anywhere else to bring her so I broke in your apartment through the window. Do you got a condom? I'm trying to fuck her on your couch."

I wasn't awake enough to be weirded out so I got up, grabbed him a rubber out of my closet, and let him go to work. Most times KUT's crazy antics were overshadowed by the pure entertainment of it all. Though, sometimes he would get out of control and his friends would get fed up with him.

There are a thousand stories I could write about SHORTKUT's nut ball behavior, but the most outrageous thing I can think of happened purely by accident and isn't entirely funny. It's more like a scene out of a Quentin Tarantino flick.

My home girl, Calla, came by my apartment one morning to talk about a problem. Calla summed her dilemma up in a simple yet complicated phrase. "Zach, I'm in love with a gay guy." We laughed. I knew she had to be talking about KUT. "You're still fucking SHORTKUT?" I said. "Don't you still have a boyfriend, Calla?" She was confused and told me she was gonna tell her boyfriend about KUT. I didn't have much advice for her.

DJ SYRUM and most of his band, LEROY SMOKES, stayed at this house on Garfield and 24th. We called it the Smokes' house and it was a regular party drug house. Four of my guys who were "jackers"...or better put..."people that rob people"... jacked the Smokes' house one night around 4 in the morning. Armed with guns and ski masks, they were looking for dough or dope I guess. Whatever they were looking for, to get it they snatched up everyone in the house and tied them up with duck tape. As this was happening, SHORTKUT, of all people, was stomping through Uptown drunk.

Coming from God knows where, he had the bright idea to stop by the Smokes' house, figuring someone might still be up and he could use their phone, crash there, or get into some more drugs. He peeked through the window to look for signs of life at 4am and saw 4 figures walking around the house with masks on. He thought, "That's cool. They're still up and they're playing ninjas. I should bust in and surprise 'em."

With four human beings tied up, bleeding, and scared for their lives on the living room floor, and four masked robbers with guns searching the house, SHORTKUT busted in the door and said, "Hey, why y'all playing ninjas?"

As the masked men flinched and turned their guns on KUT, he assessed the true situation and said, "Wrong place wrong time, huh?" To make it worse, one of the men pulled off his mask and it was Calla's boyfriend.

"Oh shit I already owe this dude one," he said. Calla, unfortunately for KUT, had just told him about her affair. KUT got pistol whipped a little, but instead of killing anyone the robbers let KUT go, finished up, and broke out.

The Smokes' house roommates could only hear voices since they were face down and recognized KUTS voice. So for months after that they were under the impression that he was involved in the robbery. Only SHORTKUT would have something like that happen to him. Since I knew all the parties involved I think I was the only one to get the whole story from all angles.

The last I ever heard from KUT, he sent me a letter from a mental institution in Wisconsin. He said that he had found God and that rap lyrics were of the devil. He told me to tell UNICUS and TRY-D. I used to make jokes that KUT would end up being the type of dude downtown saying, "Yo, you got a dollar, I'm trying to get me a sandwich." I hope that's not true. SHORTKUT was my friend.

CHAPTER 12 :
INTERLOCK AND THE INTERNET

"WU TANG is really what hip hop is," ANT said to me as I stood in his basement surrounded by like 10 million dusty records. I asked him to break it down. "They make ghetto New York rap music. That's where all this shit really came from," he continued. MUSAB sat on the couch while UNICUS and MESH were standing behind me. I think we were trying to pick out a beat to make a KANSER song. I know at least that's what UNICUS and MESH wanted to do, so they stayed quiet. My dumb ass was feeding into the argument MUSAB and ANT were trying to have with me.

The argument really had nothing to do with me, though. They were venting the state of underground rap and I was the closest punching bag in reach. "I consider myself a gangster rapper," MUSAB said. "ATMOSPHERE's audience isn't my audience."

As MUSAB said these things I could tell he had been waiting and wanting to say them to a person like me for a hot second. I was a white underground "backpack" rap kid and it was 1998. I would guess that MUSAB and his music had started to be criticized by the new breed of rap kid on the internet. Sometimes those kids are and were referred to as "backpackers". They are obviously just dumb labels but I don't think "backpacker" and "internet rap fan" are or were the same thing.

When I was in 10th grade my boy Justin Cunningham, who was one of the smartest dudes I ever met and later sadly ended up doing some prison time with my little brother, explained to me that he didn't like hip hop. I didn't understand cuz I knew he had ICE CUBE in his walkman at the time. He broke it down to me that gangster rap and hip hop weren't the same thing. Hip hop was breakdancing, KRS-ONE, AFRIKA BAMBAATAA, FAB 5 FREDDY, etc. He said he didn't really vibe on all the sound and the culture around it. He was more of a street dude who liked hardcore raps that reflected what he went through.

To try and label something that was just too big to understand, I think I, along with a million other kids, separated hip hop from gangster rap, and both from commercial rap. At that time, West Coast gangster rap out-sold East Coast hip hop considerably, so many East Coast rappers started to separate themselves as well.

"I represent the hip hop and not the rap y'all." – BUSH BABIES

"Rap is something you do / Hip hop is something you live" – KRS ONE

"Unplug it on chumps with the gangster babble / Leave your 9's at home and bring your skills to the battle." – JERU THE DAMAGER

New York hip hop invented rap, but the rest of the country that didn't grow up immersed in the hip hop culture probably found West Coast gangster rap easier to understand and more entertaining, being filled with more sex and violence. For example, compare KRS ONE's popularity with TOO SHORT's. Both are legends. If you know almost anything about rap music you know what these two have done. They both came out in the 80's and have both put out more than 10+ albums. KRS ONE's lyrics have always dealt with social issues, political issues, battle raps, and spoke of hip hop almost as a religion. On the other hand, TOO SHORT, through his long career, has talked about many things but specialized in "freaky tail" sex stories.

KRS ONE styles his delivery, using complicated metaphors and a large vocabulary, while TOO SHORT keeps his lyrics real simple to understand, funny, entertaining, and, a lot of the time, heavy on the cuss words. Both are equally great at what they do.

I'm sure TOO SHORT has sold a lot more records than KRS ONE, but that's obvious. What sells better, pro-black political literature or porn?

ANT also used TOO SHORT to explain to me the type of rap we (KANSER) did and who listens to it. In 1998, the majority of songs we recorded in ANT's basement were full of battle raps, metaphors, and big word play. You know...hip hop stuff. The crowds we were performing for at the time were into it. Our crowds were all about the underground, backpack, breakdance, and graffiti hip hop movement. "To know what we were even talking about you had to already be into the movement and have an ear for it," ANT explained. But everyone can understand TOO SHORT. He raps about girls and hustling. Even dudes like us (KANSER) hustled in our own way selling drugs here and there or even hustling our tapes.

The end of the 90's was a good time in hip hop for me. Though I had only started to make a little money here and there off it, living was far more about just being a B-boy, throwing shows, kicking it with my crew, and being us. The end of the 90's was the period in time where I felt like KANSER and INTERLOCK were in the now. We were young and just purely loved the shit outta hip hop and hadn't seen the ugly side of music yet. I don't think the original INTERLOCK crew ever did what we could have done; but, for a hot second, we were fresh.

I'm going to break down the original INTERLOCK crew. Not because our contributions to the scene were that important, but because the members of INTERLOCK are a great representation of the different kinds of kids into hip hop in the late 90's and the problems we went through represent the problems that many crews go through. The following is about the INTERLOCK crew but it is also about HEADSHOTS, UVS, and lots of other crews. Even though they faced the same problems, I feel more comfortable airing out our dirty laundry than theirs.

From the jump, there were major differences with members of our crew. First was the major difference between how heads felt about RSE (whose world we put ourselves in). FELIX and SKYE were RSE haters along with all their St. Paul FAMILY WORKS homies. They used to hate and clown on RSE bad. I think partly they were joking and partly they were loyal to the ABSTRACT PACK, being St. Paul Central alumni themselves. But while they hated, most members of CMI were kinda on RSE's dick.

They were the younger members, all of them 16-19 (DJ ANTON, DJ ELUSIVE, and BOOKA B were their age but didn't hate or jock for the most part). MESH, ILLUSION, EXTREME, UNICUS, TRY-D, CARNAGE, CONSENTR8, all 23-26, and myself, 20, were pretty good friends with RSE members at the time. Where our mistake and/or lack of wisdom fell, being a little older we should have tried to teach the younger members not to hate and not to put anybody on a pedestal. But we weren't very smart. FELIX, SKYE, and members of CMI had stronger personalities making them hard to reach. One of the biggest mistakes I ever made is that I should have never crewed up with dudes who were misrepresenting me. When you're in a crew with someone, you represent each other. FELIX said a lot of things back then I did not agree with.

Before we could even get to level two, we were hit with the most classic of all cracks in the foundation of bands or crews...a girl who tries to date more than one member of the crew. DJ DETOX, who was still in high school but a front member of CMI, had an older girlfriend who had him, like most older girls who date boys that are still in high school, sprung. I first caught wind of the girl less than three months after INTERLOCK formed. NOAH B, MU AH DIB, FELIX, the HEIRUSPECS band, and myself played a two-day outdoor rave in Somewhere-in-the-Middle-of-Nowhere, Minnesota. After we performed, I ran into this little raver girl named Rachel I knew. She was plugged into the network and got NOAH B and myself shrooms and acid. I had never taken acid before. What a better place to start than a two-day outdoor rave with three tents banging out techno music in the middle of nowhere, right?

I was so fucking high. I bought a hot dog and couldn't figure out how to get it in my mouth. I straight up forgot how to eat. NOAH B had dropped acid before so he kinda helped me through it. I had eaten shrooms like twenty times before but if tripping was compared to music...shrooms are like soft jazz and acid is like loud death metal.

Tripping that night staring at the stars on a grassy hill, I realized how weird TWISTED LINGUISTICS were... (haha) ... They're my guys but they be on some old outer space science fiction shit. MU AH DIB told me the whole story of the book *Dune* while I was tripping on the hill. He presented it to me like he was telling me stories from the Bible. I was in to Star Wars and read comic books as a kid, so I could keep up with these dudes and I had a good time.

Towards the end of the trip, NOAH brought up INTERLOCK and told me how MU AH DIB and himself had always kinda been nerds and theater kids through high school and now, all of the sudden, they were thrown into INTERLOCK and had instant popularity. He said it was weird for them being invited to parties now and being at shows where they were part of the crew. As I was tripping on what NOAH was saying he started to slip in that he had been dating this girl that DJ DETOX was somewhat in love with. Muted by the drugs I don't think I fully took in what he was trying to tell me. I should have been more on top of the situation. Even though I didn't get on top of the girl sabotaging INTERLOCK, I did learn a valuable lesson that morning: Raver girls who have been up all night on speed do not look good in the morning!!! When that sun comes up... oh shit...it's like their faces start to melt off.

Soon after that night NOAH B was kind of faded out of INTERLOCK. It's a basic rule that you don't fuck with another homie's girl in the crew. NOAH was probably in the wrong but the girl involved wasn't in the right. Plus, it even got worse with her.

The following New Years Eve '98-'99 most of the crew was at a party on 24th and Garfield in Uptown where DJ SYRUM lived and was spinning. The party was jumping and INTERLOCK kids were kicking it. About four members, who I'll leave nameless, were upstairs in the attic smoking herb or whatever when a cute white chick came up the stairs. She appeared to be about 21-22 and might have looked familiar from shows but no one actually knew who she was. Basically, without much exaggeration, she offered to give blowjobs to members of INTERLOCK. Being that it was New Years Eve, it wasn't that far-fetched and hey...why not!?

After she got some fat INTERLOCK splash in her mouth, she stood up, thanked everybody for their time, and kept it moving. As she was walking down the stairs SKYE was coming up the stairs. She said hi to SKYE so we figured that they knew each other. Somebody asked SKYE who she was. SKYE said, "Oh...that's DETOX's girlfriend."

Everybody fell out their seats simultaneously. No way we thought. The same chick that had the drama with NOAH? The homies didn't even believe SKYE. They had to go downstairs and see it for themselves. Sure enough, in the middle of a packed, smokey, noisy New Years Eve bash, there was DETOX and the same girl cuddled up on a couch.

My intentions in telling this story are not to clown DETOX or NOAH. Truthfully, I think it points out one of my young weaknesses. I learned that a true leader would have not let these events happen. A true leader would have stepped up and said something. But not SKYE, MESH, EXTREME, or myself did anything. We were half in shock and half thought it was funny. And that's why our crew was weak.

MESH still lived at 2523 14th Ave S at this time and we had huge parties over there. HEIRUSPECS, DJ DUZ IT, KANSER, the BATTLECATS, and the ABSTRACT PACK all performed in the living room with every hip hop kid from the metro area there spread out between the front yard, backyard, basement, first, and second floor. MESH and I were pretty popular party throwers on the Southside to begin with, but after INTERLOCK formed and our social circle expanded, it got nuts. There were high school kids from all over the metro, South, Southwest, North, St. Paul Central, Highland, and Roseville along with hella college kids, hella twenty-somethings, and even a few 30+ people that were around the rap shows back then.

There were a lot of wild times with the INTERLOCK crew. Lots of parties, late nights, girls, and shows. We used to bang that shit at shows. If HEIRUSPECS was performing, the rest of us would be all through the audience yelling "INTERLOCK!" every time we got a chance. We totally bit that from HEADSHOTS.

In the summer of 1999, KANSER and myself funded a compilation CD featuring all the members of INTERLOCK called *Volume One* (I don't know why we didn't think of a more original name). We all combined forces to throw a release party at the Red Sea on the West Bank; one all-age show and one 21+ show. It was a long day but we got the job done.

The show was CARNAGE, CONSENTR8, CMI, EXTREME, ILLUSION, JAMEEL SKI, TRY-D, KANSER, hosted by FELIX, and ran by SKYE. We about half packed each show and it was a good time. SKYE even booked DJ KING IXL to headline. IXL was known for being the best trick DJ in the state, but he had a reputation for rarely coming out to do shows. That was the first time I ever walked out of a show with over $1,000 in my pocket.

This girl I used to fuck with asked me to cover her while she peed behind the back of the bar because the line for the bathroom was so long. After she took a tinkle she stood up and asked me how the show was going. I told her to touch the big bulge that was coming out of my right pocket. She asked what it was. I said, "It's all 20's girl."

That might have been the worst line I ever threw at a female...ever. It didn't even impress her. She just laughed at me. But, it was still cool making that much dough at one show. We spent about three stacks to record and duplicate the CD. Combined with the release party and street sales we made it back in less than a week and sold a thousand copies of the CD that year (to us, back then, selling 1,000 copies was like bling bling!!!).

The day after the release party I got a phone call from EXTREME. He called me to tell me we did a good job the night before and I believe he called every other member of INTERLOCK telling them the same thing. EXTREME was older and more experienced than the rest of us and at different times he showed real maturity. If things had fallen different he should have been a leader and we should have done way bigger things.

The span of cultural differences between INTERLOCK members was very broad which was probably both our biggest strength and greatest weakness. For example, ILLUSION was a black dude from the Northside in his mid 20's who already had kids and TWINKIE JIGGLES was a white 17 year-old high school senior who lived on Summit Ave in St. Paul. I was right in the middle. Since I was the only one who got along with everybody and I was the one who funded our first CD, I think heads looked to me like I was suppose to lead while I was looking to SKYE who was trying to organize INTERLOCK into some sort of independent record label but had less of an idea of what to do than I did. It was really the blind leading the blind.

I was a young dumb Southside rap kid who wasn't smart enough to lead. The only vision I might have had was imitating RSE or the LIVING LEGENDS, plus I'm a real slow learner. I used to look back at early mistakes I made with the KANSER TROOP and INTERLOCK and wish I could have seen a bigger picture. Later on in life I realized the universe was preparing me for the future when different opportunities would come.

SKYE ROSSI's INTERLOCK label failed. It was run pretty poorly without real motivation behind it, but, the original INTERLOCK "crew" had some hot times. The one thing that did separate KANSER/INTERLOCK from all the groups that were smaller than us was that we knew how to promote shows, we knew how to flyer, and we knew how to throw good parties and have a good time, which drew a lot of people to us. We had our time, I guess just as UVS and HEADSHOTS had theirs. I would guess that UVS and HEADSHOTS went through similar dramas and circumstances.

I referred to myself as a backpacker earlier in the chapter. Backpack rap and backpack rapper have become sideways terms to try and label and belittle a type of kid who's into hip hop. The term has become real distorted in my opinion. Wearing a stuffed backpack properly over both shoulders was a small fashion trend for hip hop heads from maybe '92-99. I used to watch rappers like METHOD MAN and BUCKSHOT wear them on television in the early 90's and it stretched to the late 90's with the underground Lyricist Lounge artwork in New York. I don't know where it originated from. It might have came off the graffiti tip cuz we would use backpacks to carry spray paint cans around when we were younger.

My little homie Denny used to rock a backpack to carry pounds of weed around. It was an easy disguise for spray paint or drugs because the average person who sees a young person with a backpack over both shoulders just thinks "student" and don't give it a second thought. The first kids who I originally saw wear packs on a hip hop vibe were on some inner city flavor/real shit, CONCEPTS, KANSER TROOP, and lots of graf writers. But today, I hear the term "backpacker" used as a putdown. I think it's spoken with a bit of ignorance and is actually trying to refer to "internet rap kids". Kids who came from wealthier families and were less exposed to hip hop in person. But, in the late 90's and beyond, these kids dominated hip hop websites and message boards with hate and sarcasm making fun of hip hop more than trying to progress it. Somehow they got labeled as "backpackers" by rappers who were on some more street, less skill shit.

"We were straight backpacking" - EMINEM

NOMI of CMI/ODD JOBS became one of my best friends during '98-'01. He was more than a year younger than me, but from the first time we met (at an INTERLOCK meeting) I knew he had an old soul.

NOMI was a Phillipino kid who grew up in Midway St. Paul. He had come up under and around the St. Paul crowd like SESS, ST PAUL SLIM, EYEDEA, FELIX, DJ DUZ IT and many more. We were very much alike. We both knew a lot of different people. We both liked to party, do drugs, smash girls, and have a good time. We both searched for truth and struggled to understand and respect hip hop and rap as black music, and yet found popularity and pieces of our identity in a scene that was mostly white and sometimes felt like it was separating itself back then. Better put, we were both equally influenced by SLUG as we were by TRUTHMAZE. We used to stay up all night talking about life, gossiping, arguing, talking shit, trying to figure things out.

Also like me, NOMI wasn't born with a lot of natural talent for rapping but chased it hard enough till he mastered his craft. NOMI eventually became a great rapper and might be one of the most underrated rappers mentioned in the book.

NOMI and I were once at a party that got shot up. As bullets rained through the windows and everybody hit the ground, I got so scared I ran into the bathroom and hid in the bathtub.

NOMI's girlfriend at the time was a spoken word poet named MICHAELA DAY. She was a super awesome real pretty black girl who also came out of St. Paul Central. I used to, and still do, love to tell stories and MICHAELA and NOMI told me I was a griot. I asked what that meant and they said it was another word for storyteller but spiritually it was much deeper and that I would figure it out when I got older. I will speak on that later in the book.

ADVIZER was the first "internet rap kid", if you will, that I ever met and got to know. He was also the first rich white/Jewish rapper I ever knew who wasn't trying to pretend he was something he wasn't. ADVIZER was from Southwest Minneapolis (not that far from Edina and a pretty well-to-do part of town). I believe his dad was like a brain surgeon or something (I might be exaggerating that but I think he was a doctor and they were pretty well-off).

ADVIZER was a cool kid. I met him when he was still in the 11th grade. We hung around a little before he was in INTERLOCK. He was a real smart, A+ average type kid. I was older and had more street smarts, but when I was around dude I used to think his brain was firing a lot faster than mine. He stuttered a bit but I didn't know if he had a speech impediment or if his mind was just thinking faster than he could speak. What I liked most about AD was he didn't pretend to be from the hood. He wasn't a rich white kid who listened to 2PAC and tried to imitate the image. He rapped about what was real to him. To compensate for his lack of life experience, voice, and...somewhat lack of rhythm, he wrote incredibly clever rhymes filled with good metaphors and well thought sarcasm. I would bet ADVIZER spent more time on his rhymes than anyone else in INTERLOCK, or at least spent more time on his writing and less time drinking and partying than the rest of us.

ADVIZER, like the rest of CMI/ODD JOBS, sounded like SLUG. But, they were the first of a whole generation of kids who sounded like SLUG to me. SLUG was their favorite rapper, and in a way, it was cool that younger rappers were being influenced by local rappers instead of biting a rapper from one of the coasts. As soon as I met ADVIZER and his guy CRESCENT MOON, I got them in the studio to record. That might sound cooler than it was cuz all I did was bring them down to MESH's basement and have them make a song on his 4-track.

"Zach taught me how to count my bars / now
I teach MC's how to count the stars" - ADVIZER

ADVIZER was the first person who showed me the internet. He ordered tapes and CDs from online underground distributors so he always had dubs of new shit before anyone else did. He showed me where you could buy our tapes online through ATAK. He put me up on EMINEM about a year before the "My Names Is..." music video came out on MTV.

The only negative about him was I used to think ADVIZER and other internet kids would get caught up on things that weren't real. After we started selling the INTERLOCK *Volume One* CD, I heard from ADVIZER and CRESCENT MOON that it had got a really bad review online. I took that as an online magazine that reviewed hip hop had put it down and a lot of people saw the review. I could tell they both took it to heart and it really affected their outlook on INTERLOCK and the CD. I came to find out about three months later through SKYE showing me on the internet that it wasn't a review. It was a post put up by a screen name by someone somewhere who could have been joking, hating, or posting their personal opinion. I would never let a kid behind a screen name talk me out of what I felt about my own shit. Back then I didn't even know how to log on to the internet and even today I don't let it phase my game one bit.

Not pointing the finger at my guy ADVIZER, but other kids (mostly rich and white) in his position who took some sort of hip hop expert purist role I feel were responsible for the split in hip hop that took place in the late 90's and 2000. It was like they took groups like FREESTYLE FELLOWSHIP and LATYRX and put them at this god-like level and tried to lift their nose on any rapper that spoke about the streets because they couldn't relate to it. In turn, more thugged out rappers or rap kids who pretended to be thugs tried to belittle internet kids and label them backpackers. It appeared to be some sort of weird racial issue and that is what ANT and MUSAB were venting about on me in ANT's basement that night.

By age 24, I got myself an email address and figured out how to get online. Then, when Myspace.com came out, I realized how easy it is to meet girls and book shows online and I have stayed plugged in ever since.

"INTERLOCK is coming / Go and tell the neighbors" – CRESCENT MOON

*"They'd call me a backpacker / but they were
just mad that I had my mac mastered"* – SLUG

Back in those days I met a good amount of kids who worshipped groups like QUANTUM and FREESTYLE FELLOWSHIP and at the same time were real anti-gangster rappers. What always struck me sideways was if you listen to FREESTYLE FELLOWSHIP their music seems to be real inner city. Their styles were abstract and artistic but their content was definitely real. And, BLACKALICIOUS from QUANTUM made a song called "Murder, Murder, Murder, Kill, Kill, Kill" which captures everything I'm trying to say.

Fun fact: ADVIZER and DESSA from DOOMTREE both graduated from Southwest High School in 1999 and DESSA beat out ADVIZER for valedictorian by 0.1 of a grade point average or some close shit like that.

CHAPTER 13 PART 1:
I BE I AM

Some of this chapter is writing from my perspective when I was a 20/21 year-old kid. The rest of it is writing from my perspective as a 33 year-old man. In the first 12 chapters of this writing, I have tried to document events in Minnesota hip hop and its effects on me. This chapter will be more about me, events in my life, and how I grew up in Minnesota hip hop. I hope I don't make myself sound too important (haha).

I was kind of a coward as a kid. Coming from a violent, drug filled household kinda made me a little weird. My father didn't teach me much about being a man or how to stand up for myself. He couldn't teach me how to fight because he didn't know how. The only people he ever beat up were women and children.

When my mom moved me to the Cities in the 4th grade, there was an older kid that lived across the street from me named Eddie. Eddie was a black kid about four years older than me who was always getting into trouble gang banging and shit. Eddie was one of my first friends in MPLS. He was on house arrest when I was in grade school, but since we lived across the street he was allowed to come over and watch videos with us. Basically my little brothers and I were just some little dudes but since our mom stole cable, our house was the coolest spot for Eddie to be since he was on house arrest.

Eddie made attempts to toughen me up without success. Him and his friends would bring me in the backyard or the park and be like, "We're gonna make you hard, Zach." They would set me up to fight a kid who was older and double my size and offer me ten bucks if I at least fought back. I would just always bitch out, get punched a couple times, start tearing up, and then Eddie would bring me to the store and buy me a pop or something. The last time Eddie tried to teach me how to fight I failed; he looked at me real disappointed. Of course it wasn't until I got older when I realized if Eddie and his friends really wanted to hurt me it would have been easy. They were actually trying to do me a favor.

I guess since I was failing so bad God had to step my training up...so God sent me to Sanford Middle School. I don't know what it's like now but when I was young it was the worst junior high on the Southside. It's actually located in a middle class neighborhood, but because Ann Sullivan, the junior high in Seward, wasn't open yet and Anderson Open, the junior high in Phillips neighborhood, bussed in kids through the open program, Sanford was real bad. I saw fights almost everyday; on the bus, in class-rooms, on the playgrounds, and in the lunch rooms. It was mainy.

I got punked a lot, mostly by one kid in particular. To make a long story short I had a bully in the 7th grade. He bullied me most of the year until about a month before the end of 7th grade...I beat 'em up. Really all that happened was he took a swing at me, I ducked, and then I jumped on him and started wailing away in front of a full class room. I don't even think I hurt him much physically but I killed his reputation. I was sent to the office, and in front of the principle, I broke out crying. Crying real bad...like a 4 year-old who skinned his knee. The principle was so freaked out he left the office and I could hear him in the next room say, "Do we got the right kid? The slip says he beat another kid up but he won't stop crying."

In retrospect, I knew what was happening. I was crying the bitch out of me. I feel like I came a step closer to being a man that day. I never let anyone punk me like that ever again after that. Matter of fact, the only times I feel like I've been punked since the 7th grade have been because of music politics.

The next lesson I had on the road to becoming a man was when I was in the 9th grade. This big Mexican kid named Gato, who was one of my best friends at the time, beat it into me that you never run when your homies are getting beat up. Gato used to tell me, "I don't care if your boys being jumped by 30 dudes. If he gets beat up then you get beat up." He used to tell me, "If you ever run on me, I'll beat your ass so you might as well get beat up with me cuz you'll just get beat up later." I took it as kinda the rules and I think most other kids who grew up around me had the same principles.

In 1999, when I was 21, I went through a new set of lessons. At 21, I thought I was like the most popular kid in the Twin Cities, and I probably wasn't too far off. But I learned that the definition of popular does not define the number of people who have your back. From about 17- 21, I had been immersed within the local hip hop scene and caught up in high school like politics and popularity. I had hella fun. I met hella new people and got invited to a lot of parties.

I was a big figure in the little world of local hip hop that was becoming more suburban by the day. It was RSE's world, and I did my best to act as funny style as I had to to fit in with it. I first realized how fake I was being when in 1999 three of my good homies were arrested for murder. The details of what they did don't matter. The way it relates to my own personal life and the story happened like this.

I was at my crib on the phone while my friend Iris told me the story, or as many details as she knew at the time. Hearing the news that people you care about are most likely going to be imprisoned for many years is intense. It feels slightly like news of death. In one way, not as bad, and in another way, a lot worse. When murder is the case, your 99% sure your people will be gone a long time. I was mad they got caught and mad at them for doing it. I was trying to take it all in at once but it was an intense sad moment for me.

During this phone call I got a click on the other line. I shouldn't have answered it but I thought it could be more info. It just happened that it was EYEDEA. He and SID-DIQ were calling to get BROTHER ALI's number. I quickly caught myself trying to snap into funny style Zach mode but it wasn't as easy as usual. I stuttered a bit and just asked if they could call me back later and clicked back. 60 seconds later EYEDEA called again saying, "Yo, just give us the number." I wanted to snap on this dude so hard and redirect the anger of losing my friends. I was friends with EYEDEA but he didn't know who I really was.

I couldn't begin to tell this dude what I was going through at the moment. All these dudes ever did was act funny style so I always acted funny style around these dudes so I could get shows or get them to do shows for me. EYEDEA had nothing to do with it really. He just represented the happy hippity hop scene. In emotional depth I got up and dug for ALI's number and realized my own personal issues about the situation.

There was a local rap crew back then that we used to call the "HATERS". They were a group of WU TANG wannabe rappers who used to come to shows and boo or heckle whoever was on-stage. They were a big problem for all of us who were trying to throw shows or perform because they were always disrupting events. They were so fucking incredibly wack it was beyond imagination. I think if you really put these dudes through therapy you could write a paper about how hip hop can make some people real delusional.

My first and second run in with them came in defense of EYEDEA. Once at a café on Nicollet where EYEDEA was performing and the second was at the Red Sea where MUSAB was performing. Both times a member of the HATERS tried getting in EYEDEA's face or threatening him as I came to his defense. At the Red Sea show, one of the HATERS started booing MUSAB during his set so MUSAB let him come on-stage and started chopping him up. But, as soon as the HATER started getting chopped up, more HATERS jumped on-stage and totally disrupted RHYMESAYERS' show. I had a few run-ins with the HATERS at HEADSPIN Sundays too.

During one of EXTREME's sets, they tried to boo him off-stage. What made them such haters is that they wouldn't boo a rapper who was wack and who in some points of view would deserve it. They would start booing a rapper who was ripping the mic and had the crowd going, totally disrupting a show out of jealousy. Never in any of the HATERS lives had they set it off like EXTREME was setting it off when they started booing him. I used to wonder what was going on in their heads. I think they totally perceived situations way sideways from what was actually happening.

One of the HATERS tried to slap BOOKA B at HEADSPIN and BOOKA B is one of the most mellow cool cats around. I jumped off-stage to get BOOKA some space and the HATER just walked away talking shit. ILLUSION had a couple bad run ins with these dudes where they would try to start fights with him because he was Muslim, but ILLUSION, who was 6 foot 3 inches and 250, wasn't the one to pick on. I saw ILLUSION come to SIDDIQ SAYERS defense at The Whole on the University of Minnesota campus. The HATERS tried to confront SIDDIQ as if their careers were being sabotaged. To this day I can't fathom these dude's logic. I feel dumb for even giving them this much attention in this book.

The last time they ever came to HEADSPIN was during a performance by O.S.P. O.S.P. was a big rapper from over North. He had that East Coast feel to him and he was part of the spoken word/rap scene spearheaded by TRUTH MAZE. O.S.P. was a pretty dope rapper and he always did a good job every time I booked him. He'd show up on time, do a good set, and take care of business.

On this night at Bon App, O.S.P. called up other rappers at the end of his set that he was down with and had a freestyle session to close out the night. Whenever you rip a good set you can call your crew on-stage for a freestyle (I don't think that will ever get old). Anyways, it's like 11:56pm and the owner of Bon App usually wanted us to shut the music down by midnight.

So, SKYE tells me to go back and turn the light on after the next rapper and he'll shut the sound off. I fade to the back and look towards the stage. One of the HATERS is on-stage with O.S.P. and his crew. I think to myself, O.S.P. must be down with those dudes. The next thing I know, O.S.P. turns to the little HATER and starts dissing him saying that he wasn't invited up to freestyle and he ain't shit.

As soon as O.S.P. drops his last line, SKYE turns the sound off which doubles the sound of the crowd ooh'ing that the HATER just got dissed. I turned the lights on and the show ended on that note. It was pretty dope actually but that was when the HATERS marked me as an enemy. When we were trying to pack up that night, they stuck around trying to argue with us. I don't know what their point was, but I could tell then I was eventually gonna have to fight these dudes.

It was either the last weeks of '99 or the first weeks of 2000 that I slid up to First Ave real early to check out an RSE night. The night was just getting started so there were probably less than 40 people in the club that holds over 1700. I had noticed that a couple of the HATERS were there chilling back by the bar. I made a mental note that they were there but didn't put any more thought into it. Maybe ten minutes later, TRY-D comes up on me upstairs and tells me one of those HATERS just took his hat...like on some old junior high shit. He had a brand new Yankees fitted or something and I guess they just came up to TRY and took it off his head and said they were keeping it.

TRY-D by himself would get punked but I knew he would fight with me if it came down to it. I led TRY downstairs, walked up on the two HATERS, looked them both in the face, asked TRY if that was his hat, took the hat back, handed it to TRY, and then walked away. I think it stunned the HATERS for a hot minute that I had the gall to just take TRY's hat back.

They had a delusional idea that people were afraid of them. After about a 45 second delay in his small brain, one of the HATERS, who looked like a cracked out little Chris Rock, comes up on me as if he wanted to fight over TRY's hat. I was like whatever; I had been waiting for the chance to slap this little dude up. I put down the box of CDs that I was always slanging at the time and went to square up with dude.

As it caught people's attention around us, suddenly SLUG jumps in the middle and started yelling at me as if he was gonna have me thrown out of First Ave. I always thought of SLUG as my friend and he knew the HATERS were always starting trouble. In my defense I tried to tell him they had stole TRY's hat but he wasn't even listening to me. It's not hard to tell what SLUG was doing; he didn't want a fight to break out at his show and he was scared to say shit to the HATER. Well, maybe not scared, but it would have been more of a scene if he would have engaged them. I understand he was protecting his show, but that's not an excuse to front on me, especially in public. I broke out the spot with TRY-D behind me.

On the way to the bus stop I remembered that when I was 18 I was at a party where a handful of dudes were trying to jump SLUG's younger brother Nate and I jumped in to defend him. There was a gun pulled and I still had Nate's back. Now if SLUG didn't have mine like that, fuck um.

To their credit, the UNKNOWN PROPHETS were standing around the incident at First Ave and were trying to stick up for us.

Maybe a month or so after that I popped into a short-lived club downtown called Liquid. I had come there with my home girl France, two of her friends, and a few drinks already in me. It was a typical local rap night, DJ ABILITIES was on the wheels and it was all smiles, handshakes, and hugs from all the Roseville BATTLE CAT members and everyone else around the scene at that time. With some straight money in my pocket I took a couple shots at the bar and then proceeded to do one of the dumbest moves ever recorded in my personal history. I saw a couple HATERS (not the same two from First Ave) and stepped to them by myself.

I think my drunk mind thought we were gonna fight anyway, so I thought if I stepped to them first I would have had a better chance of getting a one-on-one fight or I could possibly buy them some drinks and have the beef squashed at least for that night. But that was totally not the case.

When I tried to talk to the biggest one he was just like, "na," and tried to brush me off. Not only they did they not wanna talk but they weren't trying to even deal with me. They would have totally given me a pass that night, which was what I should have taken being that I came to the club with girls and didn't have any back up. But, my dumb drunk ass forced the issue with them. From what I can remember, it went like this: I told a dude who was at least 6 foot 8 that I wasn't scared of him, he stuck me in the mouth, I splashed some of my drink in his face, his boy clocked me from the side, and then club security broke it up. I had a little bit of blood on my lip but their blows didn't phase me at all...probably cuz I was so numb from being drunk.

I went outside to fight the big one, but he didn't wanna fight me outside which didn't make sense to me. I figured that even though he was a lot bigger than me, win or lose, we were going to get the beef over with.

I went back in the club and saw through the front window that there were five of them now. The big one was just waiting for his crew to assemble so they could jump me. Before I could think of a way out of the situation, one of the workers at the club came to me and told me I had to leave since I was in the fight. That's when I followed up the dumbest move I ever made with one of the more stronger moves I ever made as a man.

In the two seconds I had to assess the situation, I realized I could dip out the door and start running (I would either shake them or they might not chase me at all through downtown on a Friday night), I could try to beg the club to let me hide inside, or I could go outside and fight five dudes. The first two options seemed too cowardly, and though the third wasn't particularly intelligent, I had to do what I had to do. I put my Corona bottle in my cargo pocket, walked outside and posted up on the wall in front of the club.

Surrounded by people from the club and others who were just walking by, the HATERS took about 30 seconds to decide which one was gonna set it off. Then, the five of them jumped me. I did pretty good considering it was 5 on 1. I think I threw a couple blows and I protected my head well. I can remember some of it like it was slow motion. I remember wondering where DJ ABILITIES, BROTHER ALI, and all the Roseville BATTLECAT members were and wondering why they weren't helping me. I saw some of their faces...their eyes were wide open frozen.

When they got me to the ground I just tried to protect my head and play dead. At the bottom of the pile being stomped out was a way more clear peaceful moment than I thought it would be. I could think pretty clear. I thought, "As soon as they back off, spring up and bust the first one you see in the face with the Corona bottle." And that's what I did. I heard a loud reaction from all the downtown spectators right after the bottle exploded on my enemies face followed by a loud and clear thought in my head, "Now I'm only fighting four dudes".

Security broke it up and dragged me back in the club to safety. I have a vague memory of Wes, the editor of *LIFE SUCKS DIE* magazine, with his shirt off outside the club being punched by one of the HATERS which always made me think he fought with me. That surprised me cuz he wasn't the type of dude I would have guessed would've... thanks Wes.

I got jumped and beat up. Nothing too bad; just a black eye and a couple scratches. The next morning I realized I deserved it. When I was younger I jumped a few dudes with my friends, trying to be hard. I could rationalize jumping people at the time but I truly couldn't justify it. It was in my karma and I was thankful that my karma wasn't worse. Being jumped at that club in 2000 turned out to be one of the most beneficial things in my development as a person. Not the fight itself but what followed and what I took from it.

First, DESDAMONA came, picked me up, and brought me to the hospital the next day so I could get a check up and make sure I was fine. That put her in a whole new light to me and I've had mad love for her ever since (even after her and UNICUS broke up...haha). Second, my dumb ass read a book. At 22, I didn't know how to read that well. I was literate of course, but had never read a book with chapters, so the night after I got jumped for some reason I decided to start a book. It was a science fiction book called *Earth Abides* and it took my slow ass forever to finish it, but when I did I felt as if I had taught myself how to read or at least comprehend what I read. Third, I redefined friendship to myself. The night after I was jumped I got a message on my machine from BROTHER ALI. He said that his wife and him had been worried about me all day and they were calling to see if I was alright. Then when I walked into work on Tuesday, one of the BATTLE CATS was standing there waiting for me. I wasn't quite sure how to interact with someone who just watched me get jumped four days before and just stood there. I just gave him a head nod and went to punch in for work.

The BATTLE CAT kid's name was Justin and he asked if he could speak with me. He said he had been waiting there for like a half an hour for me to start work. He had come to apologize for not helping me on Friday. He said he had been feeling ashamed of himself. Then he looked at me pretty square and told me he had never been in a fight before. I told him it was all good. For the next eight hours at work I thought a grip about the fight and the scene. ALI's message and Justin's apology both seemed sincere but I was still kinda salty that none of them helped me on the pure fact that I would have fought for them if the situation had been reversed.

About an hour before close, I got a call at work. It was Adam, a homie I grew up with. He told me that they were having a party over South and that I had to come through. I told him I wouldn't get outta work 'till like 2:30 in the morning. He said they would still be kicking it and he kinda pressed the issue and told me to write down the address. A party that would still be popping at 3am on a Tuesday? Adam and I didn't even kick it like that anymore. But since he was kind of insistent, I caught a cab over there after work.

When I stepped in the spot I saw a handful of cats I had grown up with. About four dudes sat me down and told me that they showed up at club Liquid about 10 minutes after I left. They said everyone was saying Zach from KANSER just got jumped. My boy SHIZ was hot, he was like if we had got there like 10 minutes earlier we would have stomped them dudes out. My guy big Philly kept using the phrase, "We been knowing you for too long, Zach." They were already on top of everything. They knew that the dudes who jumped me were gonna be at this café on Lyndale and 29th this Thursday for this open mic thing. SHIZ and big Philly were like, "Let's roll up there like 10 deep on Thursday and fuck them dudes up." I told 'em that it was mad love that they were down for me like that but that I was just gonna let it go.

I had some karma coming and actually didn't get beat up too bad. Adam then asked me who helped me when I got jumped. I told him everyone just stood there and looked scared but I thought Wes from *LIFE SUCKS DIE* might have jumped in. SHIZ said, "Zach, I was just talking about you the other day. I said I got mad love for Zach but he always be around people that don't really care about him." Then Adam told me, "Yo, those hip hop kids that be around shows, they probably respect you...but they don't love you."

That statement, "Those hip hop kids that be around shows, they might respect you...but they don't love you," was the answer I was looking for. It summed up that SLUG, ALI, Justin, and most average kids that came around the shows back then might be real good people, but they weren't like me. Or better put...I wasn't like them. The principles, beliefs, and overall way of thinking we had weren't the same.

On the ride home that night I kinda felt ashamed of myself. Ashamed that I had stopped hanging out with some of the kids I grew up with. The kids who had my back the hardest. I stopped hanging out with them at times to try and get away from the bullshit and keep myself out of trouble.

For a long while afterwards, I didn't feel safe around kids that I wasn't sure had my back. In time I've learned that people are people. You can meet someone that comes from a way different place than you and still connect with them. What I mainly took away from the situation is that there are some people you just see around and small talk with, chop it up, tell some jokes, and whatever. To a degree, they're your friends depending on how you define friends. Other people love you and are down to ride for whatever. What was harder for me to figure out was that just because someone won't fight for you does not mean they don't care about you. I would guess 9 out of 10 people totally freeze up when they see violence. I would also guess 6 out of 10 men would tell you otherwise until it comes down to it.

I'm not a good fighter and I'm not physically hard, but I can look myself in the mirror same as I can proclaim it in this book: I have heart and I have proved it many more times in my life than the stories in this book.

The members of INTERLOCK, in their own way, had my back too. In the next week, they all stopped by the crib to check up on me. One of FELIX's guys, Edger, had a real man-to-man talk with me about it. He told me to let it go and it didn't sound out of fear. He said, "Just on the strength of you being FELIX's guy, I'll go fight them dudes with you if you want, but what will it really solve? Them dudes are gonna be them dudes." I had to take my karma, be glad that some of my bad karma was off my shoulders, learn the lesson in front of me, and keep moving forward.

"If you're under 25 and you never had to ride for your crew you probably ain't got heart / but if you're over 26 and your still in the mix chances are you ain't doing your part." - KRS ONE

I was handing out flyers in front of the Red Sea on the West Bank when a couple members of RAW VILLA came up on me. It was right after I had been jumped. They ran up on me so fast I flinched back. NAES, who was about three inches taller than me, grabbed me almost in a bear hug and said, "Boy, don't you ever flinch on me. If anybody fucks with you, I got you." About a week later RAW VILLA beat up the dudes who beat me up. Not because of me, but because they had their own issues with them. RAW VILLA has heart.

My further separation from RSE's world came when RSE put up a message board on their website. The gossip and weird things I had to hear about when that was up really got out of hand and so many rap kids I knew fed into it. Luckily for me I never lived in a house that had a working computer, so I didn't know anything about the internet.

As the gossip grew, I couldn't even have paid attention if I wanted to. Around 2001, I had started to feel good about a lot of things. Kinda like I re-found myself. KAN-SER was at a bit of a low point. I feel the music we were making at that time might have been our weakest ever. We were barley getting out of town and our local shows weren't popping like they used to. This ran parallel with RSE opening the record store Fifth Element and starting to blow up, and after my altercation at First Ave we probably felt awkward around those dudes. But as my band was at a low, I was personally doing okay, had a little job, was rolling with some tight friends, and had a little confidence that, in turn, brought a few girls around.

A little prior to this time I had started to hear rumors about SIDDIQ SAYERS, the owner of RSE, talking shit about me. I heard it from many different people, none of which being him. I heard he was saying weird things like, "We don't got love for Zach anymore. He's in hip hop for the money."

These rumors really came outta the blue and I didn't understand them because I hadn't had a fall out with SIDDIQ or ever seen real money off rap. All I believed I ever was to SIDDIQ was a young dude who handed out flyers and brought people to their shows. Just a few years earlier I might have been their biggest supporter.

In the midst of this, I was at the bank in Uptown, depositing my check or some shit, when I saw SIDDIQ SAYERS. I was curious to see if we would speak so I left it on him. When he noticed me he did a double take and said, "Hey, what's up?" I said, "Nothing what's up with you." He just shrugged his shoulders and that was that. I didn't put a lot of thought into it, but I did make a mental note that we were all good. As a man, if I have a problem with someone, I will either bring the problem up when I see the person or the problem is at a level where I won't speak to the person at all.

About a week after, RSE had a big show at First Ave. I wasn't there, but something major happened between TRUTH MAZE and BROTHER ALI. Something to the extent of TRUTH MAZE and his crew jumped on-stage while ALI was hosting and brought beef to him in the form of a battle. I wish I could document this story but I wasn't there and the hearsay is all over the place. I also can't truly document what happened next because I still at this point had never logged onto a message board. What I was told from SKYE, MESH, and NOMI was that people were posting about the incident between ALI and TRUTH MAZE on the RSE message board and somehow we (INTERLOCK) were brought into it.

SIDDIQ wrote more than one long post talking tall shit about INTERLOCK, KANSER, and myself. At first, I was like, "Nah, y'all are feeding into that internet shit. I just saw SIDDIQ at the bank. He said what's up to me. He ain't got no problem with us and why would he?" NOMI and MESH were like, "No, its real. He told us we couldn't sell INTERLOCK CDs at First Ave anymore." I was told second hand that SLUG was posting things about us also. I tried to speak to ANT about the situation but he knew less about the internet than I did so he didn't even understand what I was trying to tell him.

"We do what we want / Set up shop / Sell our shit" - ILLUSION

Over the next week, that beef dominated my life. With access to the message board, all types of kids around town and on the bus asked me about it. I just denied I knew anything about it. I didn't want to talk shit about a person I had only heard had talked shit about me. But, with the message board, if he did say it, he said it to like a thousand kids.

UNICUS called SIDDIQ and tried to talk it out. SIDDIQ told him they could meet up on Saturday and talk. SIDDIQ didn't show up. SIDDIQ not showing up made me hella angry....hella angry. NOMI and MESH tried to calm me down by saying they could try and defuse the situation by posting on the message board. I was like, "What the fuck are you talking about? Defuse it on a message board, I'm smashing that dude in the face with a hammer."

NOMI and the rest of ODD JOBS were real freaked out about it. KANSER for the most part had put ODD JOBS on locally, but they looked up to RSE a lot. ODD JOBS felt I endangered their careers which put me in a very weird place. To this day (2011) I love the shit out of members of ODD JOBS, but I definitely learned then that you should never be in a crew with anyone that doesn't have your back. ODD JOBS should have had my back but they were young and put in a very strange situation.

TWINKIE from HEIRUSPECS was freaked out about SIDDIQ's post also feeling they might have traced back to FELIX talking shit, but TWINKIE, as soft as he is (haha), was a good friend to me through it. TWINKIE knew I had done nothing wrong, but understood to survive we were going to have to get punked a little.

Crazy and ironically, I ran into SIDDIQ that very Saturday night on the West Bank. I was with TWINKIE while he was being interviewed on KFAI 91.3 FM when the DJ announced that SIDDIQ and DJ ABILITIES would be on next with the BREAK A DAWN RHYMESAYERS RADIO. In my head I was like, "This feels right. We can get this over with." I figured SIDDIQ would come in and either talk it out with me or ask me to go downstairs and fight him. Either way, I was good for whatever.

When SIDDIQ stepped in the room it was the first time I had seen him since I saw him at the bank two weeks before. I was sure he was gonna let me know what was cracking. But, when he came in, he didn't make eye contact with me. We were in this tiny room so, making it pretty obvious, I stared at SIDDIQ for about three minutes as the other people in the room exchanged conversation. He just kept his head down and tried his best to pretend I wasn't there. Since there was five or six other people in the small studio room I didn't feel as if I could confront him there so I just left with TWINKIE.

I went outside via downstairs and called MESH to see what was popping for the night and MESH proceeded to tell me that SIDDIQ just posted another long shit talking message about us on the message board. I said when did he post it. MESH said 7:30pm. I said I just saw dude two minutes ago and he didn't even have the balls to look at me.

Seven hours after he stood UNICUS/KANSER up to talk out whatever problem he had with us and less than three hours before he came face to face with me and was too scared to look me in the face, SIDDIQ SAYERS hid behind his computer and talked a gang of shit about us for all the RSE fans to read. That is exactly how that day went, I did not add or subtract or exaggerate anything. In my 30+ years on earth that is by far the biggest display of being a bitch I've ever come across.

I knew then I wasn't dealing with a 7th grade bully, I was dealing with a dude who had an agenda. I was being bullied by someone who had more power than I did because he was more popular than I was. It was a weird, unique, and complex situation that not many people could relate to.

A few months after, in 2001, a 17 year-old kid named Ben walked into the record store, Fifth Element, to buy some fat caps so he could tag on shit. SLUG was working and tried to push his new CD on him. Ben didn't want to buy it and probably said something that hurt SLUG's feelings, "You used to make music for the Southside. Now you make music for the suburbs." SLUG then asked Ben what local rap he liked. "KANSER," Ben told him. Somehow the conversation got heated and Ben challenged SLUG to a fight. When Ben grabbed his belt buckle to pull up his pants, SLUG thought he saw a gun and got spooked. Then, Ben left.

That story was told to me by my friend Ben ten years later when he was 27 years old and living in California. After the kid left the store, SLUG posted on the RSE message board. He posted an apology to KANSER for anything he had done to us. Then the next day, SLUG came to speak to me and SHIZ. He told us that a KANSER fan came into Fifth Element and threatened him with a gun telling him to stop talking shit about KANSER and, at least publicly, they did. For over ten years, people have asked me if I really sent a kid into Fifth Element with a gun. These stories are all I know about that day.

I don't have to document much more of ATMOSPHERE or RSE's very successful career because it has been documented by other people. It has slightly haunted me for the past ten years that I let myself get punked publicly by them, but the principles that guide this music game are not the same rules that guide street shit or other parts of life. As RSE/ATMOSPHERE's career exploded, KANSER was basically blacklisted and did not play a show with them for ten years (1998-08). It was hard to stay afloat without major access to exposure, but we found small outlets for our music such as the Dinkytowner Café and proceeded to help as many young artists as possible. My career isn't much to brag about, but in 2011, I am the most successful hip hop artist ever out of Minnesota who did not have help from RSE, and for my own reasons, I am proud of that.

SLUG

Before finishing this book in 2011, I contacted SLUG to advance him the first draft. I offered to take the negative parts of this chapter out because they might overshadow the other stories that are much more important. But I wanted him to read it to understand how I felt more than ten years back. He read the entire book overnight and asked if I could meet with him to talk. I have known SLUG half my life, but our meeting that lasted 3 hours and 49 minutes was by far the best time I ever had with him. We talked about old friends, rappers, graf writers and how things have changed.

As popular as he has gotten, SLUG has not forgotten where he came from and had lots and lots of opinions about my book since it was documenting some of our history. There are newer younger rappers from our state that are finding big success who, without disrespect, could probably care less who SESS was. They might look at my book like meaningless old ghost stories. But SLUG took the time to read it.

Overall, I don't think SLUG liked my book (haha). He, being six years older than me, claimed he had always tried to play a parental role with me, and in his opinion, sometimes I listened and sometimes I didn't. Earlier in this chapter I told the story of how SLUG and I fell out when he yelled at me for getting into a fight at First Ave. His side of that story was he didn't care if anyone else involved got thrown out of First Ave, but he considered me to be a bigger part of everything that was being built and he was trying to stop me from getting banned from First Ave. Whether that was true in the moment or just the way he chooses to remember I'll never know, but I'll accept it as truth.

What I learned from the issues SIDDIQ and SLUG had with me was that you have to be as mature as possible when it comes to interacting with younger kids in the scene. Not to say you can't party with them, rage out, and have fun, but you should always rise above gossip, shit talking, and negativity that they are susceptible to being sucked into. I believe SLUG and SIDDIQ fed into gossiping about kids who were as much as ten years younger than themselves.

My main issue with SLUG and SIDDIQ was that I needed them to be my big homies that they initially were from 1996-1999. But after that, I was traveling this world without a map as far as this rap shit was concerned. Luckily, around that time ANT stepped up to be almost like a father figure to me.

ANT

Saying that ANT has been a father figure to me is simple. I haven't seen my real dad since I was in my mid-20's. ANT has been my older homie who likes to talk about girls, sports, and rap music. That's all I ever needed in an adult male role model. He has also been there for me when I have needed advice and when I have been in a crunch for money.

The most inspiring thing about ANT is that he didn't find success in music until later in life. In the early '90's, local rappers were starving to find beats and production. Only a few local producers existed and they were trying to charge big bucks for studio time. But ANT, free of charge, invested his time and energy into producing and developing rappers...a lot of time and energy.

When ANT was 19, he faced major prison time for auto theft. But he took a plea bargain and was put on probation for 20 years. He moved to Minnesota and got a job at McDonald's where he was employee-of-the-month one month and fired for stealing the next. After that, ANT became a janitor where he worked through his late 20's. The minute the clock struck midnight on ANT's 30th birthday, he was cleaning a toilet. Though there is nothing wrong with being a janitor, ANT told me it was a surreal moment in his life.

In the ten years that followed that moment, ANT became one of the biggest underground rap producers in the world. Along with producing records for BROTHER ALI and ATMOSPHERE, he became ATMOSPHERE's tour DJ, which brought him all around the world. Every time he gets home from tour, he has a stack of adventures that he shares with me. He has gotten to live more in his 30's than most people do in their lifetime. So if you're a pile of shit as a teenager or a dude working a dead-end job at 30, ANT is living proof that hard work can pay off.

SIDDIQ SAYERS/STRESS

SIDDIQ SAYERS is not my favorite person in the world. I'm a Southside welfare baby from a broken home who's been on my own since I was in high school. All I've ever really had in my life is rapping and hip hop. When I was a teenager, I was happy to do my best to try and help the movement he was building and I did learn from him. But when I was 20-21 years old and he was 30+, for whatever reason, it felt like he tried to take hip hop away from me. For that reason, I truly dislike him.

It pains me to give him any credit in this book...but...fuck...it pains me to type this...but SIDDIQ SAYERS is probably the most important person in Minnesota hip hop. After I type these words I will go buy myself something to eat. The money I used to buy food will be money I made from rapping. There is a good chance that I made that money off rapping because of the trickle-down effect from ATMOSPHERE and RSE's success.

In 2008, SLUG's younger brother Jordan Daily invited KANSER to perform at SOUNDSET 08's side stage. Twice during that day, SIDDIQ came over to me and thanked me for playing. It was the first time we had spoke in almost ten years. It felt ok to exchange good energy with him, but it hurt a dream that I had held onto for ten years. I had always looked forward to the day when rap was behind us and I could kick the living piss out of him...I had really looked forward to that.

What might have been SIDDIQ's issue with me is he was given the role of a "soul-seller". I don't mean I saw him sign a contract with Lucifer or some shit like that. I mean he created a business out of what we all created from our souls. The music or art that we create does not exist in this world before we create it. I believe the only logical place that it comes from is from our souls.

Most people who paint, draw, play music, dance, or do anything else creative that comes from their soul never asks anyone to pay for it. They do it for themselves. I have been selling my soul since I was 17 years old. The first time someone paid the $2 cover to come into the first show I charged to get into at a café in South Minneapolis and paid to hear me rap, I was selling my soul or, maybe easier understood, selling myself. I do not fear selling my soul for the soul can provide as much inspiration in its' existence as the sun's energy can provide light.

As SIDDIQ was chosen as a soul-seller, I was chosen as a griot along with a few other duties. My agreement with the creator was to sell my soul for food and shelter. Therefore, it was hard for me for many years to understand how to make real money off music, given the understanding that money does not exist.

SIDDIQ probably never understood me...or maybe he just wanted me to do more shows for him for free in the early years. The best story I can think of in my better interactions with SIDDIQ was in May of 1997 when I was throwing a show at the Riverside Café.

The crowd had started to show up but we couldn't get anything out of the in-house sound system. The café employee, DJ MEDEK, and myself were stuck. We had no music, no idea what was wrong, and the show was already suppose to start. SIDDIQ came in and asked me what was up. I told him we couldn't get the sound to work. He looked at our set up for about ten seconds and then turned to me. He said, "Go get me a pencil with an eraser." I didn't even ask why, I just did it. About a minute after I gave it to him we had sound and SIDDIQ played sound man the rest of the night. I asked DJ MEDEK what he did and MEDEK looked at me and said, "I have no idea!?"

CHAPTER 13 PART 2:
I BE I AM (CONTINUED)

Once you've been to one college hip hop convention, you've pretty much been to them all. They have workshops dealing with political issues in hip hop, panels, and speakers that are usually followed by a hot concert where the college money brings in some national acts. People who throw these events truly believe in hip hop as a movement and a way to save the world. I applaud their efforts because when I was younger I thought like that too.

The first hip hop convention I went to was at the University of Wisconsin-Madison in spring of 2000. The theme was women in hip hop. It was fresh. There were performances by BAHAMADIA, MEDUSA, CUTTING CANDY, and INVINCIBLE. Seeing women who could rock the stage like that was pretty estrogen awesome, and the panel discussions held my short attention span with a tight grip. During one of the discussions, one of the women on the panel told the audience that we should make the effort to tell any kids/teenagers we knew who liked rap where hip hop came from. At that point they weren't telling it on MTV so they had to hear it from somewhere.

When I returned home to Minneapolis I called my little sister who was in the 9th grade and asked her if we could hang out one day that week. I made plans to meet her after school and we would go get something to eat. I brought her to a Thai spot over on Southside. We sat down, ordered some pad thai mock duck (my favorite food in the whole universe) and I asked her what her favorite type of music was. She said she liked all types of music but mainly rap. I already knew that and had a fully-prepared speech to give her about the origins of hip hop; GRAND MASTER FLASH, AFRIKA BAMBAATTAA and the ZULU NATION, New York, the Bronx, turn tables, break dancing, everything. I was ready to school my little sister on where rap music really came from and how the radio rap she listened to was just an exploited version. Blah blah blah...I was ready.

I started by asking her where she thought rap and hip hop came from. The question took her off guard and she took a second to think. Her eyes on her young face moved around showing the silent movement in her mind. Then, as if she made a final decision on which answer to use she looked at me with a small bit of uncertainty in her voice and answered, "Africa right? Hip hop's from Africa."

I was stuck for a hot second. Her answer seemed ten times deeper and truer than what my answer was. I scrambled to pick my thoughts back up and still went through with telling her the whole routine. But mostly, I was blown away by her answer.

I started to see hip hop different after that. I listened to all the music that I had recorded and was currently selling and realized how weak I was. I rhymed words but I didn't speak. I started to pay more attention to local poets like TRUTH MAZE and FRANK SENTWALI (EDUPO), two older emcees who had mastered their flow and turned it into spoken word poetry. They didn't babble. They said statements in their rhymes.

I started working on my craft day and night. Working with my odd voice and my weird Southside slang filled accent. I felt like I was 16 again rapping to myself in my bedroom constantly.

I studied different religions and read books about reading peoples energies and how energy moves through the world. MESH gave me his favorite book, *The Celestine Prophecy*, which changed my life (the movie sucked ass though). It felt like I was re-membering instead of reading. I was learning more than ever before, learning more about myself.

I was once at an open mic where the sound system crashed and I watched a local poet named BRO SON capture the room by loudly saying, "I don't need a mic, Jesus didn't need a mic when he spoke to hundreds of people who had gathered to listen to him on the hills." Several years later KANSER was performing an all-age show in South Dakota when the sound went out. To save the show I stood atop a chair and told the crowd "I don't need a mic, Jesus didn't need a mic when he spoke to hundreds of people." I then broke into a giant acapella freestyle about the World Trade Center on 9/11. It saved the show but I felt like a biter. I had totally ripped that off from BRO SON.

I saw BRO SON after that standing outside of my local Southeast Minneapolis hangout/hip hop spot, The Dinkytowner, and weakly started to confess that I had stolen that Jesus line from him. Before I could get halfway through he cut me off and said, "Dude, I stole that from KRS ONE. My little brother and I saw KRS speak when we were kids and the sound went out and that's what he did...man, ain't nothin' original Zach."

Those words from BRO SON changed my look at the art of emceen'. I started bit-ing more, but adding on, giving everything I took my own twist. Making a strong effort to improve, I got tips from FELIX when it came to controlling the energy of the crowd and how to put the spotlight on UNICUS when he was doing a solo. I figured out when your on-stage you can feel the energy of the crowd almost physically like a 6th sense. It's as though you can almost feel their thoughts and when you make them laugh with a punch line or agree with a statement they shoot their good energy at you which you can reflect and shoot back at them with greater power. It's really magical and is the best feeling and highest high I have found in my life. Its even stronger than love.

I could tell I was surprising MESH, UNICUS, and KANSER'S DJ ELUSIVE. My rhymes were better, my stage presence was better, and my energy was better.

At the end of 2001, my little homegirl Sarah broke up with her boyfriend. I could guess she was on sad mode so I called her and asked if I could pop through her crib to holler at her. Sarah was a 20 year-old black girl from the Southside. She was kind of an Uptown girl. She liked to party, drink, and go to shows. In her teens she fucked around with a lot of extra-curricular drugs, but when she hit 20 she quit cold turkey. That impressed me. I had tons of friends and family who have been stuck on drugs for years never able to shake the addiction. So Sarah's self-control represented strength to me.

She was living in a basement bedroom of a house in Uptown just off West Hennepin. I asked how she was dealing with the break up. It had just happened maybe three days earlier so she was feeling down. Down the same as how most 20 year-old girls feel when their boyfriend breaks up with them. I told her I was gonna give her some rap lessons. She laughed and so did I but I told her that I thought it would help keep her mind off things and give her something to focus on.

I knew Sarah wrote rhymes here and there. Her friends would play me the little raps she would record on their voicemails. I noticed right away that she had a good voice; it was real low. We used to give her shit that she sounded like a man. After a little pressure I got her to read me some of her raps out of her notebook. Like most untrained EMCEES, the rhymes were all over the place and she had a hard time saying them to the beat. We took one of her rhymes and dissected it. I showed her how to write rhymes to bars, simple rhymes like RUN DMC.

"Years ago a friend of MINE
Asked me to say some mc RHYMES
So I said this rhyme I'm about to SAY
The rhyme was dope and it went this WAY"
- RUN

I told her she had to master simple bars before she could add more style to it. On a sheet of paper I drew out the bar structure and showed her where the words that rhymed should go. I told her to do it as an exercise and not to be too concerned with content. Less than five hours later she called me from work and read to me her first 12 bar. I swear to God, it was better than the rhymes of a third of the rappers I was doing shows with at the time.

Every few days for the next three months we worked on her rhymes. Not only did she suck everything I told her up like a sponge, but I was getting her to do shit I couldn't do. She was naturally good at making words rhyme that didn't really rhyme like BLACK-THOUGHT from THE ROOTS does. We sat and listened to women rappers like LAURYN HILL and LADY BUG from DIGABLE PLANETS, trying to find the right approach for her delivery and voice.

I used things that ANT had taught me. I told her to rap in her bedroom full volume when no one was around. I sat with her a lot and asked her who she thought she was? What did she believe and what did she want to say? ANT always said if you didn't know who you were you came off confused on the mic. Sarah was honest with me; she was a 20 year-old girl in the middle of a heartbreak. She wasn't quite sure who she was but the more she wrote it down the more she figured it out.

During the period of time I was working with Sarah on her raps I was kickin' it full-time with my homie SHIZ. SHIZ is a pretty unique dude. He likes to refer to himself as "The SHIZ". He's part Irish, Native, and black. Every other person that encounters the SHIZ thinks he's a different race. SHIZ has a long unidread and kinda sticks out in a crowd. He grew up in the housing co-op in Riverside, an extension of the West Bank in South Minni. At this time in his life, SHIZ was part gangster, part hippy, part Rasta, and 100% B-boy.

He loved hip hop even more than I did. He also loved soul music, jazz, reggae, and rapped with an old school feel and old school beliefs. I had to talk him out of some of the old school. He thought there were kids that shouldn't be allowed to rap or even listen to rap cuz they didn't understand where it came from. I would explain to him that I now believed hip hop was for everybody and that I had performed for thousands of different kinds of kids of different backgrounds and places. Through music I had been given a chance to meet all types of kids which opened my mind. Sometimes I feel inner city kids can be just as ignorant as rural kids can be, trapped inside their own world without true knowledge about what's on the outside.

The SHIZ was pretty ignorant to the music game, but at the same time pretty spiritually advanced. I didn't have to ask him who he thought he was. He and I already knew.

Playing with ideas, I asked Sarah and SHIZ what they thought about starting a new group with me. I said I wanted to do something different than KANSER. I didn't tell them at the time, but some of the reason I wanted to start a new group was because our government was going to invade Afghanistan after the 9/11 bombings. I was consumed with political thoughts but MESH had formed different political views than UNICUS and me, so I couldn't really express all my thoughts in KANSER's music.

SHIZ, Sarah, and I were on the complete same page when it came to a lot of things, so I thought we should make a group with a platform like PUBLIC ENEMY. We sat in my room and came up with a politically conscious, spiritually aware stance with a drip of Southside flavor. That would be our platform.

We got some beats from DJ ANATOMY and MEDIUM ZACH and wrote two songs, "Spark" and "It's Alright". Sarah was supposed to sing the hook on "It's Alright" even though she didn't claim to know how to sing. We figured since she was a girl she could figure it out. Sarah wasn't real big on the tracks back then. She kinda wanted to mess with a live band. I hollered at some of my guys from over South and at TWINKIE JIGGLES from HEIRUSPECS. TWINKIE and I, through INTERLOCK, had somewhat of a friendship and dug each other's work but never had the time to work together.

From practicing with my guy IKE and his band over South and TWINKIE with some ex-HEIRUSPECS members, I got to really see and compare the differences in bands. There are two types of live bands you can work with:

TYPE A: This is IKE's band. Real relaxed, bring of case a beer to practice, smoke herb, kick it, and play music while other people come through hanging out during rehearsal. If practice is at 6pm, that really meant 7pm. The end result is a good time and long sessions where it takes everybody a lot of takes to get the bar counts right, possibly get something accomplished, but more likely just a good time.

TYPE B: This is TWINKIE's band. That shit is like a government, no beer, no drugs and small talk to a minimum. No one else is allowed at the rehearsal. If practice is at 6pm, that means be there by 5:45pm to set up. The end result is songs being made, music being learned fast with few repeat mistakes. Practices aren't fun, matter fact, they suck to even think about but make much more sense.

We rolled with TWINKIE, his drummer "KOOL" KEVIN HUNT, and guitarist JOSH PETERSON. We did one song at a HEIRUSPECS show at this little theater called the Bryant Lake Bowl and our first full performance at Intermedia Arts for DESDAMONA's monthly Encyclopedia of Hip Hop series.

Right before we went on at the Intermedia show, I asked JOSH and KEVIN what we should call our band. We had a couple of ideas but we had to finalize something in the next 90 seconds so we could announce ourselves. We decided to roll with TRADITIONAL METHODS. It had been written on a box of wine at TWINKIE's parents' house. Along with that, Sarah was still undecided on what her MC name should be. She was playing with "MC GASP" but I said just stick with your real name, SARAH WHITE, a black girl calling herself SARAH WHITE...sounds fly. She was like...whatever.

Still rough around the edges, we stepped on-stage with a low tone energy stage show, political and spiritual lyrics over semi-dark instrumentals presenting a pretty clear message of left wing beliefs. Oh, and most important...a girl rapper! In 2001/2002/2003, it was right on time, and locally, we got pretty popular. TWINKIE and I gave it credibility while SARAH and our message made it interesting.

Around town our draw became thick fast being bigger than KANSER's and just a bit smaller than HEIRUSPECS. Our draw was different. It wasn't just hip hop heads, it was a lot of women who might not have been that into rap but wanted to stand behind SARAH and political activism. Our shows were like Southside anti-war rallies. People were trying to book us faster than we could produce songs.

To keep up, I had to crash course school SHIZ and SARAH on how to deal with music politics while, at the same time, TWINKIE was schooling me. I was older than TWINKIE and had been on the scene longer, but he was much more successful when it came to dealing with club and bar owners, press, soundmen, colleges, etc. TWINKIE was a rich white kid whose dad was the president of a college. He could totally speak their language.

TWINKIE was stunned that I didn't know how to do a sound check. I explained to him that for the last seven years I had been doing shows with KANSER. We would step into a bar with turntables and the soundman would never respect us as real music. Soundmen would just say quarter-inch out to RCA's and that we didn't need to check. Same as running a CD. On top of all that, I had the habit of speaking with a lot of slang while TWINKIE spoke very proper and communicated better with people who didn't grow up in the city.

I got into arguments with TWINK, but truthfully I learned a lot from him and brought that knowledge over to KANSER, plus practicing with a band once a week took my breath control to a new level.

We had the basic band problems like KEVIN and TWINKIE being in love with SARAH, KEVIN and TWINKIE being scared of the SHIZ, me sleeping with all of SARAH's close friends, SARAH, SHIZ, and myself trying to explain to TWINKIE that we weren't FELIX (from HEIRUSPECS), and finally...JOSH. JOSH was a lot cooler than the rest of us and he never had any problems (he's a Gemini, male Geminis are cool, and he kept his other side private).

The weirdest problem was everybody wanted to get their hands on SARAH, both metaphorically and physically. But she handled herself well. SARAH's good with people. She had natural instincts to hustle and enjoyed being popular. I think for at least a year of her life SARAH was the most popular girl in Minneapolis, at least in Uptown.

As SARAH took singing lessons and her raps continued to mature, I had to learn my role in the band. I was the front man and did most of the talking, but SARAH WHITE was the focal point. She was better than me, or at least sounded better on the mic and was more talented. In KANSER, not one of the three MCs stood out far enough from the others to notice. Night to night, depending on who was coming off the hardest between the three of us would decide who we had step out front. I was never jealous of SARAH, only proud. Though at times I was scared, I realized that if SARAH didn't show up for a show, we were fucked. If UNICUS had to cancel on a KANSER show, I just had to step my game up. But the TRADITIONAL METHODS crowd didn't care how good I could freestyle or do any of my other magic tricks. They wanted to see the METHODS and they wanted to see SARAH WHITE.

TRADITIONAL made some noise around town for almost three years. It was a lot of fun and it was something different for me. I got to record a project with TWINKIE like I always wanted and I got to put on two of my close friends, SARAH and SHIZ.

But the true reason I gave TRADITIONAL half a chapter in my book, with maybe more details than KANSER got, is cuz of two personal problems I had when I was with the band.

About a year into TRADITIONAL, somewhat of an offer was put on the table for us. It wasn't a guaranteed super big Sony Music cash advance/just sign the contract offer, but it was a chance. I'd been rapping in KANSER for almost a decade and I knew what we were. We were an underground rap group. There's little to no ability to market KANSER. We're just pure B-boy hip hop, skills, beats, life, experimental recordings, and real live party rocking emceen' over instrumentals. That's what we are, that's what we're good at, and that's what we set off in the beginning to be. But TRADITIONAL had something different, something more in the now of 2002.

I was sat down and told that if we took the live band, put them slightly to the background, took SARAH WHITE, myself, and another black male a little more developed than SHIZ and gave it everything, we (them and us) might be able to do this for real. They even suggested that we replace SHIZ with UNICUS. That implied leaving MESH & DJ ELUSIVE out and breaking up KANSER. I tried to explain that SHIZ just needed some more time to develop. He wasn't as naturally talented as SARAH was but he wasn't wack. They knew that already but they said the time is now...right now.

My initial reaction, of course, was no. But it was the afterthought that fucked with me. The more I thought about it the more I knew it was right. SARAH WHITE had something that people wanted. What I lacked in fashion I made up for in skill, and UNICUS was a fully developed black MC with a lot of talent. With TWINKIE's organization and discipline I knew at the least it could get as big as HEIRUSPECS with maybe some potential for more. But it didn't feel right. ELUSIVE, MESH, and SHIZ were my brothers and the more I thought about it I realized...SHIZ was TRADITIONAL METHODS. I never even brought up the potential deal to UNICUS or SHIZ for that matter. Sometimes I think that was my one chance in life to break big. But most of the time, I'm like who cares. When people say it's business not personal, that's just an excuse to be a bad person.

Sadly, parts of my beliefs were crushed during the time in TRADITIONAL. We did so many anti-war shows and protests and spit lyrics about how going to war with Iraq was wrong. I felt like we were fulfilling a higher purpose for ourselves and God was working through us. To sum it together in my idle mind, I thought because so many people were coming to our little Minnesota rap shows, we were stopping our government from going to war with Iraq to the point that when we did invade Iraq I was crushed. It has been hard for me to write political lyrics ever since.

In 2004, MESH and SKYE left us to take different journeys in life. I was totally ok with it and even felt like it was overdue. DJ ELUSIVE started to fade away slowly after that which I also understood. ELUSIVE and MESH are family to me and that will probably never change. Their reasons for leaving and putting down their pursuits of hip hop music represents the lives of the majority of other people in this book. They grew up and started families. And the world needs good fathers way more than it needs broke rappers.

After they left, UNICUS and I have been able to push on and find new levels of success. TWINKIE JIGGLES once made a joke/comment about us; "KANSER has took what should have been a five year career and stretched it out to fifteen plus years." Even though we are small time in the big picture I feel blessed almost every day for what we've been able to accomplish and I feel even more blessed to have found a partner in rhyme like UNICUS. Someone who loves the music and is as dedicated and takes it as serious as I do.

"Love what you got or you'll lose what you have" - Pigeon John

Soon after SKYE left, our friends DILLON PARKER, Mike Campbell, and Chris Cloud got involved in INTERLOCK. They learned as much as they could about music by working with INTERLOCK artists then DILLON PARKER and Mike Campbell later started their own record label, STOPHOUSE MUSIC, which I'll talk about in chapter 24.

I try and communicate with the Creator as much as possible. Whether you call it God, Allah, the force, Buddha, or just the good energy that's around us, I try and communicate with it. I feel it communicates back with me when it needs to and I believe while praying over the decision about TRADITIONAL METHODS it told me as long as I speak the truth and practice the art form of emceen' properly I would be always taken care of when it came to food and shelter. That's when I became a full-time broke rapper.

"We are the voice the government would love to suffocate" - SARAH WHITE

CHAPTER 14 :
THE LORING PASTA BAR
BATTLES: VESH vs A-QUIL

Battle rapping...an MC battle in relation to rap music is kind of like comparing the slam dunk contest to the game of basketball. John Stockton holds the all time assist record in the NBA; however, at 6 foot 1, I don't even know if he could physically dunk a basketball. If he could, I never saw him do it in a game. Just the same, not every great rapper can freestyle battle. Battling and dunking just happen to be the flashiest parts of the games.

In the first few months of 2002, Adam Garcia of the BATTLE CATS and his friend, Abhijit Misra, started a weekly hip hop night at the newly opened Loring Pasta Bar in Dinkytown. Their 18+ Monday night show was located just half a block from where Bon Appétit was located and on the same block as the Varsity Theater. The place was pretty huge, with two floors, water fountains, an expensive menu, and modern art on the wall. I thought this place was a little too fancy to have a rap night. Plus, I thought the city wasn't ready for another weekly rap show after Bon Appétit got shut down.

The first night started slow and for the first few months that followed it was tough to get a crowd in there; it didn't help that it had a 650 person capacity. You needed 100 people on the first floor alone for it not to look empty. DJ AARON MONEY was the in-house DJ, and slowly, through the first few months they started to pull a small crowd, mostly dancers who really enjoyed the giant smooth floor on the first level.

In July of '02, Adam (who was my roommate at the time) asked me if I would host an MC battle at the Loring. Adam said they were gonna start havin' a battle tournament every third Monday of the month with a $150 cash prize for first place and $50 for second. There would be no entry fee and I would get paid $60 every week to host it. I was surprised how diverse the battle was the first month. I'm not even sure how they got the word out, maybe the internet, maybe flyers.

I expected all internet white kids with real weak raps, but, to my surprise, it was real diverse: TRY-D, MIC CHECK of the VERBAL ASSASSINS, and this new dude named ILLICIT; a TUPAC type rapper from the Eastside of St. Paul who was with his homie

YOUNG HUSTLE. They brought a teaspoon of street to the contest. ERNIE RHODES and GEOFFREY WATSON from the newly formed DIALOGUE ELEVATORS CREW also came out. VESH, a 22 year-old white cat from the Northside (who looked liked Dylan from *Beverly Hills 90210*) was a little rough around the edges with his raps but he had some nice punch lines.

None of the rappers stood out as great battlers. Battles hadn't been the main focus of our scene for years so no one that entered the first month was that experienced. ERNIE RHODES ended up beating MIC CHECK in the finals. ERNIE basically won the battle with mic control. He kept his rap steady, clear, and never fell off. That alone beat every other rapper he went up against.

The battle was funnier to host than I expected and looked like it might have some potential. The only truly ill moment that stuck out in my mind was when MIC CHECK battled SYST. SYST was a young art student who was a giant hip hop purest. He had started out in a group called CENOSPECIES (with P.O.S.) but had broke solo and put out his own CD. He had come to the Loring Pasta Bar slanging his CDs out of a cardboard box but was having trouble getting them off. MIC CHECK said:

> *"You brought your CDs to clock, but at the end of the*
> *night your gonna leave with a full box."*

It was a semi-hot line but the reason it sticks out in my memory is because the street hustle of CDs/tapes had been INTERLOCK's bread and butter for years. Between CARNAGE, UNICUS, TRY-D, MESH, myself, and others, we had sold thousands of pieces of product at local shows. Being somewhat in the shadow of RHYMESAYERS' success, our main hustle was going to as many hip hop events as we could and walking around with a box of CDs/tapes/t-shirts. We were the only ones doing it constantly with a somewhat quality product. We hustled a little but half the time the CDs just sold themselves. People would ask what was in the box and if it was local rap. We must have made it look too easy or something because around this time everybody and their mom started trying to sell some sort of burnt CD, and about 99% of them were so weak that it gave the whole hustle a bad name.

If you risk $10 on a local CD from someone you've never heard of once and its weak...most likely you'll never do it again. I hope I'm not coming off bitter, but the 2,000 different rappers that sold their CDs at the Pasta Bar were destroying CARNAGE/INTERLOCK's hustle. It's never been the same for us since. But I guess everything must pass.

The next month, AUGUST of '02, I got a phone call from DIALEK, a St. Paul rapper who had gone to Central with SKYE, FELIX, and others around me. SKYE and I had a good business relationship with DIALEK and his group PUREST FORM. The members of

PUREST FORM had gone straight to college after high school and only focused on doing shows when they returned in the summer. As a promoter, SKYE and I felt the PUREST FORM guys were real easy to work with. They were good, they showed up on time, didn't complain, and most importantly...they brought people. Not a million but a good amount. They had their own little following of fans and friends from St. Paul that was kinda separate from what we had going on. Anyways, back to the reason DIALEK called me.

When they had come in to town for the summer they got ahold of SKYE and I looking for at least one summertime show. SKYE and I just referred them to the Loring Pasta Bar Mondays and this dude Jamie who was helping to book Wednesdays at Gasthof's. We figured they would get plugged with shows no problem. Well, DIALEK had called to tell me that it was now August and both spots had fronted on them. They wouldn't return their phone calls. DIALEK didn't sound super upset, he just sounded like a dude who felt he had been hated on a little.

I told him I would holler at the promoters of both spots and see what I could do. I called SKYE, told him the demo, and we were both pretty surprised. We figured since we had vouched for PUREST FORM someone would have put them on. The next week I went to both spots and asked why PUREST FORM hadn't been put on and I received the same answer, "I didn't really like their music." Verbally, I replied, "For real, you didn't dig 'em that much?" But in my mind I was like, "What the fuck? PUREST FORM is at least 10 times better than whatever weak ass group you got on-stage tonight!!!"

To each his own I guess, but it was official...PUREST FORM had been hated on. The 3rd Monday of August fell the day after the first annual Twin Cities Celebration of Hip Hop, where VESH won the MC battle.

The next day at the Loring Pasta Bar, Adam Garcia and I were there early. Right when they started charging at the door, DIALEK hit the spot with a full band of homies behind him. "Hey Zach, can we get in the battle?" he yelled from the door. Adam waved to the doorman to let them in and he came and signed about 20 names on the list (well, maybe it wasn't 20 but it was a lot). DIALEK said they had to bounce real quick and asked what time they needed to be back. I told him to be back by 10:30 and that we would only have 16 spots for the battle so I asked him if we couldn't put all his homies on which ones should we take. He said, BDF, A-RON, and himself. That night DIALEK and his PUREST FORM clique pulled off the hardest statement moves I had seen in rap since UPSET ran through four rappers in the South High lunch room when I was in 11th grade.

The three of them destroyed everybody! Not even one battle was close. DIALEK himself beat ERNIE RHODES in the 1st round, who was last month's champion, he beat MIC CHECK in the 2nd round, who took second the month before, and he beat his partner A-RON in the 3rd because of how the bracket was set up. A-RON, skill wise, should have taken second.

Later, he finished by beating VESH in the finals who, just the day before, had won the MC battle at the Twin Cities Celebration of Hip Hop. As far as I saw it, the statement they made that night was, "We're better than all of you! Even if you hate on us and won't give us a show at the Pasta Bar we'll come and take it!" To add to the tightness, DIALEK never entered the Loring Pasta Bar battles again...end of story.

After I announced DIALEK as the winner and told the crowd to come back next month, same time same channel, another member of the PUREST FORM click approached me and said he had signed up for the battle but didn't get on since it was full. He asked how he could guarantee a spot in September. I asked him his name and he said A-QUIL. I wrote it down and told him we would have a spot for him. A-QUIL came back in September but only did so-so.

Two months later in October the battle was kind of slow. We had maybe 140 in the audience and seven entries. Before the battle began I had to beg the crowd to produce one more rapper so we would have at least 8 (a number divisible by 4 to hold a tournament). TRY-D ended up beating VESH in the finals but only because I made them go about 5 rounds to entertain the half asleep audience. TRY ended the 5th round with a hot line but if I had ended the battle during either of the previous 4 rounds the crowd would have gave it to VESH. I later apologized to VESH. I told him I didn't mean to cheat him I was just trying to give the crowd their money's worth. He didn't sweat it at all. He said he just came to battle so he could talk to girls when he got off-stage. He didn't give a fuck. VESH was a pretty easy-going dude. Let me date this again, October of 2002 we had a crowd of 140 and 8 emcees.

On November 8th of 2002, EMINEM'S blockbuster movie, *8 Mile*, hit theaters in the Twin Cities. The third Monday of the month in November of 2002, the Loring Pasta Bar was sold-out at 650 people by 11pm and we had over 50 rappers try and sign up which we had to cut down to 32 for time. It stayed this cracking for the next year and then some.

The rappers who had been coming for the previous four months crushed all the newcomers. The battles had started to get better too because the MCs were getting more experience. I started to feel like an NBA ref. I would give calls to the vets and I would always make the new jacks go first. The battles were supposed to be judged by the crowd, but if it was close or a tie I would give it to the MC who had been coming longer. Sometimes if the battle was really one sided but the losing MC had a pocket full of friends in the crowd that made a lot of noise for them I would overrule it. And, as the battles went on for months, Adam and I would make the brackets to produce the most entertaining night.

At about 10:30pm we would stop taking entries and go upstairs and draw out the night.

- We would put the best MCs against the worst in the first round, and pick who we thought were the top four and give them the easiest road to the final four.
- We would try not to pin rappers from the same clicks against each other.
- We would try our best not to let a really weak rapper slide to the final four by not having to beat anyone good.
- We would never directly cheat anyone. If you were new to the Loring, you would just have to beat a good rapper in one of the first two rounds to pay your dues. If you paid your dues we would give you an easier schedule.

A common occurrence would be when some rapper from some click from somewhere's boys hyped him up like he could really compete after they saw *8 Mile* and he would sign up to battle. These guys would step on-stage barely able to hold a mic and just get obliterated. There were at least 5-10 of those per night. 9 out of 10 would never return. Once in a while a kid would come back after taking a beating the month before, do a little better, maybe a little better the next month, and so on. I used to root for those kids in my mind and before they got off-stage I would tell them they did good (off the mic), look 'em in the eye, and nod my head. Battle rapping is more of a sport than an art form and some cats just weren't born with the talent to play the game. But, you gotta give it up to the cat that gets humbled in defeat and comes back and gives all he's got.

There was a wide range of rappers who would come to compete at the Loring:

SHAWN SKIE: A black dude from the Eastside of St. Paul. In his late 20's, I had known SKIE as the best rapper out of the Eastside. SKIE would always come right off the head. I don't think he ever premeditated anything. Half the time he wouldn't even be ready for the next battle. We would have to call his name over and over while he was at the bar getting a drink and not paying attention. He would beat MCs with straight up freestyle skill and usually made it to the final four if he didn't win. I liked his flow...it reminded me of SESS.

MALO: A young Mexican kid from the Westside of St. Paul. He had a hardcore freestyle that would shatter kids. He later was part of a group called ST. PAUL KINGS.

ICE ROD: The goofiest white dude around. He would show up to the battles in old school Reebok pumps, funny orange stretch pants, and a ski mask. He was so goofy. Sometimes he wouldn't even rhyme words; but, the crowd loved him and I learned to as well. His hottest line ever was when he told VESH, "You're less significant than a little poop taken by a treasure troll." He didn't even rhyme it with anything.

PHAT D: An older black dude who was, I would guess, in his early 30's. He was a lot of dude. Must have been about 280 lbs. He had old school punch lines and once the fat jokes had been played out he crushed kids. His best highlight was he beat EYEDEA in the second round the one month EYEDEA came and entered.

SLIM CHANCE: A mixed kid from the suburbs who never did that great in the battles but later became a dope emcee as the front man of the Mankato/Twin Cities based band PARALLAX. SLIM CHANCE might be the most successful emcee to come out of the Pasta Bar battles and he credits the Pasta Bar as the place he got his start.

PRATIS RAIN: A heavy set dreaded black kid who had a lot of punch lines that went over people's heads. I saw many months where I felt the crowd cheated him. He would drop complex punch lines that nobody must have understood and then he would get beat by an old stupid, "He looks like Bob Marley with those dreads" line. Or, "He looks like DAS EFFEX." I used to think he got overlooked a lot but he eventually won it in April of 2004.

META: Another MC out of St. Paul Central who came with a lot of skill mixed with punch lines. META had good confidence and good stage presence. He looked like an emcee if you know what I mean.

YOUNG G: I think he might have been in one of the African American frat houses at the U of M. Or, he was a U of M athlete or something, because when he came to the Pasta Bar, he always had what seemed to be a whole fraternity with him. He had charisma, a good voice, and lots of confidence.

ELLIOT: A skinny light skinned dude from St. Paul who had some cool raps. He was such a nice dude without an ego. I used to wonder how he said mean things in battles. After I stopped hosting he actually took over.

MEDUIM ZACH: Of course he got his name because of me. He also gave me the nickname BIG ZACH. M. ZACH was good and would come strong the first two rounds but always seemed to throw in the towel by the third round.

SONRA: A suburban white kid who showed no fear going up against inner city cats of all shapes and sizes. The only time I might have ever cheated anyone in the battles I took away a win from SONRA. He had gone neck and neck with SHAWN SKIE into an extra round. The crowd called it a tie and I was gonna give it to SONRA but SHAWN SKIE said in my ear "Give it to me Zach" and I did. It was like a NBA referee giving a call to a veteran over a rookie. (Sorry SONRA)

ROMES: A kid from rural Wisconsin who must have been hungry. He would drive about an hour and a half every night just to compete in the battle.

BDF: A dread from St. Paul with the original B-boy flavor.

CANNON: A rapper out of Duluth, MN who would come down to compete.

The crowd was from all over the place; every hood, every suburb, Eastside, West-side, Frog Town, Midway, Southside, Northside, Northeast, and plus a good amount of U of M students who lived on campus would slide through. It was definitely the hottest spot to be in the Twin Cities for over a year. It got to the point where there would be a line down the block and around the corner by 9:45pm. I was 24-25, and for the second time in my short life, I was the host of the hottest night in MPLS. Hosting the Pasta Bar wasn't always fun, it did not have the grass roots, organic, community feel that Headspin Sundays used to have. It was way bigger than that and sometimes it was pretty hectic.

When I perform or host other events I feel somewhat in control. Like everyone is listening to me and if I have to force the issue they will do what I ask them; calm down, pay attention, or whatever. But, I never felt in complete control at the Pasta Bar. I always felt like the whole place was on the brink of a riot.

The main reason I think people are attracted to battles is they generate the same feeling or energy that a fight does. But most times no violence actually occurs... but it can. And, its more likely to get hectic when you have 30 different clicks from all over the metro area who all think they're the toughest homies out of whatever hood they come from. But, since they're from different places, there is no food chain established and every click has one representative in the battle who has a 31 in 32 chance of being totally humiliated in front of 600 some people while representing their clique, gang, rap group, whatever.

Every night I ever hosted the Pasta Bar I had some sort of weapon on me. Mostly it was brass knuckles that I kept in my right pocket. The rappers most likely to start any trouble or have their friends start trouble were the weak inner city rappers. The weak suburb or rural rappers were usually nerds or kinda nervous to be up on-stage in the first place.

I had the most problems with the super weak inner city rappers whose raps always sounded like a weak version of whatever was on the radio. They would never freestyle and their egos were in such a state of fana-land they couldn't even comprehend when they got beat. The most common excuse was, "Play some beats." As if we would've played a better beat for them to rap over they wouldn't have just got chopped up. I didn't take much shit though. The first few months I tried to reason with weak rappers. After that, I just ignored them...and their little friends. Believe me, there is almost nothing worse to deal with in the world than a wack rapper who doesn't know he's wack at a giant MC battle.

There were so many moments at the Pasta Bar I would have to write another book to document them all, but the moment that best describes the whole thing was when VESH met A-QUIL in the January finals of 2003.

The Pasta Bar was built on VESH. In order to have a successful battle night, you have to have MCs that the crowd wants to come back and see. VESH was a skinny, funny white dude from the Northside of MPLS who had caps for days. VESH didn't have good rhythm, but his raps were on beat just enough to get by. His voice and delivery weren't that tight, but this dude said the most outrageous shit. I've been around rap more than half my life and I've never heard another rapper come up with caps as good as VESH. He was like the most witty freestyle stand-up comic you'd ever heard. He barely had filler rap between punch lines. Each round was just 30 seconds of straight punch lines. In the 23 months we held the battles VESH entered it 15 times, won it 6 times, and took second another 5.

Lifetime, I would guess VESH was 49-9 at the Pasta Bar and every time he got beat it was an event. The rapper that beat him hit him with everything he had. It got to the point that when I would announce a battle and say VESH's name on deck in the first round, the crowd would "OOOOOOOH" louder than they had all night just in anticipation of what he was about to do. I could probably write a third book about the punch lines VESH used over all those months, but the one that sticks out as the most clever through all the battles was when he was up against SHAWN SKIE and he said,

"You look like you got hit by a city bus with wet paint." - VESH

The whole crowd along with myself had a two second delayed reaction as we focused in on SKIE's white sweater and realized it was the same pattern and colors as the front of a Twin Cities metro transit bus. The crowd exploded about two seconds after he dropped the punch line cuz it took all of us that long to figure it out.

A-QUIL on the other hand was kind of the underdog. His first two attempts at the Pasta Bar only saw him get as far as the second round. His confidence was not high and his punch lines came off practiced but not memorized. His third attempt was in November of '02. The first battle after *8 Mile* was released. With the crowd quadrupled in size and the number of rappers doubled, A-QUIL stood out that night slicing through four different rappers in the first four rounds. He reached the finals only to run into VESH and be taken out by the king of the Pasta Bar.

The next month A-QUIL showed up early, came over to me, gave me dap, and told me he was gonna run and get something to eat. I didn't think much of it. It was in one ear and out the other. But later that night, when we had gotten to the second round, A-QUIL approached the stage and asked why we hadn't called his name yet. I looked over at Adam who kept track of the brackets while I hosted and asked why A-QUIL was skipped. Adam said he didn't sign up.

Holding up the battle, I looked at A-QUIL and asked if he had signed up with Adam and he replied, "I thought I had to sign up with you. That's why I came and told you I was getting something to eat." I was like, oh fuck. So by the way of the universe A-QUIL was left out that month which VESH also won.

The next month, January of 2003 fell on Martin Luther King Day which should have been a day of peace and love, but the Pasta Bar was the most hectic ever. I had rappers from every angle yelling at me, homies threatening to rush the stage cuz they felt the crowd cheated their boy, arguing with Abhijit and Adam...all types of shit. It was the usual procedure for VESH. He cut through some nobodies and TRY-D (he was always eating TRY-D up). He did run into a tough battle with META that I had to put into over-time but he came out on top. A-QUIL, on the other hand, was havin' a so-so night. I don't think any of his rounds were easy. All his battles were close, but round by round he made it to the finals: VESH vs. A-QUIL January of '03.

From jump it felt like the crowd was right on top of me when the finals began. After the standard two 30-second rounds apiece, I did a crowd check and it was dead even. If there were 600 people screaming it was 300 apiece split right down the middle. Plus, there was booing that I couldn't ever differentiate from cheering. It all sounded like noise to me. After a first overtime I tried to do a hand check by getting the crowd to raise their hands instead of making noise but that was also too close to count. The crowd, all 600+ seemed pushed against the stage like in a giant concert and they were all screaming at me from the second floor, the right, the left, and behind me. I didn't know how to call it. I felt like whoever I gave it to didn't matter.

Half the crowd was going to be real upset. DJ STAGE ONE was sitting on the side and I SELF DEVINE was in back of the turntables. They were kinda being grumpy because they felt like the crowd cheated their guy BUDAH TYE back in the second round. I turned to them and on the mic asked them who they thought won. Half of the reason I did it was to take the pressure or blame off of myself, and the other half was I figured they were so respected that the crowd would argue with them less. I SELF pointed towards A-QUIL but STAGE ONE asked for the mic. With a 600+ person angry mob all around us, STAGE ONE said into the mic, "I think they need one more round." The crowd reacted in dangerous agreement with STAGE ONE and I signaled to the DJ.

The DJ dropped a beat and I handed the mic to A-QUIL and he pulled the dopest line out of his ass. Matter fact it was more of a statement because I don't think he rhymed it with anything. Everyone knows that the Northside of MPLS has the hardest hoods in Minnesota and their hoods are mostly African American. VESH is a clean cut kid who just happens to have grown up there and represents it on the mic every chance he gets. He had won enough battles that black kids had started to yell out, "Northside!" when VESH stepped on-stage.

Well, A-QUIL in the fourth round of the Jan '03 finals said, "You claim the North-side but the Northside don't claim you." A deep "OOOOOOH" went through the crowd and VESH came back with, "All they got in St. Paul is Snoopies," referring to the statues placed around St. Paul to remember Charles Schultz. Well, that line sounded like he was dissing St. Paul in general, not just A-QUIL for being from St. Paul. With that VESH lost just enough of the audience that when I did the noise check, I paused for a second and said, "I think A-QUIL got it."...History.

In the 23 months the Pasta Bar battles ran, there were hundreds of rappers that entered but there were only 14 different winners. The Pasta Bar was four times more popular than HEADSPIN Sundays down the block had been just four years before. But, hip hop was four times more popular in general. To win the Pasta Bar you got more than the $150...you got props. For the next month around town, you were the shit. I've had my picture in the paper a handful of times and it was almost the same. People treat you a little bit different for that month. It was kind of like your 15 minutes of fame. But, as soon as the next month's battle went down and there was a new winner it was over.

It was a big deal, it wasn't like you won a rap contest in front of 100 people and it wasn't like you played a show in front of 500 of your own fans. You beat five rappers in one night, and in a way, you beat 31 rappers in one night in front of 600+ people of whom you didn't know. Added was that there was another 100-400 people that tried to come but weren't let in. The word of your win spread through the gossip and hit the streets. It was all over the internet by the next day. Since there were only 14 different winners you were kind of in this elite club if you won, I can tell the story from the view of the host, audience member, and also as a winner.

In February of 2003, the month after A-QUIL defeated VESH in the finals, Adam and Abhijit doubled the prize. It was the one year anniversary of Monday nights and in celebration they put up $300 for the winner and $100 for second place. Abhijit had asked me about two months prior if I would enter instead of host on the one-year anniversary. I told him yes with complete confidence that I would win. I had been battling for years on the street, high school, and house parties. Even though I had never been in a real tournament I was pretty confident I could. Plus, as the host I knew what I was up against. For the last seven months I had hosted, seen, and scoped out every rapper that came through.

The month before the battle I practiced a lot in my room. Practicing battle rapping is weird and kinda sucks. I don't like doing it. You have to sit by yourself, turn on a beat, pretend you're battling a pretend person, and come up with raps on command. I tried going over to SKYE's house where he would play coach with a stopwatch and turntable. He would say battle Michael Jordan, drop a beat, and I would do my best to come up with a 30-second verse. Most battlers have some premeditated material, myself included. But I've found that if you over-prepare it will fuck your game up. Instead of freestyling you will stumble over premeditated lyrics that you haven't truly memorized. So I tried to go into the battle with at least one punch line on every rapper I knew memorized but not more.

I did feel I was in a political position that gave me a good chance. It would have been real hard for a completely unknown rapper to win because he would've had to first win the crowd over and then defeat popular rappers. Being popular could also hurt me. It gives a rapper who is less known way more to go on and more to make fun of.

This might sound corny but that EMINEM song, "Lose Yourself", was real motivating. I worked part time at this pizza spot in Uptown and the day of the battle I asked if I could slice meat in the basement. The owner looked at me odd cuz nobody ever wanted to slice meat in the basement. It was hot, sweaty, and it sucked. But it gave me a couple of hours of practice. I turned the radio dial back and forth from B96 to KDWB at the time they were playing EMINEM's song four times an hour. It was "Lose Yourself" until you "lose your mind" rotation. The song is about getting ready for a battle and I was downstairs pumping myself up rapping every word. The owner of the pizza spot came down and caught me and told me to get back to work. I probably looked like the most typical white boy rapping EMINEM lyrics by myself in the basement... (haha), but on the real...I think it helped my confidence. (haha)

I dressed as basic as I could. Plain shirt, baggy pants, and a black skull cap giving my opponents not a lot to go on. I also had a button-up that I took off after the 2nd round to throw opponents off, in case they had thought of a hot line to use against the button-up. I felt pretty prepared but what I didn't expect was that the year anniversary battle would be big. Bigger rappers came out to enter; BDF, A-RON, BUDAH TYE, BROTHER ALI and to watch; SLUG, I SELF DEVINE, SARAH WHITE, TOKI WRIGHT, CARNAGE, P.O.S., BIG WIZ, MASTERMIND, ST PAUL SLIM, and DIALEK. The Southside was definitely in the house. Girls were everywhere, including like five girls that I thought were the shit at the time. The place was packed full of different characters from my life and the Cities. Status wise and audience size, it was the biggest MC battle ever held in the Twin Cities.

Up until the battle began, most of the other rappers wouldn't know I had entered and wasn't hosting. I eventually went behind the stage to hide and meditate. The bigger rappers shook me for only a brief second. Then the competitive nature in me came out and I started to focus on if I was pinned against a VESH, BROTHER ALI, or BUDAH TYE. They would be hard to get by but they weren't even who I was most worried about. A-RON and A-QUIL from PUREST FORM along with their boy BDF were who I considered the most dangerous.

They were dope freestylers, they were dope battle rappers, and they had status but there wasn't a lot to go on when it came to trying to clown them. I sat behind stage and I watched A- RON and A-QUIL bump themselves up for the battle, giving each other some sort of secret PUREST FORM hand shake. I stood up, walked over to them, looked them both in the eye, and said good luck. I started to walk through the crowd when my little brother Eli came over to me. My little sister and him came through to support me and I was glad they were there. Eli pulled a coin out of his pocket and told me that it was his lucky coin given to him by our late grandfather. Eli told me to put it in my pocket and it would give me good luck for the battle, then he gave me a hug.

The host of Ohio's giant MC battle Scribble Jam was there as the guest host, KEVIN BEACHAM. He prepped the crowd for the event, told them that the prize was doubled, blah blah, blah. He announced me first. Right off the bat I was like here we go. There was some reaction from the crowd when they realized I had entered. As I stepped on-stage I thought that Adam would have given me someone easy for the first round and I think he tried but most of the rappers out of the 32 had been invited special for the year anniversary so there wasn't many weak rappers. First round I pulled this young kid CYPHER.

Off jump he wasn't a super scrub. I had seen him battle around town and I knew I had to take him serious. VESH sat on the right side of the stage and gave me dap when I got up there. He laughed and kinda looked at me with a look on his face like, "What's Zach gonna do?" I think the whole crowd did too. CYPHER came at me pretty good but two bars into my verse I hit him with a killer crack baby punch line that blew up the crowd. Quickly, realizing that I had already won, I stopped aiming at CYPHER and I used the last 15 or so seconds of my verse to address that I was gonna win the battle and started calling out other rappers, VESH, TRY-D, and A-QUIL. Then I told the crowd that the first rapper who made fun of my beard was gonna get it bad (my beard is the easiest thing about me to make fun of so I thought I would threaten anyone who went for it). Instead of letting it be my first battle I made it my opening statement, as the first battle in the first round the crowd ate it up.

Four battles later, BUDAH TYE hit the stage and totally crushed some young kid that probably regrets ever trying to rap after that night. To end BUDAH's really one-sided battle he said,

"That nigga Zach looks like a white boy Bin Laden"
as he looked directly at me in the crowd. The whole place exploded!!!!!

Replying to my beard challenge might have been the biggest line of the night. Luckily for me, it wasn't on me. I mean, it was calling me out but since it wasn't used against me in a battle I survived.

As I watched, I saw that the competition was tough. I saw good MCs like SHAWN SKIE, JAYECHS, and ILLICIT get beat in the first round. I eased by my second round beating SYST. He had been in a group with P.O.S. right before P.O.S.'s career took off so I hit him with,

"You used to be in the CENOSPECIES crew / and now
you're just mad cuz P.O.S. is more popular than you."

I finished the round by saying, "Somebody tell Budah Tye that I'll be waiting for him," letting the crowd know I wasn't scared. But, in truth I was kinda scared to battle BUDAH. The way the crowd reacted to his Bin Laden line? I didn't know what he had in store for me. Plus, I would have to dis I SELF DEVINE and the UVS crew and that could lead into a fight or real beef with these dudes.

As the second round went on, BUDAH's name was called against VESH. In my head I was like yes!! I thought there was no way that BUDAH would get by VESH. I watched hoping that VESH would just hit him with some fat jokes and knock him out. BUDAH was wearing a Paul Pierce Boston Celtics Jersey and VESH said,

"Hey, he ate Paul Pierce and stole his Jersey." - VESH

That along with a few other caps I thought BUDAH was gone for sure. But BU-DAH came back and ripped the shit outta VESH with straight up tough hard battle raps.

"On the mic you ain't no beast / the closest you've ever
came to the Northside is Northeast." - BUDAH TYE

The crowd went bonkers. The echo of I SELF DEVINE banging on the stages plywood went through the building with about 200 heads jumping up and down in the front rows. BUDAH took his jersey and shirt off and threw them into the crowd. As almost 700 people went nuts all around me all I could think was...oh fuck.

TRY-D, VESH, and last month's winner A-QUIL all got beat in the second round. In the third round I got put against PRATUS RAIN. He had some good lines but PRATUS just so happened to work at the Popeye's Chicken on Pleasant and Lake Street right by where I lived at the time so I just clowned him on that and got through. BUDAH's battle was next and it felt like the whole place was just in anticipation of when I would meet BUDAH in the next round and then the winner of our battle would meet BROTHER ALI in the finals. But BUDAH and BROTHER ALI kinda ran out of gas. BUDAH got beat by A-RON and ALI got beat by BDF.

I was acting real cocky but A-RON was who I most feared coming into the battle. He was a better freestyler than me and had more to fight for. Beating BUDAH TYE and NEW MC from KANSER would be a major statement. Instead of havin' an attack plan I just thought I would react to what he would come at me with.

I talked last chapter about my small fallout with RHYMESAYERS that had never really been resolved but when I stepped against A-RON in the semi finals, BROTHER ALI was in the front row cheering for me and SLUG was on the side of the stage yelling, "NEW MC!" I knew St. Paul was deep in the crowd and there was at least 50 heads there that had gone to St. Paul Central that would be rooting for A-RON. So, to try to sway some of those people to my side I said,

"I got a lot of love for St. Paul Central / but why you give a rapper with no potential?"

I could hear small laughs in the crowd from the ones that understood. I went first, A- RON went second, and then A-RON went third (Scribble Jam style). As A-RON finished his second verse I realized that I wasn't winning. A-RON wasn't eating me up but it was close and A-RON had a good amount of friends in the crowd that would cheer for him. I had one last chance to win over all the neutral people. A-RON's last statement was that I wasn't really from South MPLS, and in a blink, I grabbed the mic and flipped it around on him saying he was dissing the Southside. That awoke all the Southsiders who were the majority.

"He's trying to dis where I'm from I got pride / I'll show you how its done"

I put down the microphone and with both hands threw up the SS hand signal used by Southsiders that only Southsiders would know and yelled out "SOUTHSIDE!" I yelled it as loud as I could without a microphone. All the Southsiders threw up the SS back at me and yelled it back...A-RON was done. A-RON didn't really dis the Southside, he dissed me, but I had to do what I had to do, kinda like a low blow. By the look on his face when he got off-stage I could tell he knew.

The few minutes I spent off-stage before the final round is a deep memory in my life. I thought about the EMINEM lyrics to "Lose Yourself"..."One shot." I thought about when I was in the 8th grade and my basketball team lost in the city championship. We played together for three years and finally made it to the playoffs. Then when we got to the finals and I had a bad game. I scored 0 points and had 2 major turnovers in the 4th quarter. At 25 years old that dumb game still haunted my memory. Not because we lost, but because I choked and didn't do my best under pressure. So I thought to myself, I could make up for it right here. I was gonna win, and if I took second I was gonna do my best.

When they called my name for the finals I got lucky, META had beat BDF to get to the finals. META was a real ill rapper who had just jumped on the Pasta Bar scene. He was also from St. Paul Central and had that crowd behind him. But, I had grown up with this kid who tagged META, so I used to rap for him all the time and flip his name around. All I did in the finals was flip and rhyme the word META all over the place that I think even impressed him. After the crowd gave it to me and KEVIN BEACHAM announced me as the winner I hugged META and in his ear told him he was a real good rapper. He came back the next month and won. Later in META's career he was able to tour the country a few times opening for DEVIN THE DUDE.

That was the first rap tournament I ever won. The Pasta Bar closed at 1am, so about a fifth of the crowd went down the block to the Dinkytowner from 1am-2am like they did every Monday. I went there and got something to eat to celebrate the victory. Then I got a ride home, sat by myself for about 20 minutes, and then walked to the gas station at like 3 in the morning to get a juice. On the walk back I stopped on Lyndale and 33rd, looked up at the streetlight to talk to God for a second, and felt the most healthy pride inside myself that I have ever felt.

When I got home my little brother Eli called me. He was high on coke talking crazy about how good I had done, letting me know he was proud of me. Less than three months later he went to jail for accessory to murder where he remains to this day. The memory of that phone call has always meant a lot to me.

The next day I got to work at the pizza spot a little early, like 10:45am, when I didn't have to be there 'til 11am. The boss asked me what I had done the night before and

I told him I won a rap contest for $300. He looked at me sideways like he had looked at me the day before when he caught me rapping in the basement. He was probably debating if I was lying or not.

Then, at 11am, Sarah Lajon, who was the other pizza maker and also the most beautiful girl in my personal universe at the time showed up for work. As soon as she stepped in the door she said, "Zach, that was so cool last night. I was in the crowd when you won the battle." After hearing that the boss looked up at me and I could tell he thought, "That story was real?" Sarah had a boyfriend and never threw me the "Girl Energy" if you know what I mean, but I had to work with her cute ass everyday at that pizza spot for two years. She was part Mexican, white and Philippino, looked like Angelina Jolie, and was the sweetest nicest girl ever. Impressing her if only for a day was almost as cool as the $300 I won.

I know in the big scheme of things I might have made that battle out to be bigger than you might think, but at the time in our little world it was big. I'm sure all the winners have their personal story about the night they won. MASTA I won the Pasta Bar right after his father passed away and he later told me he talked to his dad between rounds. The month PRATUS RAIN won he told me he woke up in the morning and looked himself in the mirror and thought he was looking at the champ. The day after ILLICIT won I ran into him in Uptown and he was glowing. He looked at me dead in the eyes and said, "Dog you don't know how good I feel right now." But I did know how he felt cuz I had won it too.

I first started to get to know ILLICIT in the beginning of 2004. The first night I really kicked it with him I talked him into taking shrooms with me after a Pasta Bar night. Combined with a blunt we got real high and sat in the living room of this cute girl Gillian's house and talked about battling at the Pasta Bar. We talked about the level of intelligence it takes.

Getting deeper in our trip we talked about how infinite the mind really is, about how human beings can think up spaceships, take it from their imagination to the drawing board, through mathematics to a blue print, construction, and actually build a space shuttle. Personally, I can't comprehend how a space shuttle works. Something that weighs that much is the last thing I would think could fly into space. My mind must just not fire that fast or work that way. But ILLICIT pointed out that if you took anybody at NASA whose IQ score is probably mad higher than ours and dropped them on-stage at the Pasta Bar where they would have to come up with insults against a person they saw for the first time 10 seconds ago that all had to rhyme while also be entertaining to the crowd, make sense, and be delivered on time to a beat...Who's mind would work faster? And who would look stupid? On the drugs we were on that night, that thought kinda made me feel smart.

THE LORING PASTA BAR
MC BATTLE WINNERS

DATE	1ST PLACE	2ND PLACE
JULY '02	ERNIE RHODES	MIC CHECK
AUGUST '02	DIALEK	VESH
SEPT '02	SHAWN SKIE	ICE ROD
OCT '02	TRY-D	VESH
NOV '02	VESH	A-QUIL
DEC '02	VESH	TRY-D
JAN '03	A-QUIL	VESH
* FEB '03	BIG ZACH (NEW MC)	META
MARCH '03	META	VESH
APRIL '03	VESH	PHAT D
MAY '03	VESH	PHAT D
JUNE '03	VESH	ICE ROD
JULY '03	ILLICIT	MALO
AUGUST '03	ADAM	SHAWN SKIE
SEPT '03	ICE ROD	VESH
OCT '03	TRY-D	PHAT D
NOV '03	SHAWN SKIE	YOUNG G
DEC '03	SHAWN SKIE	MASTA I
JAN '04	VESH	ICE ROD
FEB '04	MASTA I	PRO
MARCH '04	PHAT D	MASTA I
APRIL '04	PRATUS RAIN	PHAT D
MAY '04	MASTA I	O.C.

year anniversary

CHAPTER 15 :
P.O.S.

I've heard other rappers hate on P.O.S. because of his punk rock background, saying he just came out of nowhere. But I can remember P.O.S. coming to our shows like Headspin Sundays for years. Being a black punk rock kid who came to hip hop shows back in '98, he was kind of memorable.

If you can believe this or not, the first time I ever talked to P.O.S. was when he came to the second ever INTERLOCK meeting in 1998. With a demo tape he asked if he could be down with the crew. MESH, FELIX, and others told him no. I think CRESCENT MOON was the only one who voted yes. To put it in perspective, P.O.S. wasn't that tight back then, and since it was only the second meeting of a crew that never could keep their shit together, there wasn't a lot we could do for dude. But, it's still ironic that P.O.S. asked to be down with us and we said no. P.O.S. has now sold more CDs than us...all combined...times at least five. (haha)

In 2002, INTERLOCK was contacted by a company doing advertising for the Minnesota Timberwolves. They told us that the Timberwolves had some of the lowest attendance of African Americans to home games in the NBA. Aiming at the black audience, they were gonna run a string of commercials with a beatbox cypher being held in front of the Timberwolves arena with emcees rapping about the Timberwolves (they should have just gotten a better basketball team).

The audition was held in a building downtown and several INTERLOCK members, P.O.S., and I took turns standing in front of a camera with people watching us behind glass. We would state our name and then kick a flow with no beat.

After the audition, everybody broke out and P.O.S. asked if I wanted to get some grub. I was like, "Sure, where you wanna eat?" He said, "We can get some free food from my work."

Free food always tastes good so wherever he worked I was down. I can't remember what I thought, if I thought he worked at McDonald's, a fancy downtown restaurant or what, but the next thing I know he wants us to duck into Rick's Cabaret, a downtown strip club. I said, "Whoa, you work at strip club dog?" P.O.S. replied, "Yeah, and the foods good."

P.O.S. got me a veggie burger and a good half hour watching fake boobs. Even though he couldn't hook up a lap dance, it was an okay lunch. I asked P.O.S. what he did there. "I work in the bathroom," he said.

"What you mean you work in the bathroom?" I replied. He brought me in the men's can and showed me his station. He had a chair next to the sink and he offered dudes towels after they took a piss...in a downtown strip club. It was wild. "You could probably move a lot of drugs out this station," I said.

"Oh, people ask me for drugs everyday," he replied. I told him I had a plug on pills and that I was broke. He said he could use some money too...so...I made a phone call. End of story. We didn't get the Timberwolves commercial. It was given to a short-lived young beatbox trio called the 3KINGS. We did receive a phone call that went,

"Hey, this is Marty from the Timberwolves audition. We decided to go with some young kids for the campaign but we wanted to thank you guys for coming down. Tell that Zach "NEW MC" guy that he didn't have the look we needed but his freestyle was so fun to listen to we want to give him two sets of 4 lower level tickets this season, they're in the mail."

That's all I truly wanted anyway.

CHAPTER 16 PART 1: ANYTHING CAN HAPPEN

2003 was the hardest year of my life. In twelve months and one day I had four close friends die and my little brother went to prison for murder. A bright spot in this year was TOKI WRIGHT and Larry Lucio asking me to volunteer and help with the Twin Cities Celebration of Hip Hop. When TOKI first left me messages asking if I would come to meetings, he said I would be working with teenagers through an organization called "Yo! The Movement". This at first sounded like something I wouldn't be into. At 24, I wasn't, and still do not claim to be, good with kids. But what I soon realized was the teenagers that were part of the "Yo!" weren't normal teenagers...they were rap kids. Kids that were into rap were easy for me to relate to and hella fun to be around.

It was through Yo! The Movement that I first met the next generation of our scene, ILLUMINOUS 3, DJ SNUGGLES, DJ GABE GARCIA, Adam Davis, and many more beautiful young kids. TOKI and Yo! The Movement's basic vision was to diversify Minnesota's hip hop scene which I believe, then and in the long run, they did.

In August of 2003, I entered the MC battle at the 2nd annual Twin Cities Celebration of Hip Hop. It was held at Intermedia Arts, inside and outside. The festival ran all day Saturday & Sunday and the battle would be held on the main stage outside unless it rained. In the giant resurgence of battle tournaments that followed the release of *8 Mile*, the Celebration of Hip Hop's MC battle was the second biggest crown to capture locally besides the Loring Pasta Bar battle. Since I had won the Loring six months earlier I really wanted to win this tournament.

Hosted by FIC and the PHAROHS, it ran in the usual format with 30-second rounds. One round per battle until you got to the third round where it was two rounds per battle. Along with many entries by many rappers I didn't know, some Loring regulars, MEDIUM ZACH, VESH, ICE ROD, and GENE POOL showed up for the battle. On top of that, REASON, who won the teenage MC battle held at the Walker Art Center, and two rappers out of Oklahoma City, QUESE and DUO, who by chance were driving home from a Native reservation show they had played up north the day before and came across the celebration, signed up as well.

I was on fire that weekend; it was probably the best performance I ever had in a tournament. After the battle was over, FIC would keep both rappers on-stage, see what the crowd thought and then announce the judges' decision. I was moving so fast. I would slaughter my opponent so bad that it was more than obvious I was the winner and then run off-stage to make the statement that I didn't need to wait and hear what the crowd or the judges thought.

After the 2nd round was over, FIC and TOKI WRIGHT announced the names of the eight finalists and said the rest of the battle would be held the next day at 5pm. I was like, "What the fuck? I'm ready to chop whoever you put in front of me right now, bring it on."

Never have I felt that confident about anything, my blade was sharp and my mind was moving at top speed. I felt like I could have ate 30 more rappers up right then and there...line 'em up.

I sat on the ticket table at the front gate and vented my ego to SHIZ. Right then, DUO and QUESE walked by on their way out. They gave me dap and props on the battle. I did the same and told them I would see them tomorrow with a little competitive, but friendly, smirk. SHIZ, with a tone of voice that made me pay attention, told me, "Those are the two you have to worry about tomorrow, be prepared to battle them."

From what we saw that day they were both upper level emcees with strong free-styles and seemed like veteran battlers. They had unique appearances, QUESE was Native American with glasses, big white earrings, and I think a small pony tail. DUO was a tall black cat with crazy long dreads that he had wrapped up in a bun at the top of his head, jewelry on his hands, and black finger nail polish on his nails. I felt like both of their appearances gave me a lot of ammunition to work with. I took into account what SHIZ said but still felt confident.

TWINKIE JIGGLES had an after-party for the celebration that night at his house. I went there woofing and talking shit how I was going to win the battle the next day hands down, guaranteed. I left the party early to go home and practice a little and get some good sleep. I was so confident when I counted my money that night, I subtracted the $250 prize from the battle that I had not yet won from my bills.

When I got to Intermedia the next day I looked over the schedule for the main stage.

3pm-4pm	DJ Battle (which I was to host)
4pm-5pm	ILLUMINOUS 3
5pm -6pm	Emcee Battle
6pm-6:30pm	MAC LETHAL
6:30pm-7pm	TRADITIONAL METHODS/ KANSER
7pm-8pm	The CORE
8pm-9pm	BROTHER ALI
9pm-10pm	CAMP LO

I thought to myself, perfect. The later the night goes the fatter the crowd will become. I'm going to host the DJ battle, tell the crowd to come back in an hour and watch me win the MC battle, win it, and run off-stage so I'm not there when they announce me as the winner. The host will be like, "Where's NEW MC?" for at least a couple minutes. Meanwhile, I'll hide in the back room of Intermedia during MAC LETHAL's set so no one sees me 'til I pop on-stage an hour later to perform with TRADITIONAL. I'll make it all dramatic and theatrical and then rock the house with TRADITIONAL/KANSER. If I pulled this off I knew it was gonna be a dope day!

Well, I pulled off part one. SKYE, DJ FRANCISCO, and I ran the DJ battle and it went pretty smooth. Somewhere in there I slipped in that I was gonna win the MC battle. That was the easy part. Part two started off according to plan. In the 3rd round of the MC battle I had to battle a female rapper. I crushed her but made sure to keep it silly so the crowd and the judges wouldn't think of me as a bad guy.

"I better chill on the sexist jokes, shit I've already lost DESDAMONA'S vote"
- BIG ZACH (DESDAMONA was one of the 5 judges for the MC battle).

The final four rappers were ICE ROD, DUO, QUESE and myself. I was put against QUESE. Even though I was still hot, QUESE was the first real comp I had faced and his first verse was pretty good.

Jumping back in time about four years, there was a rumor that the ABSTRACT PACK had gone to play a show in L.A. and got into a confrontation with ABSTRACT RUDE (a popular underground L.A. rapper) over the name "abstract". Supposedly when RUDE dissed the PACK on-stage he took a lotta shots at them for being from Minnesota. I wasn't a fan of ABSTRACT RUDE after that. I felt he dissed my state and I thought it was unfair to dis a rapper from where they were from on your home turf...that was until I had to battle QUESE, a dope ass rapper from another city who had a good chance of beating me in my home town if I didn't come tight on my second verse.

Hey, call it home court advantage. I let the crowd know he was from Oklahoma, took hella shots at Oklahoma, and then called DUO out who was standing off to the side of the stage.

"And your boy from Oklahoma, dude to your left /
that's right, you. I'm gonna serve you next"

Saying it, I looked DUO in the face and pointed at him. DUO looked up in shock at first and then just nodded his head to imply it was on as the crowd ooooooh'd real loud. It was over after that. It didn't even matter that QUESE's next verse was hot. By placing myself in the finals to the crowd, I placed myself in the finals.

I jumped off-stage before QUESE even finished his verse. Out of nowhere SLUG grabbed me and tried to coach me a little. SLUG was a battle vet and this was the finals. I should have stopped, calmed down, and listened to him more but my mind was moving so fast. I didn't chill and take it in. Instead, I ran to a corner and started rapping to myself while DUO defeated ICE ROD.

They finally called me back to the stage for the finals. When DUO and I made eye contact I gave him a wink with my left eye that the crowd couldn't see to let him know it was all in fun but to also signal it was on. He gave me a head nod back and we grabbed the mics. FIC made me go first because I called DUO out. The first two rounds of the finals were kind of plain. We both freestyled okay with no giant hits and only slight crowd reaction. Just as planned, I jumped off-stage when DUO completed his last verse, ran quickly through the crowd into the building, through the inside areas and into the backroom. It wasn't until I sat down and took a breathe that I questioned myself, "Did I win that?"

Either way it was close, if I did lose it wasn't bad. I thought if the judges gave it to him I didn't want to be up there anyway to watch them announce him as the winner. But it didn't feel like I lost. As I argued with myself, a young rapper named BONEY LINBURG came through the back area. Looking at me weird he asked, "What are you doing back here?" I just smiled. Then BONEY said, "I think they want you back out there."

Thinking he meant so they could announce the winner, I told BONEY to chill. I told him that I was cool and I knew what I was doing. He tried to tell me to come back out there again and then left. I could kind of hear what I thought was TOKI WRIGHT's voice on the mic, talking to the 300+ people in attendance outside but it was muffled in the back room. Since it wasn't FIC's voice I figured the battle winner had been announced and TOKI was introducing MAC LETHAL.

I would guess at least 5 minutes went by, but maybe up to 10. I had started to go over the TRADITIONAL METHODS/ KANSER set in my head since we were on next.

I thought the band would be mad at me for not helping them set up the equipment. But I had to stick to the plan. Right before we were scheduled to go on I would walk out as the MC champ. My lame ass had by now just figured since I was the hometown hero the judges probably just gave it to me. Then, BONEY LINBURG popped open the loading door that connected the back room to outside. "Yo, he's in here," BONEY said from the outside in.

I was like, "Fuck, what's going on?" I stepped outside amongst 300 people who were all looking at me with giant question marks on their faces. I took a longer than normal walk to the stage through a sea of people all staring at me.

What had happened was the judges called the finals a tie. TOKI WRIGHT stepped on-stage and told DUO and myself to come back for one more round. DUO had never left the stage but I was missing. For the last 10 minutes, which was an eternity, TOKI had been calling me to the stage. With the crowd in a question mark it must've looked...pretty dumb...or...I looked pretty dumb.

Getting odd looks from TOKI, the DJ, the judges, and everyone else, I was quickly told the summary and that I had to go another round. Completely out of my rhythm I spit a shaky 30-second freestyle. Then, with triple the energy as his first two verses DUO started rhyming something nice. He finessed the crowd with a joke about my beard calling me teen wolf and then looked me eye to eye. That's when I knew, he knew, that I knew...I was getting served. That shit felt horrible.

I kept my head down and went through the motions on-stage as they called him the winner. Besides a very close loss in a tournament in San Diego, California, the last time I really got beat was when I was 17 years old in September of '95. I had forgot how bad it felt.

DUO and QUESE were real cool dudes. We chopped it up for a second but they were in a hurry to get on the road back to Oklahoma. I talked them into staying for at least one song in the TRADITIONAL set so they could see what I do.

TRADITIONAL METHODS was one of the hottest groups in the city then, but the crowd barley reacted to me. I felt dumb to even being up there.

In Chapter 9, I said the only time I had ever seen SLUG look dumb was when BUDAH TYE beat him at the 7th Street Entry and he stayed on-stage and kept talking on the mic. That's how I felt that day. Once you get beat in a rap battle you should no longer touch the mic that day. There's always tomorrow but today is over. A crowd that sees you lose bad doesn't believe in you anymore.

15 years on the mic, that was probably the dumbest I ever looked. That might be saying a lot cuz I've looked dumb more than once. In the long run it ain't nothing. It stung for a couple days, now it's just a fun story to tell.

"Say what, say what, say anything can happen." - WYCLEF

CHAPTER 16 PART 2: ANYTHING CAN HAPPEN

My homie SHIZ, short for SHIZNON, is a unique dude. He is part Native, part Irish, and part African American. Being of mixed blood, his skin tone and features are the most beautiful in the human race. But, sadly, he has had to walk with those features his entire life in a world that looks upon him with racism. That racism he has felt, combined with growing up on the West Bank in South Minneapolis, has made SHIZ kinda tough. He ain't scared of shit. I'm not that tough and have been shocked multiple times in my life when SHIZ showed no fear in fighting dudes who were way bigger than him. SHIZ has stepped to some monsters.

I tried to teach SHIZ everything I knew about the local rap game, and for the most part, he'd listen. But, there was one thing I tried to tell him that was kinda complex: If you get in a fight when you are a local rapper who does shows in front of local audiences, you will be recognized. People, including the police, will be able to identify and find you afterward.

SHIZ is my brother. I would die for him and I am loyal to him. But, I do not have blind loyalty to anyone that I claim to love. If they are in the wrong, they are in the wrong. In 2003, SHIZ was dealing with a lot of pain. Three of his best friends died that year. To relieve some of that pain he went down to the Dinkytowner on a Saturday night to have some drinks with some people he knew. Saturday nights at the Dinkytowner were called the HOOK UP. It was spun by DJ STAGE ONE and hosted by UNICUS. One of the people SHIZ was with, who he didn't know well, went into the bathroom to snort some coke. He came out the bathroom claiming he had been robbed. That dude hyped up his friends and, for whatever reason, singled out DJ STAGE ONE as the dude who robbed him.

STAGE ONE was in the DJ booth where he had been all night and had not robbed anyone for coke in the bathroom. So, when four random dudes stepped to STAGE aggressively accusing him of robbing someone for drugs, I doubt STAGE had any idea what the fuck they were talking about. As the confrontation heated up, SHIZ and my friend Curtis claim that they stepped to the situation to defuse it and protect STAGE.

When the four dumbass dudes attacked STAGE ONE, STAGE's brother, BRO SON, trying to come to STAGE's defense, attacked SHIZ. In the corner of a packed Dinkytowner hip hop night, a violent scuffle set off by some coke head dude got outta control. And, for some reason never perfectly explained to me, SHIZ punched STAGE ONE in the face.

I had gone to some punk rock party over Northeast that night so I wasn't at the Dinkytowner when this went down. But in the morning, STAGE ONE's homies started blowing up my phone because "The mixed dude who raps with BIG ZACH" was the only one they could identify at the scene. They were hella angry and for good reason.

At 4pm that Sunday afternoon, I put on an all-age rap show at the Dinkytowner. On the hunt for SHIZ, STAGE ONE and 15 of his guys, including Chaka (commonly known as I SELF DEVINE) and BUDAH TYE, rolled through my show. Frustrated that SHIZ wasn't there, I SELF DEVINE eventually approached me and asked where I was hiding him. I SELF DEVINE is a pretty big dude and he was angry. I thought they were going to beat me up so I asked if they could do it outside so it wouldn't happen at this all-age show full of teenagers. BUDAH TYE, trying to settle the situation, asked me to give them SHIZ's whereabouts. Out of my loyalty to SHIZ, I refused. BUDAH TYE then asked me for SHIZ's number.

Out of my fear of being jumped at the all-age concert I was throwing, I gave BUDAH SHIZ's cell number. When the show was ending, BUDAH, I SELF, and STAGE spoke to me and told me they were gonna beat up SHIZ. Nothing too bad but he was gonna get what he deserved for what he did to STAGE. They told me if I stayed out of it, they would not have beef with me. Because I consider STAGE ONE my friend and because I felt SHIZ might have been in the wrong, I agreed.

The next night at the Dinkytowner, I ran into the dudes who had actually attacked STAGE ONE. They were kinda bragging about it. Then, BUDAH TYE and I SELF DEVINE came in the Dinkytowner, probably still on the hunt for SHIZ. BUDAH and I SELF didn't know who these dudes were because SHIZ was the only person recognized when the fight went down. This is what I tried to emphasize and explain to SHIZ.

These dudes were kinda talking shit about BUDAH and I SELF as if it was funny they were looking for SHIZ even though SHIZ was really trying to break up the fight and it was them who attacked STAGE. They only laughed because they knew that no one knew who they were. None of them could have lasted more than 10 seconds in a fight with BUDAH or I SELF. Part of me wanted to jump up and tell BUDAH and I SELF who they were but I knew that would not make the situation better or get SHIZ off the hook. Me saying something wouldn't change the fact that SHIZ still punched STAGE. BUDAH and his crew stayed on the hunt for SHIZ for months and I stayed out of it.

Without SHIZ's knowledge, they spotted him at Pizza Lucé downtown one night. They decided to give SHIZ a pass because SHIZ was eating with his girlfriend. Also on the hunt for SHIZ, I SELF DEVINE told our friend SARAH WHITE that he was looking for him. I SELF DEVINE, not knowing much about SHIZ, was unaware that as soon as SARAH WHITE told SHIZ that, SHIZ got heated and started looking for I SELF.

Later on, SHIZ spotted I SELF DEVINE eating dinner with his woman at the Red Dragon in Uptown and stepped to him. I SELF DEVINE, probably a little shocked that SHIZ had the nuts to step, said, "You really gonna do this in front of my girl, man?"

SHIZ and I SELF went outside and fought one-on-one. I SELF got the best of him before the bouncer came outside to break it up. I SELF DEVINE felt very disrespected that SHIZ would interrupt a date with his woman, especially when SHIZ had been given a pass when they spotted him eating with his girl not too long before.

Sometime after 2am, I was woken up by my phone ringing, it was BUDAH TYE and I SELF. They were hella angry. BUDAH briefly told me what had happened before I SELF got on the phone. He told me to give him SHIZ's address. When I tried to talk with him he told me intensely, "No words, no vowels, no nouns, no adjectives, just his address, just numbers." Out of my loyalty for SHIZ, I said no and I SELF hung up on me.

The next day I went to work. I was there for about an hour before I saw BUDAH TYE and I SELF DEVINE drive up on my work and park across the street. Knowing that BUDAH and I SELF were hard enough dudes to walk up in my work and snatch me over the counter and whoop me in broad daylight, I immediately picked up the phone.

Because I grew up in South Minneapolis and because I have never snitched on no one in my life and because dudes I grew up with love me as much as I love them, I was able to make a phone call and, within four minutes, two other men were also parked across the street from my work with guns ready to protect me. As BUDAH and I SELF sat in their car, one of my friends walked into my work and asked, "Is that them in that white car that looks like a cop car?" I told him it was. He then brought me in the bathroom and pulled out a little 22 pistol and asked me if I knew how to use it.

I told him I didn't so he showed me where the safety was and how to shoot it. He told me if they came in to shoot them in the lower body and that doing so would help me fight the case in court. He told me that they would stay parked outside and he would come protect me if needed.

This was a very surreal moment in my life. Even though I had never earned their respect I had grown up looking up to both of these men who were now parked across the street.

"I used to watch BUDAH TYE battle on cable access / high school
classes tagging in my text books" - BIG ZACH (NEW MC)

They were deciding if they were going to use force to get SHIZ'S whereabouts out of me. I am not trying to paint a picture of either of these men as bullies or villains. They are just men with principles. They live by principles the same as me and my homeboys live by principles. The only difference is they are a little harder than we are.

The root of the issue was they had their friend's back and I respect that. But if they would have stepped out of the car and came into my work they would have been stepping outta bounds. They would have broke the agreement they made with me at the Dinkytowner to stay out of conflict. By the principles that me and my homeboys live by we would have had the right to defend ourselves. I was scared. Not like piss my pants go hide in the basement scared. But I did feel fear.

At this very moment I was not in control of my life. I SELF DEVINE was in control of my life. If he would have gotten out of that car and came into my work, my life as I knew it would have been over. BUDAH and I SELF stayed parked across the street for somewhere between 20 minutes and a half an hour. I'm not sure because time was hard for me to comprehend at that moment. I don't know what they talked about or what they thought about, but they were strong enough to make the decision to drive away.

That night, KANSER played a show downtown and one of my best friends, DILLON PARKER, who was also good friends with BUDAH TYE, came through with a couple of big homies, including my homie ANT-DOG, to watch over me. Right before we went on, not knowing about the conflict earlier, DJ ELUSIVE played a record by I SELF DEVINE. It was ironic.

I walked around with that little baby 22 for the next three days. On the fourth day, I took it out of my backpack and prayed for God to protect me before I left the house for work. I was only half a block away from my work when someone yelled from behind me. It was I SELF DEVINE. He had black leather gloves on and I figured he was gonna smash me. I laughed to myself when I remembered I didn't have my gun. When he approached me, I stepped back, looked him in his eyes, and said, "I don't wanna fight you, Chaka."

"I don't wanna fight you either," he said. We talked and he told me he didn't have a problem with me. I SELF DEVINE is the hardest and strongest dude I have ever met growing up in Twin Cities hip hop. His energy is so strong that sometimes it takes all my strength just to look him in the eye. Soon after that, SHIZ was spotted having some drinks at a bar in Uptown. Several men ran through the bar and put a little whooping on SHIZ. They didn't kill him or put him in the hospital. They just gave him what he deserved for making the mistake of punching STAGE ONE in the face.

Now, that beef is long behind all of them and they shake hands when they see each other. I pray that STAGE ONE, BUDAH TYE, I SELF, and especially my best friend

SHIZ will understand why I put this story in my book. In their opinions it might not have anything to do with hip hop. I heard a lot of people in the hip hop scene gossiping about the beef. But no one I heard gossiping would last more than 10 seconds in a fair fight with SHIZ or I SELF DEVINE.

A few months later, one of the friends that came to protect me righteously gunned down another man who was beating an innocent girl in the street for no reason in front of a bar called Azia on 26th and Nicollet. I saw it with my own eyes. The friend who came to protect me spent the next three years in prison during which time I only wrote him one letter. I am a bitch for that. A few years after that incident, I was with the second friend who came to protect me. We were being dumb and got into trouble. Neither of us snitched on each other but, for maybe 30 seconds, the possibility that he would snitch on me crossed my mind.

I am a bitch for that as well.

CHAPTER 17 :
PEACE TO SHAWN NEIS

In June of 2003, a friend and ally of the KANSER TROOP, 23 year-old Shawn Neis, passed away from a drug overdose. None of us appeared at his funeral because we were on tour in California at the time of his death. Shawn opened the first underground hip hop shop in Minneapolis, MINDSTATE.

For the record there has always been URBAN LIGHTS in Midway St. Paul, a record store that sells 12 inches, CDs and tapes. They have a good record pool for DJs but cater to mainstream radio rap and R&B. There is also Michael's Hip Hop Shop on Chicago and Lake Street in South Minneapolis, which has stood for years 15+ years, (I bought two pairs of shorts there last summer) but they are strictly a clothing store.

The RHYMESAYERS store FIFTH ELEMENT is now the hub of underground and mainstream rap, but I believe MINDSTATE opened about 5 months before them.

MINDSTATE is located in the Dinkydale mall in Southeast Minneapolis. They sell clothes and underground rap. Shawn helped push a lot of KANSER/INTERLOCK product for us out of MINDSTATE. He was good at selling music and spreading the word about music he liked.

Shawn was also an ally because he ran a live rap night at Gasthof's bar in Northeast Minneapolis every other Wednesday from 2000-2003. Gasthof's was a pretty cool basement spot that had good sound and big glasses of beer. Its only flaw was that it didn't look like the type of place that would have hip hop. On a busy street in an otherwise pretty peaceful neighborhood, it appeared to be a closed German restaurant if you drove by it on a Wednesday night. There were no signs of what was cracking in the basement. But down below, a good amount of drunken nights, good shows, battles, and a few fights took place every other Wednesday.

Shawn's Gasthof's shows were real social and hosted by CARNAGE. With in-house DJ EXCALIBUR, it was a spot to chop it up, get drunk, and chill. You had to be careful cuz the door man was known for not ID-ing young girls. I once met a girl at Gasthof's that told me she was a high school junior. I was like, "How did you get in here?" She's replied, "It's Gasthof's on hip hop night." As if I wasn't in the know.

Not only did Shawn have local acts but they brought in tons of semi-big underground acts from Chicago, New York and the West Coast. Shawn dug a lot of the West Coast underground like Z-MAN, SACRED HOOP, LIVING LEGENDS and others.

Eventually, Shawn sold MINDSTATE and moved to Duluth, Minnesota where he was about to open another underground shop that was above a live music café. The last time I saw Shawn he brought us up to Duluth to play the café where he showed us his new store up above. It was almost ready to open with murals already painted on the walls. If the store would have opened, combined with Shawn throwing live shows downstairs, it would have done a lot for Duluth and a lot for us moving product up there.

Shawn went to Columbia Heights High School, in a suburb of Northeast Minneapolis. But he was originally from Alexandria, Minnesota, a small town between Minneapolis and Fargo off Highway 94. The story I would like to tell about Shawn happened almost a year after he passed away during my first trip to Alexandria. But first, let me jump back to Dinkytown during the time of the Loring Pasta Bar MC battles.

I was leaving the Dinkytowner bar with my home-girl when I saw ILLICIT, a regular from the MC battles standing out on the block with a small boombox freestyling to himself, or so I thought. He approached us on some street performer shit asking us if we had any change for his cup, telling us his landlord gave him two days to come up with $250 for late rent or he would be homeless. He told us all that in his freestyle and then asked if we wanted him to rap about anything in particular cuz he would rap about whatever we wanted if we would drop a dollar.

We took a pass but in the back of my mind I thought that takes heart. Matter of fact, that takes balls I don't even have. Maybe a week later I saw ILLICIT again on the street and I asked him if he made his rent. He told me he did but it took him two and a half days of standing in Dinkytown rapping on the corner all day for U of M students. He won me over with that shit. I asked him if he had anything going on the next weekend. He said no so I told him he was in my crew now (INTERLOCK) and that he had four shows this weekend in Minnesota with us.

Our first show that weekend was in Alexandria. We played a show dedicated to Shawn thrown by three female friends of his. It was a dope show and there were lots of people there. Way more than I expected and they seemed to be hip on who we were and hip to the underground in general. I traced the knowledge of the culture that existed in the small town of Alexandria directly back to Shawn.

I learned he moved back and forth from the Twin Cities to Alexandria for years bringing back tapes, CDs and the overall knowledge of the hip hop culture. Between sound check and our performance, the girls brought us to the spot they had arranged for us to sleep at, but instead of a hotel or someone's house they rented us 3 two-bedroom cabins. Plus they made us hella good food, bought us lots of liquor, and paid us in advance pretty well. We got the full treatment.

UNICUS, DJ ANTON, NOAH B, myself, and now ILLICIT came to Alexandria to represent INTERLOCK but when we got on-stage I realized we were doing more than that. We were representing what Shawn had found in the underground of the Twin Cities and was never fully able to show his friends and family back home. In one world, Shawn loved underground hip hop and he loved and supported INTERLOCK. In another world, he loved all his people he had grown up with in this small town. I feel that some way from beyond the grave he brought us together.

When we were on stage that night it was special. The energy between the crowd and us was way deeper than some regular show. I've been on the mic over a thousand times in my life and felt all sorts of different vibes from whoever was listening, but that night I could feel something inside myself and all around us that words can't describe. It wasn't about us; we were just playing our part.

Towards the end of the show I fell back while DJ ANTON was running a routine. I looked over at ILLICIT who at this point I still didn't know that well and said, "Man, I ain't trying to come off weird but I feel like Shawn is here with us tonight like I can feel him." ILLICIT looked me square in the eyes real intense, and with complete confidence like he already spiritually understood what I was trying to say, said, "Dude I didn't even know Shawn and I can feel him right now. Peace to Shawn Neis." What ILLICIT said in the mic became the phrase for the rest of the night.

By the way...we all got laid by Alexandria girls that night...thanks Shawn.

Peace to Shawn Neis, a friend and ally of INTERLOCK.

CHAPTER 18 :
CRAYOLA COLOR KIDS

Race issues in hip hop start conversations that make me want to shoot myself.

I apologize to the reader for how much I have talked about race in this book. I did my best to describe how our world of rap has changed, race included, and what I saw or how I felt at the time. This chapter will sum up how I feel now.

Rap music is black music, in the sense that it was created by African Americans same as Jazz and Rock & Roll. This should be common knowledge but just to add on to it, Minnesota rap music is black music in the sense that the first people to make this music in Minnesota were African Americans.

"Hip hop started on the Northside" *- TRUTHMAZE*

We all know who started this shit, we all know who invented it, and we all know where it came from. We also know that large groups of different kinds of kids support it and all types of people love it.

When I was younger I probably got caught up trying to understand what had happened to the scene. It felt like I walked into a room that was playing one kind of music and was taught how to play it by a group of people. Then, I watched 95% of the group of people who taught me leave the room and hundreds of new people come in and pay to watch me make the music that I was taught. Furthermore, a "few" of the new kids in the room started to claim they made a better version of the music than the people who had originally taught me how to make it. I tried to tell them that that was disrespectful but not all of them believed me and there was a small split.

LIFE SUCKS DIE magazine, a locally run graffiti/other weird stuff publication that INTERLOCK actually used to share a studio with, could be my best example. LSD had a column called "Cooking with Chef RAEKWON" poking fun at the WU-TANG member. Now I'm sure the LSD crew was clowning. But these dudes were computer kids who were all raised in upper class house holds. If by some chance they were to come face to face with RAEKWON, I would imagine they would get the shit slapped out of 'em and probably not even fight back. The way I grew up, you don't talk shit about people publicly that you're not prepared to deal with.

The viewpoint from their side I'm sure is that kids like me who held hip hop so sacred were taking it too serious. LSD writer DJ ANDREW used to do record reviews on the BEATBOX radio show. I would listen to him and almost always disagree with whatever he was saying. But, sometimes, it was funny.

In 1999, when MOS DEF dropped the record *Black on Both Sides*, I thought it was the dopest shit to come out in a minute. To this day I would still call it classic. Well, DJ ANDREW hated it. He might have reviewed it two weeks in a row just to make more fun of it. The LSD review was just as bad.

BROTHER ALI, who probably felt the same way I did about the record, told me he went up to the radio show and told DJ ANDREW he would stick him in the mouth if he made fun of MOS DEF again. ANDREW, who was kind of a frail kid, not the type to have a physical confrontation, supposedly got pretty freaked out about it. When ALI told me this over the phone I couldn't help but laugh a little.

Two days later, DJ ANDREW came in my work to get some food. He said what's up so I said what's up back, but before he left I signaled for him to talk with me for a second. I told him I had laughed when ALI told me what happened so I felt a bit two faced saying what's up to him without asking his side of the story. ANDREW got slightly emotional as he explained himself. He said he was just trying to have fun and open people's eyes. ANDREW then left the BEATBOX radio show.

DJ ANDREW had a lot of skill behind the wheels. He wasn't afraid to be stupid either. He once beat DJ ABILITIES in a battle by mooning the crowd in the final round. He started DJing for this group called the PIZZA BOYS; two white dudes who were doing 80's retro rap and fashion before it was cool to do 80's retro rap and fashion. They played right before us (INTERLOCK ALL STARS) at First Ave once.

They did corky things and moved around weird on-stage. It wasn't my thing, but I did think the members of the PIZZA BOYS were alright dudes so I didn't want to hate. But the longer they rapped the more I took them as making fun of hip hop. Since we were on next, it was as if they were making fun of us. Not aimed directly, but they were making fun of what we were about to do when we got on-stage. As they got off-stage and we were being announced, CARNAGE confronted them about it. "So what are you guys trying to do exactly? Are you doing hip hop or making fun of it?"

The conversation would have ran longer but I was trying to drag CARNAGE up on-stage. In defense of himself, DJ ANDREW said, "Is BIZ MARKIE making fun of hip hop? We're not doing anything that he's not doing."

*"A year ago you were into raves hanging with gays / now you got a new
label hip hop purest / trying to tell veterans how to drop lyrics"* - *MUSAB*

For years I have heard black and white rappers say they believe it is easier to
be a white rapper in Minnesota then a black rapper and that it is harder to succeed as a
rapper whose music reflects the black inner city experience because the press, venues,
and fans in Minnesota don't relate to black rappers as much as they do to white rappers.
I wasted a good amount of time (mostly in my head) pondering this.

Sad but true, ATMOSPHERE didn't blow up until SPAWN (the former black
rapper in the group) left or was faded out the group around 1998. But that just happened
to run parallel with a time where SLUG was busting ass and getting a lot better at writing
songs. Since the time I knew SLUG, I was pretty sure he was part black, white and Native.
I asked him once at his crib why he didn't represent being black and Native in his songs.
He said that since he looked white, he didn't have to go through the same problems that
blacks and Natives did. He said he had never been denied a job because he was black. I
thought that was a good point. Then he jokingly said, "And shit, this white rapper thing's
about to blow!" (haha)

If SPAWN not being in the group had or has anything to do with ATMOSPHERE'S
giant popularity, that is a heavy question I don't know the answer to. I do know the top
three most successful rappers out of Minnesota are white (if you count SLUG) SLUG,
EYEDEA, and BROTHER ALI. The 4th would be P.O.S, who is black but his punk rock
background pulls him a predominantly white punk/hipster crowd. The 5th is FELIX
who's mixed and is a part of the band HEIRUSPECS whose members are half white and
they have a pretty big white following. Over the years, I have heard disgruntled local rappers bring up these race questions about those five rappers, but never bring up the fact
that those five rappers music, talent, and work ethic might be the highest in the state.
And that even though on the surface all their crowds appear to be suburbian white kids,
thousands of people of all colors have enjoyed their music over the years.

I couldn't tell you that some of my minor success hasn't had something to do
with me being white or that my main rap partner UNICUS being Haitian has not helped
us because the population of Haitians in Minnesota that are into underground rap is
under ten people including UNICUS, his brother and cousin. (haha) The truth about all
that shit is, I don't know. I really don't know.

"Watch all the white kids eat it up like mayonnaise" - *SLUG*

Things have just changed, and back in the mid-90's none of us knew what our crowds would look like in the future... shit we were just trying to get anyone to listen to or care about our raps in the first place. In 1995 SLUG needed the co-sign of black rappers like D-SPAWN, MUSAB, and the ABSTRACT PACK to be accepted and be able to survive the times. But he also needed real skills to survive. With my own eyes, more than once I saw SLUG and URBAN ATMOSPHERE step on-stage in front of a black, inner city, hardcore hip hop crowd and perform, kill it, get props, and survive in the mid-90's. Most people/rappers who have ever hated on SLUG in front of me never saw that era and probably are too bitch to have been able to survive it.

I have been to two rap shows at the Cedar Cultural Center in my life. The first was the 2nd Mic Check Showcase which featured ten local groups and the BOOT CAMP CLIK in 1995. It was a pretty tough crowd in all definitions of the phrase. Mostly black, urban, hardcore hip hop heads, and there was a lot of hating on the local talent. The second show that I went to there was seven years later in 2002. The line up was HEIRUSPECS, ODD JOBS, and P.O.S. and SLUG opened with a little set. Now this crowd might have been the most high school white girl softest crowd I ever saw in my life. There were probably only five people in the almost sold-out audience that weren't white (if you don't count performers).

I sat back in the cut and thought a lot about the way things have changed. All four of these artists (or groups) were more successful than any of the ten groups that opened for BOOT CAMP in '95 (with the exception of SLUG who played both). But, if you took ODD JOBS and P.O.S, put them in a time machine, sent them back to' 95 and let them open for BOOT CAMP in front of the '95 crowd, they would have got boo'd off-stage. The type of music P.O.S. and ODD JOBS made was way too abstract and soft for the '95 crowd.

I tossed this back and forth in my head all night. These kids at the 2002 show were really supportive, they were fans, they were having a good time. They were the outcome of the scene built by SLUG and RSE. Then I had to remember I had a lot to do with this too. I helped white kids become comfortable in local rap. The white kid hip hop scene here was mostly created by RSE and INTERLOCK.

Towards the end of the night I realized that there were three people who were at both shows, SLUG, UNICUS, and myself. SLUG played, he was the king of this shit, I would assume he had a good night. UNICUS was kicking it. He was getting a little drunk and hollering at a couple girls. Then, I thought, "Why am I in the corner thinking about these racial, urban issues? Why do I care?" Then I decided fuck it, it's just the way it is and I shouldn't think about this dumb shit anymore. What I finally came up with was ...... it is what it is. Going in circles debating race issues in hip hop is a waste of time.

One time when I was hosting at the Pasta Bar, a white kid dropped the N word when he was battling. The front five rows were made up mostly of black kids and they tried to snatch him by the legs off-stage. I grabbed the kid so he didn't fall into the sea of ass whooping that awaited him and just ended the battle and disqualified the white kid. BUDAH TYE was pretty close to the front and was somewhat leading the charge for the kid. I think after I disqualified the kid BUDAH wasn't tripping but yelling at me to get my attention. He told me to say on the mic, "If you ain't black, you can't say nigga!" Doing what I was told I put the mic up to my mouth and almost said the whole sentence. I caught myself and tossed the cordless mic to BUDAH and said, "Maybe you should say it."

It would be impossible to sum up a talk about racism in general and racism in hip hop is even more complicated. But I have a final statement. I thought of it when I was at Scribble Jam in 2004 and then it was reinforced the next week at our own Twin Cities Celebration of Hip Hop.

I looked over the sea of people at both events and I clearly saw all the diversity. All different colors, all different religions. People from different hoods and classes, suburb kids, city kids, rural kids, all in the same place, all hanging out together. I thought it was most likely that these kids' parents were not hanging out with people from other races. I could almost guarantee that their grandparents and great grandparents weren't. Then I thought, "This is all because of hip hop." I think hip hop has helped to fight racism... That's what I think.

CHAPTER 19 :
TEACH ME HOW TO RAP

One morning when I was 27 in 2005 the phone rang and I didn't recognize the area code on the caller ID. I answered and a girl's voice asked if Zach was there. Always suspect of crazy girls calling my crib I replied, "He could be, who's this?"

She told me she was calling about a television show on MTV called *Made*. Since I quit watching MTV when FAB 5 FREDDY stopped hosting *YO! MTV RAPS* like ten years ago I had no idea what that meant. I asked if it was that the show where they punk celebrities? She laughed and said, "No, it's a show where a young person who has a secret dream of doing something they have never tried before gets a three week crash course in their dream. What I'm calling about is we have a young kid from your area that would like to become a rapper. Do you think you could teach a kid who has never rapped before how to be a rapper in three weeks?"

I said, "Fuck no, you can't learn how to rap in three weeks." She then said, "We'll pay you." After a pause, I said, "Well, maybe I can teach him how to rap in three weeks."

Through the rest of the conversation I didn't get a lot of words in. She was talking real fast and I could tell she knew little or nothing about hip hop. She told me that they found a nerdy white kid from a rich suburb and basically explained to me the story line. Even though it was "reality" TV they already had the story sketched out. Drilling me with questions but not letting me answer, the conversation froze when she finally said, "I know you're white, but beyond that, do you have street credibility?"

On general principal I should have just hung up right then. The definition of "street cred", the way mainstream big businesses such as MTV see it, is a fashion image of "being from the hood" that they can sell to kids. It's deeper than that but its too disgusting to break down further.

She was not asking me about my little brother being in prison for murder. She was not asking me about the other friends I have that I send Christmas letters to in prison. She wasn't asking me about being raised in the inner city of Minneapolis. She wasn't asking me about when I saw my homie get shot the summer before. She was asking me if I wore a gold chain around my neck and if I could dress like 50 CENT.

The next day KANSER left for a weekend of shows out of town with the CORE. One of the rappers in the CORE, AD, drove us in a 20 passenger bus so we had plenty of room. The other rapper, TOKI WRIGHT, talked with me about the MTV *Made* offer. He said they had contacted him also along with a local rapper, MASTERMIND, from GUARDIANS OF BALANCE. I told him I thought it was weird and felt kind of funny style, but TOKI and the CORE's manager, LARRY, talked me into returning her email. TOKI said he and MASTERMIND were gonna go for it and if one of the three of us got it we should try to include the other two. They made it sound cooler than the lady on the phone did so I completed everything in the email MTV *Made* sent me.

TOKI was chosen to be the kids rap coach, which I thought was pretty tight. TOKI is a good representative of the Minnesota rap scene. Besides being in the CORE, he also ran the once a year TWIN CITIES CELEBRATION OF HIP HOP that happened every summer and was always one of my favorite parts of the year.

But TOKI didn't end up to be the main coach; MTV sent an underground rapper from New York, C-RAYZ WALZ to be the front coach for the kid. TOKI was used as the plug to the Twin Cities scene.

I didn't know who C-RAYZ WALZ was. But, for the few weeks he was in town I saw him around. He asked me if I could get him a show anywhere on short notice so I plugged him with UNICUS who got him on at the Dinkytowner Saturdays.

Also, the following Tuesday at the Dinkytowner, BIG QUARTERS and their crew FAM FUED had a CD release for an instrumental mixtape. I SELF DEVINE, TOKI WRIGHT, ILLUMINOUS 3, BROTHER ALI, and myself were on the bill to do two songs apiece. Songs we had recorded over FAM FUED beats.

After I did my couple songs, TOKI asked me if I would host the MTV *Made* kid's first performance this Sunday which was also at the Dinkytowner (the Dinkytowner got a lot shows in this story). TOKI was trying to keep his word hoping that I would get on TV if I was the host. He also had GUARDIANS OF BALANCE booked to open the show to keep his word about MASTERMIND. I told TOKI I would do it.

The BIG QUARTERS show was so packed, it was crazy hot just off body heat alone. I saw C-RAYZ WALZ there that night. He seemed kinda pumped up and told me he had watched my performance and he was real mad about my mic levels being low. "I couldn't even hear you spit, son!" he said, seeming more amped then he should be.

The next thing I know C-RAYZ is on-stage about to do a song. Since I had never heard him rap before I slid up front. It looked as if it was unplanned and C-RAYZ just handed a CD of his beats to BRANDON ALLDAY of BIG QUARTERS. C-RAYZ'S beat came on and I don't know what happened. He started swearing at the sound man, rapped a few bars, and I think said something disrespectful to BRANDON ALLDAY who then stopped the beat. Then, C-RAYZ WALZ yelled at the crowd, "Fuck this, I got 200 dollars in my pocket if anyone wants it!" He then threw the mic down and walked off-stage. It was real awkward since only four or five people knew who C-RAYZ was. I heard voices in the packed house say, "Who the fuck was that?"..."What was that about?"

Maybe I took it wrong, but I felt like he really disrespected my homies FAM FUED. I wasn't gonna let an out-of-towner step in our house and say he could serve any rapper here for $200. With no music and the crowd still with a question mark on their faces, I stepped on-stage, grabbed a mic, and said, "Did dude say he'll battle anyone here for 200 dollars? Cuz if he did, I'll battle him."

FREEZ from ILLUMINOUS 3, a 17 year-old rapper who was probably the illest high school emcee in the state at the time grabbed the mic and said, "Yo, NEW MC vs. C-RAYZ WALZ!"

The crowd was half anxious and still half confused as C-RAYZ stepped back on stage. Not fully sure what C-RAYZ's initial statement was all about, I gave him a chance to get out of it. "Yo, I'm not calling you out. But if you were saying you would battle anyone here for $200 I'll battle you." Not having $200 in my pocket I looked over at MEDIUM ZACH of BIG QUARTERS who I knew made way over $200 that night at the door and asked if he could spot me. MEDIUM ZACH looked at me like, "Ahh man."

Everyone's confused eyes were on C-RAYZ now. He stood there for about 10 seconds without saying anything before FREEZ busted out a little giggle on-stage. C-RAYZ then physically put his hands on FREEZ.

C-RAYZ WALZ putting his hands on a 17 year-old brought the night to a stop. The fight was broken up and I went home thinking, "What the fuck was that all about?"

I had dinner with TOKI and MEDIUM ZACH a few nights later where I told TOKI that I didn't think it was a good idea if I hosted the MTV *Made* show anymore after the altercation with C-RAYZ. He told me C-RAYZ wasn't tripping and said he still wanted me to do it. We all talked about what happened and I could tell TOKI was in a real strange position. Being on MTV *Made* was the biggest opportunity of TOKI's life so far, and the drama it was coming with was unexpected.

ANT brought me to an RSE show the next night where I ran into C-RAYZ. He was cool at first but the longer the night went on he got weird and kept saying weird shit in my ear like, "I'll hit you with these darts son, I'll hit BIG ZACH with these darts." Eventually I just kinda told dude to get away from me. ANT saw some of it and when the show was over we hung out for a few hours.

He brought me to the crib to listen to some new songs he had made or something. Afterwards he sat me down and tried to tell me not to host the show. About 96% of everything ANT has ever told me has ended up to be real. I should have listened to him on that one.

The day of the MTV *Made* show was also May Day. The Minneapolis May Day celebration is held at Powderhorn Park and is one of the best days of the year. I saw mad friends that day at the park and asked a few of my Southside homies to come through the Dinkytowner. "This dude (C-RAYZ WALZ) might be acting funny, so just come down there to cover me," I said. About ten of my homies including DILLON PARKER and some LONG DOE dudes came to hold me down.

What was presented on MTV as a "downtown hip hop night club" was really the Dinkytowner at 6pm in the evening and the Minneapolis crowd was really just made up of the MTV *Made* kid's high school friends.

TOKI told me how the night was suppose to go. They had to hurry things up because the kid's dad didn't want to be out too late. C-RAYZ gave me bad vibes from jump so I just avoided him. When he got on-stage and started rapping with the kid, my homies started instigating, challenging him to battle me, and threw like $500 up in the air. The crowd that was there wouldn't have even understood what a rap battle was so I didn't really know where this was about to go. C-RAYZ then, on the mic in front of a high school audience, starts talking shit to all my homies...crazy type shit.

Long story short my homies tried to jump C-RAYZ WALZ. When I say long story short, I mean it. The whole incident lasted about 15 minutes. What saved C-RAYZ was TOKI WRIGHT. C-RAYZ hid behind him and just talked shit while my boy DILLON, BIG WIZ and other homies tried to get open to take swings at him but couldn't manage to get around TOKI. Of course none of that drama aired on the MTV episode, but I would guess that whoever did the editing got to watch some funny shit.

Besides TOKI getting some props that he deserves, I wish the whole thing would have never happened. Even though I wasn't in the wrong, I'd like to apologize to C-RAYZ WALZ. I don't believe the fight was our fault or his fault. I believe it is the result of when you take something as pure as hip hop and dilute it with something as fake as MTV.

CHAPTER 20 :
GOD'S LOOKING RIGHT AT US

In 2006, KANSER played an outdoor, all-day festival at Harmony Park Campground in Geneva, Minnesota called Hip Hop & Harmony, maybe an hour and ten minutes south of the city. LYRICS BORN, SAGE FRANCIS, HEIRUSPECS, DOOMTREE, the CREST, and many more were out there with us.

KANSER was supposed to play at 4:30 right after the UNKNOWN PROPHETS. During the PROPHETS set it started to rain a little, and then a little more, and then a dust storm which I could see coming from about three football fields away blew through Harmony Park blowing over trash cans and people's tents, forcing most of the crowd to run back to their camp sites and take cover. For a second, it got pretty scary, or at least I can say I was scared. It felt like a tornado might be coming through and when I realized a couple hundred kids were out here with no real shelter, I knew the outcome of it could be real bad. I took cover in one of the trucks that the speakers had been brought in behind the stage. I watched as the rain came harder and the PROPHETS finished their set to about 60 die hard kids who were somewhat protected by the roof of the stage.

I figured the show was over, or at least we couldn't go on, as we waited for the storm to pass. UNICUS, myself, and our band, MORE THAN LIGHTS, hid backstage hoping the weather would get better. The storm lightened up a little and at 4:30pm, the soundman told us to go on. As the rain fell behind them, maybe 20 kids still pushed to the front of the stage. The first song on our set was called "Solar". It was a song about being able to do anything and the chorus went,

"You were born to shine like solar / she was born to shine like solar."

UNICUS said to me, "It's kind of weird that we're about to do that song in the rain." I grabbed the mic and spoke to an empty, open, and rainy campground. Fifty yards from the stage, there were trees that hid a couple hundred kids from the rain. "Hey," I said. "I know you can hear me back there. It's kind of inappropriate that were gonna start our set off with a song about the sun, but if any of you kids back there smoking herb and barbecuing mosquitoes wanna come out here, we're still gonna do our thing."

Matiu, our guitarist, started playing the intro and we just started rapping in the rain. People slowly started appearing, coming from all sides out of the shadows of the world. When we got to the solar part in the chorus, I swear to God it stopped raining.

I did the second verse and when we hit the second chorus, the sun came out. It was real magical and the kids in the crowd reacted as if we had all performed a miracle together.

KANSER's set was fun. When it was over, I wandered through the woods until I ran into someone who had some magic mushrooms. He broke me off a bag big enough to feed the whole band and KANSER got high. Tripping through the woods with a growing number of kids at a hippy rap concert was crazy fun.

I stopped and talked to everyone I could, making conversation with everyone I walked by. I watched DOOMTREE's set, which was the best rap set that ever happened in the history of the universe. The sun had come out and it was perfect outside. This was the moment when I realized how dope they had become. I looked over at my boy, DJ TREY TAYLOR, and said, "Am I trippin' on shrooms or are they dope as fuck right now?" The members of DOOMTREE who were there were:

SIMS: A James Dean style white dude with a strong rap.
DESSA: A tall Puerto Rican/white chick. Her rap style has a spoken word base and her singing voice is of a fallen angel.
MIKE MICTLAN: A Mexican kid originally from Los Angeles who, along with his abstract DOOMTREE style, had a taste of street in his rap.
PAPER TIGER: The DJ on the wheels.
LAZERBEAK: Producer of monster like original beats, LAZERBEAK started off in a young popular punk band from Hopkins, MN called The Plastic Constellations.
CECIL OTTER: Rapper with a smooth, abstract, and poetic rap style.
P.O.S. : A black punk rock kid with one of the most original rap styles I've ever heard.

Prior to that moment, I liked all these dudes as people but hadn't given them much credit as rappers, beat makers, and DJs. But, at that moment, I realized how dope and original they were.

Almost at the peak of my trip, I cut backstage to eat some of the free food. Back there I saw the HEIRUSPECS' band writing out a set list. TWINKIE started to ask me when he thought TRADITIONAL METHODS should come on-stage and how many songs we should do. I was tripping hard enough that I had totally spaced that

TRADITIONAL was supposed to play. The man who was running Hip Hop and Harmony had tried to book TRADITIONAL METHODS but we couldn't get our shit together.

So, yesterday he had contacted HEIRUSPECS special requesting if SARAH, SHIZ, and myself could guest appear in the HEIRUSPECS set. "Have you talked to SARAH?" I asked, knowing she and SHIZ were here but not knowing if anyone had talked to them. TWINKIE gave me that look like, "Zach, go figure out what's going on and quick." I was like, "Ahh fuck." I thought SARAH was mad at me about some other shit that had happened a few days ago (it wasn't nothing but I didn't want to have to talk it out right now on mushrooms).

I walked through the woods looking for her. When I saw her, I just punked out and walked by her. Then...I did it again. "Zach!" she yelled. She came up to me with real pleasant energy that let me know we probably weren't in a fight. "Are we gonna play with HEIRUSPECS or what?" she said all smiling.

"Man, are you still mad at me about the other..." she cut me off before I finished, "No, your so weird," she said. "I was just tired when we spoke and..." she cut herself off, looked at the size of my pupils, and asked, "Are you high Zach?"

I said, "Yeah, I'm on shrooms." We started laughing and she asked, "Are you gonna be able to perform? Will you remember your lyrics while you're on shrooms?" I said "Yeah, I'll be cool but we better find SHIZ so we can go over the old songs behind the stage."

I told SARAH I was cool so she wouldn't worry. But the truth of the matter was I never performed high, drunk, nothing. Like once in my life I smoked weed before a show and up until that point I had never drank anything (six months later I did a show with YONI and DESSA and I had three beers before I went on and lost my voice halfway through the set. I'll never do that again.)

HEIRUSPECS started playing, we weren't suppose to jump on until almost the end of their set and we were only to do two songs, easy enough. The only problem was we hadn't practiced or played together in almost a year. The three of us tried to go over our lyrics but kept forgetting them. We kept forgetting who went after who and where the choruses were. For a second we were like, "oh fuck." Then we stopped, mapped out both songs, and, to the background beat of the HEIRUSPECS band, we performed to each other. It felt like holding hands with an old love.

SHIZ, SARAH WHITE, and my high ass flipped the lyrics to both songs in a perfect energy triangle that reminded me of the old high school cyphers I learned how to emcee in. As we remembered the songs, we remembered how fresh the lyrics were as they came out.

We started to sneak on-stage just as I was totally peaking on mushrooms. It started to get intense. The crowd had doubled in size from when KANSER was on and the mushrooms were making me nervous. HEIRUSPECS were banging away, the music was loud and clear, the crowd was into it, and I was tripping balls! The sun was setting and the stage lights were so...colorful. I wish I could describe it better.

FELIX signaled to me that we had about 20 seconds as he had the crowd clapping to the beat. I stood on the side of the stage and tried to shy away from the 400+ pair of eyes with their focus on the stage. Tripping harder than I had in over a year, I got ahold of myself and stepped into the open with SARAH and SHIZ. I would only guess a third of the crowd knew who TRADITIONAL METHODS was but their reaction to us combined with how high I was made it feel like THE FUGEES in the DAVE CHAPPELLE block party movie.

Performing on shrooms to that crowd in that environment was sooooooooooo fresh!!!!!!! Soon as I touched the mic my mind linked into the songs. I was still tripping but my perspective on everything going on around me didn't effect the lyrics coming out my mouth at all. Looking at the crowd through my eyes, it felt as if we all had a strong connection. Like we were out here together enjoying life, nature, good weather, and good music. After the first song, I couldn't take it anymore! I said the most classic ridiculous thing I have ever said live at a show.

"Yo, I don't want to set a bad example about drugs. I don't do speed, I don't do coke, and I don't do heroin...but I'm on shrooms right now and I'm tripping my balls off!!!"

I would guess 150-200 people in the crowd were either on acid, ecstasy, shrooms, really drunk, and/or on whatever new drugs the kids are doing these days cuz of the way they reacted to my off-the-wall statement.

The outdoor stage had a roof that came to a point in the middle directly above us. Halfway through the next song I looked out beyond the crowd into the fresh night sky and saw a star or planet perfectly lined up with the point of the roof. My eyes looked from side to side looking for other stars until I realized that it was the only one out. I looked behind the stage, no stars had appeared in the night sky behind us either.

What appeared directly over the stage and crowd at Harmony Park that summer night was one giant star; as if God was especially looking at us. I wanted to stop the music and tell everyone but I double-thought, "Is that really there? Maybe I'm just high."

Not wanting to make an ass out of myself I asked SHIZ if he saw it too. When he said it was there I had to tell the crowd. It was one of the most spiritual moments I've ever had and I'm glad I didn't have it alone. People still approach me about once a month and say, "Yo, I saw that star at Harmony Park too."

UNICUS, the MORE THAN LIGHTS band, and myself were geeking for days about how much fun we had at Harmony Park. I assumed the feeling was mutual amongst the other performers until I found myself at a party at the DOOMTREE mansion soon after.

At the party I overheard a conversation between SIMS and DJ TREY TAYLOR. They said something like, "What did you think of the Hip Hop and Harmony shit"…"Um, it was alright"…"We got paid"…"Yeah, it was okay." I thought to myself, "What the fuck! That was the funnest day of my life!"

I then had a meeting with UNICUS and the MORE THAN LIGHTS band and we decided to separate MORE THAN LIGHTS as a different group that was more than just KANSER with a band. MORE THAN LIGHTS would pursue playing more and more festivals. We contacted WOOKIEFOOT and CHRIS (Bella), who throw the festivals at Harmony Park every year, and have been riding that roller coaster ever since.

Eventually, MORE THAN LIGHTS signed with MJG, the premier festival booking agency in the Midwest and have found a whole new scene and new "trip" to take. Since it strays from hip hop I'll leave it at that. But if I ever write a second book, maybe I'll record the adventures and new world that MORE THAN LIGHTS was able to find.

I truly believe that Harmony Park is a magical place and that the tree's hold special energy. It was that energy that directed us on a new path. I believe Harmony Park is my home.

CHAPTER 21 :
SPOTS

This chapter is small write-ups of rappers or groups that I didn't get to mention or mention enough of during the stories in the book but shouldn't be left unrecognized in Twin Cities hip hop.

STEREO TYPE CLICK/SP STYLES

The CLICK is the front-cover group of Eastside St. Paul. They've been around over twelve years and hold their own niche in the city. Their company ST STYLES does a lot of mainstream club events, giant boat parties, and even run a trip to Mexico every year. DJ D-MILL is a good promoter and a good club DJ. SHAWN SKIE is one of the illest emcees in the state.

EG BAILEY

EG BAILEY runs the Minnesota Spoken Word Association. Spoken word poetry has always had a close relationship with hip hop and EG has kept that tradition strong by managing acts like TRUTH MAZE and getting him tours out in Europe. EG has always been a positive nice dude to KANSER and even gave us an opening slot for KRS ONE in 2007.

HEIRUSPECS

The HEIRUSPECS band is like a machine. They used to be the most "sober" band I've ever been around and they operate totally different from any other rap group or band that I've ever dealt with. There has been a revolving door of members/musicians since they first got together at St. Paul Central High School in 1997 with the two staples being the lead MC, FELIX, and the bass player, Sean McPherson aka TWINKIE JIGGLES.

TWINKIE is the coolest rich kid I've ever met. His family is stupid rich. But TWINKIE and his family have not once ever acted snobbish or pretended to be something they weren't around me. The relevance of TWINKIE coming from money to the story of HEIRUSPECS is that he didn't grow up around hip hop and didn't find the music/culture 'till he was 16-17 years old. With that being said, he had more excitement and resources to drive a live hip hop band to local popularity and beyond.

Also, being a bass player, TWINKIE saw things different. He could pin point what sounded good in rap outside of what the words were while still being real big on lyrics. He can dissect them bar for bar. He's told me things like, "If your 5th bar was written better that verse would be perfect," after hearing me rap a 20 bar verse. When I would look over my lyrics I would realize...he was right.

Out the box, HEIRUSPECS had popularity. Since they started out in high school they had a St. Paul Central following. Young kids who might not necessarily have been into rap would come out to see HEIRUSPECS because their shows would double as Central High School social events. After FELIX and TWINKIE graduated, the Central crowd still followed them, and HEIRUSPECS shows grew into St. Paul social events.

When they linked into INTERLOCK in 1998, they picked up the South/Southwest Minneapolis rap crowds through doing shows with KANSER and ODD JOBS and repeatedly blew us off the stage with their live show.

To me, it was somewhat embarrassing to play before HEIRUSPECS back then. FELIX was a better MC than any of us when it came to live shows and HEIRU's live band carried three times the energy and volume than our music (back then we were still using badly recorded DAT tapes).

In 2001, the HEIRUSPECS band did a show backing TYPICAL CATS (Chicago) and ODD JOBS at the Bryant Lake Bowl Theater. SLUG, who was right between DJ's at the time saw them and asked if they would back ATMOSPHERE for a couple local shows along with a show in Chicago.

Even without FELIX being represented, the shows where HEIRUSPECS backed SLUG, along with the live recordings that were later sold, brought HEIRU to a new level of popularity. It's funny, HEIRUSPECS had been together and pretty relevant to the scene for over four years but there were articles written in Twin Cities' local papers with quotes like, "HEIRUSPECS, not just SLUG's back-up band anymore." But press is press and exposure is exposure so they just rolled with it.

HEIRUSPECS still has one of the best live shows I've ever seen in any genre of music. I've seen them probably 9,000 times give or take the exaggeration, and played with them doing guest spots or performing as the second MC in the group about 20 times. Having the live band and FELIX keeping most of the lyrical content non-offensive and light goes over extremely well with people that don't like rap. They kind of are the "happy rap" group to book in the underground. I don't say that in a bad way. I say it meaning they can get gigs that the rest of us can't. For example, free outdoor all-age events where you can't swear. They also cater to college crowds as well as, at the same time, an underground rap crowd with ease.

Through all the different members the solid five that has been the most successful are:

FELIX as the front MC
MU AH DIB as the second MC/beat boxer/singer
TWINKIE JIGGLES on bass
PETER LEGIT killing the drums
DVR keeping it cool on the keys

With a ridiculous live show and sharp business sense, HEIRUSPECS is one of the top 5 or 6 most successful rap groups ever out of Minnesota. It has been a lot of fun being a part of their movement.

"This is movement get your squadron and take aim." - FELIX

THE UNKNOWN PROPHETS

The PROPHETS are to Northeast Minneapolis what I guess I am to the Southside, the semi-popular veteran rap group that's been on the scene for a long time. The PROPHETS bring a good "happy rap" feel to the city. Their vibe is good, lyrics are easy to understand, and BIG JESS' beats are beautiful. There aren't more stories of these dudes in the book because when I was doing drugs, throwing parties, and chasing girls, BIG JESS was raising a child. JESS got a girl pregnant when he was still in high school. His dream of chasing rap always came second to taking care of his responsibilities as a father.

BIG JESS - only second to ANT as a producer in Minnesota rap
MAD SON - MC
WILLIE LOOSE - DJ

LEROY SMOKES

The SMOKES were around for over ten years and have packed major venues around town. Their CD release shows were like city-wide events. What I believe held the SMOKES back doesn't have anything to do with themselves. What held LEROY SMOKES back is the existence of HEIRUSPECS. The city already had a popular live hip hop band. That spot was already filled, even though both groups sounded nothing alike. Over the

years, Leroy Smokes went through lots of members, ups and downs, drugs, shows, girls...
you name it. To me they will be best remembered for the parties they used to throw when
most of the members lived and practiced on Garfield and 24th in Uptown.

THE BLEND

I would say the same thing about the BLEND that I said about the SMOKES. Being a live hip hop band in the same city as HEIRUSPECS is hard. Frontman, TOUSSAINT, is a good singer and spoken word artist. THE BLEND attacked the University of Minnesota campus getting lots of college gigs. They also played lots of shows with rock bands.

TOUSSAINT MORRISON really tried to separate himself and the BLEND from the local hip hop scene. He took a shot at TOKI WRIGHT at an open mic which further separated them from the scene for many years. But I'm glad to say that just before the release of this book, they were able to patch things up and throw a successful show together. The first time I saw TOUSSAINT sing, I told him he was a better rock singer than a rapper.

"My man Zach from KANSER / Said I'd make a better rockstar than a rapper"
- TOUSSAINT MORRISON

THE BLEND started at South High where PROF got his start as the 2nd rapper.

DJ DUZ IT/DJ ABILITIES/DJ BLASTA/DJ BJ/DJ ANTON
DJ JUDO/BOOKA B/DJ ESPADA/DJ ELUSIVE/JUSTIN TIME

In the mid-90's, a grip of local DJ's came out of St. Paul, the most successful of them of course being ABILITIES. But in the early days they were all on the same level and in the same circle of friends. ABILITIES and DUZ IT were young homies to SESS. Throughout the book when I talked about going to parties in St. Paul with NOMI, NAMELESS, SKYE, and the BATTLECATS, these dudes were always there probably DJing the party.

BOOKA B, JUDO and ANTON were all in INTERLOCK for short periods, and of course, ELUSIVE was KANSER's DJ from '98-'08. ESPADA was a little older than the others and I think came from a different area, but I met them all around the same time.

ODD JOBS

The adventures of ODD JOBS...the things these dudes went through would take up way more than a page in my book. I thought I knew enough about them that I could write in their part without asking but I met up with CRESCENT MOON to play basketball and fact checked. In less than a 15 minute conversation I realized that these dudes needed a book purely written about them. Maybe not even a paperback book with chapters. Maybe a 12-part comic book mini-series.

Odd Jobs started out as a B-boy crew called CMI that included lots of kids who were into hip hop ages 15-Try-D from Southwest Minneapolis to Midway St. Paul. CMI was then adopted by the INTERLOCK crew that protected them inside of the local scene in their beginnings.

They stripped down to ODD JOBS with two producers, DETOX and ANATOMY, and two rappers, CRESCENT MOON and ADVIZER. They released their first full-length CD, *Conflict & Compromise*, when they were all still in high school. Then, they sold 1,000 copies before they went to college. Along with fellow CMI member, NOMI, they threw it all on the line and moved to New York City. While in New York, DJ DETOX was picked for a "white hip hop boy band?" He then found himself in the short-lived group BAD RONALD which had a video in rotation on MTV in 2001.

BAD RONALD's debut album hit stores on Sept 11th 2001, the same day as the World Trade Center bombing, and their sales and existence got lost in the mix. But DETOX was fronted advance money from the record label that he used to help fund ODD JOBS' next project.

ODD JOBS busted ass in life working jobs and the studio for months to come up with their next release, *Drums*. With a small indie record deal and a whole lot of work, ODD JOBS went on tours opening for such groups as DE LA SOUL, DJ SHADOW, ZION I, JEAN GRAY, and THE LIFE SAVAS. All the while, ODD JOBS hustled. CRESCENT MOON toured in and out of the country with EYEDEA & ABILITIES as well as ATMOSPHERE doing backup vocals. ATMOSPHERE repaid them in 2003 by bringing ODD JOBS on the *Seven's Travels* tour.

To the home town, ODD JOBS looked on top of the world. And maybe they felt like it themselves for a hot minute. Then, they took it to the next coast, the West Coast, re-locating to San Francisco, California to work on their next record. The break up that followed is their own business and there is a lot more to the story I just told...a lot more. (Members going to the army, car accidents, money owed to them, and girls...I would guess lots of girls).

I consider a few members of ODD JOBS close friends of mine, and when you bring ODD JOBS up to them you get the vibe that they feel like they failed. But if you ask me, if you step back and look at the big picture, ODD JOBS made it. There are millions of bands and artists that are trying to "make it" (whatever that means) and less than 1% of them could move to New York City from a Midwest state and accomplish what ODD

JOBS did. I'll speak for myself, but I think I would represent all their friends, fans, and family by saying that I was proud of them.

SHOTTY BOO

SHOTTY is a St. Paul street rap legend. More than being known for shows and releases, he is known as a monster freestyler/battle rapper all over St. Paul. Like most of the elite from St. Paul, he came out of St. Paul Central High School. I would hear stories about him from FELIX, SLIM, NOMI, and others.

Back in '98-99, SHOTTY had his picture in The Source when he was running with LITTLE BUDDY and his crew. Rumor has it, SHOTTY BOO won and/or did well in some big battles out on the East Coast. I wasn't around for the events that created the myth of SHOTTY, but I did get a small taste once outside of the Blue Nile Bar off East Franklin (right by where I grew up).

I watched this nerdy hippy white cat actually pick a battle with SHOTTY. I watched a small crowd gather and SHOTTY tear this dude to pieces. SHOTTY played and entertained the spectators real well and used the fact that he looked a lot harder than the dude he was battling to his advantage. Whoever the dude he was battling was trying to say that SHOTTY wasn't real cuz he was rapping about guns and street shit. SHOTTY came back with the freshest reply I ever heard to that attack.

*"I'm real hip hop quote unquote... I said, I'm real Hip Hop quote unquote /
but if the records don't sell, I'm back to selling dope"* - SHOTTY BOO

CONTACT

CONTACT is a rapper from the Northside who has been around for years. He even had a release that featured national guest stars like KURUPT and LIL' JOHN.

TOP TONE

TONE had a rep for being from the streets. His hustles included many different outlets besides music such as owning property and selling houses. People who know TOP TONE probably have a tough image of him so I think it's unique that my main memory of him is when I was 21 out back in the alley of a video game arcade he used to own off Lake Street. I was on some emo shit hung up on a girl I was fucking when he popped his head out back and asked me what was wrong. I told him I just fucked this girl who I was hung up on but she had a boyfriend, a dude I knew but wasn't super close with. TOP TONE then sat down and broke me off some real solid advice, big dude to little dude. Even though TOP TONE was known in the street rap game and probably doesn't remember my little emo moment, I thank him for the advice.

DJ STAGE ONE

I grew up listening to STAGE ONE on the radio. When I was 19 and hungry, to understand the history of our scene I got ahold of STAGE and told him I was writing an article for a website on the history of Twin Cities rap, which was a totally lie. I didn't even know how to log onto the internet. I just had to make up a reason to be asking so many questions. STAGE told me he was born in Dayton, Ohio before moving to Minnesota. He told me he was down with SCHOOL OF THOUGHT and UVS. He talked about the Northside graf scene and spoke a lot about the community over North. Lots of B-boys he had come up with got sucked away from hip hop and into the streets. I remember him using a term "The streets have a way of sucking you under." It was then when I first noticed the differences between Southside hip hop and Northside hip hop.

The best memory I have of STAGE ONE is at my 29th birthday show. The homie BIG WIZ showed up and gave me some shrooms. I was having a great time when I started tripping. I got on the mic and started spilling intense emotionally driven theories onto the crowd. I think I started out by saying that the rap on the radio was all fake and that MOS DEF was the realest rapper when it came to describing the streets. That went into how hip hop was black music, into how I was from South Minneapolis, into how much I loved P.O.S. I was intensely losing it and had everyone's attention. I was no more than 30 seconds away from spitting my theory about how the human race is half ape and half alien when STAGE ONE stepped on-stage to save me. With very soft energy, he took the mic from me and calmed me down (haha). I thank him very much for it cuz I don't know what I would have said after that.

GOLDEN

A transplant from Pennsylvania, GOLDEN paid a good amount of dues in Minnesota with his group SUSPECTS. SUSPECTS were just a couple years late behind RSE. They attempted to throw many of the same style shows that RSE had put on just a couple years before SUSPECTS moved here from the East Coast. What they were trying to do had already been done. But with a readjustment, JEYECHS of SUSPECTS fell back to play the hype man and GOLDEN stepped up to the front spot. They made a good attempt at attacking from a clean-cut pop music angle. They had a sound that could be compared to the BLACK EYED PEAS, and through a good connection, even toured with the BLACK EYED PEAS for a brief stint. I like JEYECHS and GOLDEN a lot. They are very talented. I've always quietly rooted for these dudes to succeed at what they're trying to do.

DJ CHUCK CHIZZLE/OSP/CALLUS

CHUCK CHILL is a mainstream hip hop/R&B Northside DJ who has been a radio host on KMOJ and B96. Though CHUCK mainly messes with mainstream music, he pops his head in on the underground to see what's cracking whenever he gets a chance and has DJ'd for acts like CALLUS and OSP.

CALLUS was a pretty hard street rapper from the Northside. He should have won the 2006 Twin Cities Celebration of Hip Hop emcee battle, but he got too tough with a small young looking kid name BLISS. I was judging the battle and knew that CALLUS was the best rapper in the contest but I couldn't freeze time and tell CALLUS he was using the wrong tactic.

OSP stood for "On Something Personal". I first saw him in a half spoken word/ half rap group called FUWAS along with TRUTH MAZE, GENESIS and MICHAELA DAY. OSP was a powerful strong rapper from the Northside who believed every word that came out of his mouth. KANSER made one song with OSP called "Beaut-e" that I'm still pretty proud of.

ERNIE RHODES

ERNIE RHODES' heart and drive way exceed his natural talent. If you see ERNIE in concert twice, you may or may not like his music. But, you probably can't deny that he was better the second time you saw him. He gets better all the time. The freshest thing about ERNIE is that he doesn't pretend to be anything he's not. He's a 30+ black male from an upper class family that lives, works, and hangs out in Uptown, wears funny socks, dates lots of cute Uptown girls, and has a rap style somewhere between BIG DADDY KANE and EYEDEA. It's the weird emo Minnesota style laid on top of an old school foundation.

Most MC's that succeed start in high school. When I say start, I don't mean write their first raps on paper. I mean start pushing; open mics, battles, shows, and getting their name out. ERNIE graduated high school, college, toyed with marriage, got a 9-to-5 in a cubical, and then, at age 27, dropped everything and put it all on the line to pursue a small dream of becoming an underground rapper. I respect that a lot, and in scale, I consider ERNIE successful.

PEEWEE DREAD & DRED I DREAD

ANT once made a joke to me saying the only people who had true musical talent in Minnesota were PRINCE, SLUG, and PEEWEE DREAD. The rest of us were just faking it. It was a joke but he was trying to make a point on how talented PEEWEE is. PEE-WEE DREAD is by far the freshest reggae MC in the state. Originally from New Orleans, PEEWEE can rap and sing in any style you need. His band, DRED I DREAD, was pretty popular around the state in '99-'00 and PEEWEE continues to always be a presence in the scene.

THE CORE

The CORE is the group that TOKI WRIGHT got his start in along with fellow rapper AD. In the era of emo rap they brought the fun back.

In February of '03, I buried one of my closest friends who had a surprise death from a blood clot in his leg. After the funeral, five close friends and myself went to the CORE's CD release show at the Quest Club and had possibly the most fun ever which was very therapeutic to all of us. They had the HOUSE SQUAD dance team behind them on-stage and their set was the shit.

GUARDIANS OF BALANCE

ST PAUL SLIM and MASTERMIND. Originally called the CUT out of St. Paul Central in the mid-90's. The GUARDIANS re-introduced themselves in 2002. They are the hardest/most intelligent rap group in Minnesota.

SANDMAN

He was all I heard about coming out of the Northside for years. I wish I could tell you more about him but somehow we have never crossed paths.

DJ DAN SPEAK/BROTHER JULES

Like SANDMAN, DJ DAN SPEAK and BROTHER JULES are dudes who by the way of the universe have never crossed my path. Both of them are old school DJ's who I have listened to on KMOJ and seen their names on flyers for years but don't know much about them. I do know they deserve many props.

ILLUMINOUS 3

These kids define the word fresh. FREEZ of ILLUMINOUS 3, at 17 years old, was the most developed high school rapper I had ever heard in my life.

I consider these kids like little brothers to me. They are on the bridge of underground hip hop and pop culture in the way they rap, dress, and act. Hopefully, they are the future. They also invented the term "wag" which I'm too old to know the definition of. (haha) "Wag" seems to mean and stand for something big to all the young people in the movement in 2011.

TRAMA

As a transplant from Queens, he brings the East Coast street flow but adds humor with everything he does. His street promotion ideas and hustle make the rest of us look bad. I first caught wind of TRAMA when he wheat pasted posters of himself all down Lake Street and other parts of the metro. As a former tagger, I was hella impressed. No one has hit the city with gorilla promotion like that before or since.

DJ SNUGGLES

He was a teenage wonderboy on the beatbox. He won Scribble Jam in '06 and is the only dude in my lifetime to be able to challenge TRUTH MAZE for the local title.

FIC

Originally out of a group called the PHAROHS, FIC has a good cadence, smooth flow, and has done songs with members of the R.O.C.

MARIA ISA

The front woman for the reggae-tone hip hop movement in Minnesota, MARIA has nick-named our state "Sota Rico". She is extremely talented and a very hard worker. Though I do not know MARIA well, I share one terrible memory with her. I am obsessed with NBA Basketball and my favorite player of all-time is Kevin Garnett. I rooted for him for years while he was with the MN Timberwolves and in 2007 when he was traded to the Boston Celtics, spiritually I went with him to Boston and became a huge Celtics fan. In 2011, the Celtics were defeated in the playoffs by the evil Miami Heat and it was a tough day for me. I felt as though my generation had finally gotten too old to win championships anymore. I walked down to the Nomad World Pub and sat in sadness. Then, MARIA ISA comes in the bar wearing a Dwayne Wade Miami Heat jersey!?! MARIA came over to me to say hello and to give me a hug. I couldn't even look her in the eyes. I just put my head down and walked out the bar. I walked all the way home and held my head down for weeks..... until my boy, Dirk Nowitzki, and the Dallas Mav's defeated the evil Miami Heat in the 2011 NBA finals!

BIG QUARTERS/FAM FUED

When I was 19-21 I had a roommate, Andrea. She told me she had two little cousins who just moved to the Cities and were into underground rap. BRANDON ALLDAY and MEDIUM ZACH who keep the record buyer tradition of making raw hip hop beats alive. They are more focused on production than lyrics or live shows and their grind is hard. They work with inner city youth teaching production classes, keep their lyrical content very politically correct and conscious, and help lots of local musicians with odds and ends. Overall, these dudes are such good people that I feel like a bad person when I hang out with them (haha). They are very good at coming up with new ideas to promote themselves and are very good at getting good local press. Personally, these are two of my favorite dudes.

They created a production crew in 2005 called FAM FUED with dynamite beat makers like BENZILLA and KING KARNOV. Both later went on to produce beats for famous rappers such as RAEKWON, BLACK THOUGHT, MURS, and BUSTA RHYMES.

OUT OF BOUNDS

OUT OF BOUNDS came out of the rave scene and the hip hop scene at the same time blending the two types of music. The rapper CAESAR can flip words like a machine gun over high-tempo beats. KANSER did a lot of shows with these dudes at the Red Sea at the top of the century. I had always stereotyped raver kids as being soft and I had these kids pinned as raver kids. I don't know which theory was wrong, but one late night at the Red Sea when I had a small beef pop off, OUT OF BOUNDS and their crew stepped up to have my back. They were pretty organized about it and three of them even escorted me and the two girls I was with to our car to make sure I wouldn't get jumped outside. I have had mad respect for them ever since and have never stereotyped kids who listen to techno as soft again.

JON JON SCOTT/RAW VILLA/BLACK CORNERS

When I was 14 to 15, my friends and I would catch the bus to hang out in Uptown all the time. On Lake Street and Hennepin, there was a record store called Applause. They would let us crack open CD's and listen to them at the listening center. This older black dude (mid-20's?) named JON JON who worked there would let us listen to stuff for as long as we wanted even if we weren't gonna buy anything. JON JON was in a punk band at the time and told us they had once done a show where they called the MICRANOTS on-stage to freestyle. I thought that was super awesome. JON JON was the first person I ever met who worked at a record store and knew about hip hop. He was up on everything new that came out and was always super cool to talk to.

During the same time I met MUJA MESSIAH in high school. MUJA had his own street B-boy style that was unique at South High. My boy ASK and I approached MUJA in the hallway and asked him if he tagged "ALADA", a tag we saw around town. I can't remember how we figured out that was his tag. We probably saw it on his school note-books or took a wild guess. MUJA and I have been somewhat down with each other ever since that day.

MUJA is a super dope rapper, he was already getting props from older rappers when we was in high school. During the age of CONCEPT, HEADSHOTS, and OMAR, MUJA already existed with his own flavor. After high school, KANSER did shows with MUJA's group RAW VILLA at the 7th Street Entry for RSE events. That's where I met other members of RAW VILLA, REAL SPIT RIC, NEAS, and DJ MASHOUT.

RAW VILLA was more street and had more of an edge than most of the groups we did shows with back then. Even back then, I always felt kinda square around RAW VILLA. These dudes are always the coolest dudes in the room, they always dress clean, are sharp with speech, and never seem broke or uncomfortable.

JON JON SCOTT became a pretty big blogger/music critic and started working with RAW VILLA under the label name BLACK CORNERS helping them book shows and promote themselves being somewhat of a bridge from their street style of rap over to the local music scene.

RAW VILLA has probably felt frustrated at times because the national image of Minnesota rap does not reflect them. In MUJA's most popular song, "Get Fresh", he spits

"Like it's all backpack and hippy / Like it don't be cracking in my city"
– MUJA MESSIAH

That lines about me. Not in the literal sense where MUJA was taking a shot at me but it's about the culture I have been able to eat off. I make "backpack hippy rap" (haha). That's what I do and I love what I do, but I'm aware that it's probably been easier for me to find outlets and an audience in this state than it has for MUJA when he's a doper rapper than I am.

Even though we're different RAW VILLA has always seemed to like me. They're some of my favorite dudes to see out at the bars or clubs and talk shit with. MUJA's career is still on the upswing and I wish him more success to come.

DJ MASHOUT used to try and punk me downtown when I was younger, but over the years I've grown on him and he has saved me from getting beat up now at least once.

The best memory I have of a member of RAW VILLA is during an open mic at Bon Appétit. NAMELESS of CMI was freestyling and passed his turn to NEAS of RAW VILLA. NEAS reached out his hand to shake NAMELESS' who was holding the mic with his right hand and NEAS spit:

"We cool you my man we tight / but next time you
shake my hand you better make it your right"

Simultaneously as NAMELESS reached his left hand out to shake NEAS' right hand.

OMAUR BLISS/YONI/NEGATIVE ONE
These dudes have been down with KANSER for years. They came out of the HEADSPIN era. OMAUR started off in a group called the POETRY, the same group that DESDAMONA started off in. OMAUR and YONI later formed a group with DESSA early in her career called MEDIDA.

WOOKIEFOOT, the biggest festival group in Minnesota, used to have a party house in Uptown (later known as the Playhouse) on the corner of Garfield and 32nd. My homies and I would hear about the parties through either YONI, OMAUR or NEGATIVE ONE. WOOKIEFOOT parties were super crazy weird to us. UNICUS, SHIZ, and I used to be posted up like, "wow." There were dudes in animal costumes, girls covered in glitter and fake fairy wings, different rooms with different DJ's playing different kinds of music, full bars, pot food, and disco balls. It was energy that we weren't hip to yet, but OMAUR, YONI, and NEGATIVE ONE, who we knew as rap kids, seemed to be a part of the whole thing.

Like I mentioned in the last chapter we were later invited to play at a festival called Hip Hop and Harmony in 2006 where we found a spiritual home at Harmony Park (home base of WOOKIEFOOT). We (MORE THAN LIGHTS) have done very well for ourselves as Minnesota's new festival hip hip group, but we credit these three rappers, along with a jam band rap group called the 420 ALLSTARS, as the ones who built the bridge between hip hop and Minnesota's jam band/festival culture.

ECID/CAPACITI/KRISTOFF KRANE

Every time I bump into ECID he tells me what he's been doing, where he's been touring, and how many records he's selling. In full humor I want to yell at him, "Ecid! I respect you already, shut the fuck up!" He has that approach with me because he has found some success with his music but has not gotten his props.

KRISTOFF KRANE came up under EYEDEA as his Padawon and CAPACITI came up under CARNAGE.

All three carry on EYEDEA's abstract rhyming style. It's a rap style that has no street influence in it therefore it's not accepted by many hardcore rap kids. Even though it took me a while, I understand now that it has its place. Their style of rap is just the furthest left. I think KRISTOFF KRANE is a great freestyler and I think all three are hard workers and have, or are, mastering their own styles.

If ECID does feel like he's been shorted on his props I'll publicly give him some right now. In early 2010 someone started talking shit about ECID to me like it was high school so BIG ZACH slapped dude in his face. The dude didn't do shit but apologize to me on Twitter about it (true story minus some details).

BONAFIDE/EMS/DJ GREEN

When I think of these dudes I think of the Fineline Music Café. It's one of the premiere venues in the state and EMS is their best soundman. Matter of fact, I would say EMS is the best soundman in the state when it comes to hip hop because he understands how rappers hold their mics. The average soundman who has been taught how to mix a singer is always under the impression that every rapper is cupping the mic which is not always the case.

PARALLAX

PARALLAX was a rock/rap group fronted by one of my favorite local emcees, SLIM CHANCE. All hailing from different metro area suburbs, the band members met at college in Mankato and became the biggest band in Mankato before they brought it back to the Cities. I partied with this band and they were truly a modern day American band. They partied, toured the country in a Winnebago, rocked hard, drank a lot, and everybody loved their girlfriends. They were the best girlfriends ever for a band. They were at every show, supportive, cool as hell, and always gave me food or bought me drinks (haha). Sadly, PARALLAX split up in 2011. Lucky for me, their last show was opening for us at the sold-out MORE THAN LIGHTS release party at the Fineline in downtown Minneapolis.

RED'S CLASS AT CENTRAL

Like I mentioned again and again throughout the book, St. Paul Central High School produced the majority of dope emcees, DJ's, and producers from St. Paul. I can't document this in detail but I have heard from many people over the years that there was a music recording class you could take at Central way before it was common to have recording programs at local parks and schools. Many of my peers who went to Central, FELIX, ST PAUL SLIM, DJ DETOX, and others, praise a teacher named RED for helping the development of their talents. I've never met RED but if half of what I've heard about him is true I would like to thank him for what he has done for us.

WIDE EYES

I think KANSER can take credit for putting these kids on. UNICUS and I gave these kids some of their first shows but I gotta be honest, it was because they were nice kids not because we thought they were dope. They were just a couple of dirt ball teenage white kids from Mound, one of the furthest suburbs. I didn't think they were good at all... but... I did see they had the heart for this shit. I probably saw in them what ANT saw in us. Kids who didn't have it but had the drive to get it. Six years later WIDE EYES is one of the dopest groups in the city and SEAN ANON has the potential to be the dopest rapper in the state if he keeps focused.

WIDE EYES brought with them from the outer suburbs a young little dready folk singer/graphic designer named DALIA who has the prettiest voice I've ever heard in my life and now does the majority of our artwork, including the layout of this book.

USUAL SUSPECTS

All the rappers in this group have separate styles and different talents that they bring to the table. I was super excited when this group appeared because one of the original members, ABDUL, is of Somalian descent and was a huge hip hop head. Our city has a huge Somalian population, but by 2011, we have yet to build a bridge and Somalian kids are almost non-existent at underground rap shows. ABDUL lived down the block from me on the West Bank and we used to get late night eats at Hard Times Café and chop it up. I prayed that he was the first of many Somalian rappers to sprout up, but ABDUL moved to Toronto soon after.

I play basketball with three of the remaining members along with every other local artist that hoops at our "rap scene Wednesday night open gym". IBE from USUAL SUSPECTS can jump out the gym and attack the rim something terrible. He has viciously dunked on over half the rappers in Minnesota (I shouldn't say no names...but CRESCENT MOON, ILLICIT, BENZILLA, and I SELF DEVINE. Fuck ..... they all might punch me in the face for telling the world IBE dunked on them so if your reading this please don't tell them). Luckily for me, I'm old enough to know to get out the way when IBE comes to the hole.

M.ANIFEST

Originally from Ghana, Africa, I believe M.ANIFEST came to St. Paul for college (Macalester). I was first exposed to him because he used to do shows with PROF & RAHZWELL at the Fineline early in all of their careers. Ashanti, who was then PROF & RAHZ's DJ who later became M.ANIFEST's manager, booked me to host their shows. M.ANIFEST brings good energy and diversity to our scene.

DJ VERB X

An old school DJ that has held down Thursday nights in First Avenue's Record Room for years. Real cool cat. When I was 22, VERB used to throw good warehouse parties off Central and Broadway over Northeast. At one of those parties, an older raver girl brought me home and taught me a few things about life I didn't know.

DJ KOOLHANDS LUKE

An old school DJ and party thrower. LUKE is the type of DJ who plays what he wants more than he plays to the audience. His crates include a lot of reggae, dancehall, jungle, and underground hip hop. Luke's a few years older than me and has some great stories of his own from back in the day.

He once told me he threw a party on 14th and Lake in like '91 where a bunch of gangbangers and skinheads got into a fight at his house. He told me he was on acid and couldn't handle what was going on so he ran down to the basement to hide while his windows were getting broken out. He can tell the story a lot better than I can recap it.

SPECIAL DARK/THE SESSION

SPECIAL DARK hosts a rap radio show that plays early on Sunday mornings before the sun comes up.

EMPIRE

A rap group from the late 90's who performed with crazy energy and theatrics.

MAD ESSENCE

A Chicago transplant who made beats and worked with RAW VILLA and CONCEPT. MAD ESSENCE was a street dude but I always got along with him. He did shows for me back in the HEADSPIN days.

DETEK

He made a lot of beats for people back in the days. I don't know why we never made a song together. I did go to his parties on Chicago and Lake above Robert's Shoes. I made out with a pretty hot girl on the rooftop one time...but she ended up being kind of crazy. (haha)

DEPTH/TCHHA

The Twin Cities Hip Hop Awards has been thrown yearly since 2007 by a St. Paul rapper named DEPTH. I feel a lot of people take this event too seriously. Because of that, I have never attended. But I appreciate that DEPTH has nominated me for several categories every year.

DJ K.A.

He's a Chicago transplant who was featured in the book, *Bomb the Suburbs*, written by UPSKI. He came up tagging with UPSKI.

STREET LEGAL

STREET LEGAL is a white kid that grew up on West Lake in Minneapolis. He could be seen at open mics and battles when he was a teenager. He had an energy about him that was a little loud for his age. Not knowing how strong hip hop was inside of him, TOKI WRIGHT made a comment to me that someone should go talk to him. He was implying that I should reach out and offer him some guidance.

The next day, STREET LEGAL stopped in the pizza restaurant where I was working at the time and grabbed a slice. I went around the counter and sat with him to try and feel him out. Looking in his eyes, right away I knew he had hip hop inside of him. It just needed time to grow. I then asked him to act out a high school lunchroom freestyle skit with other young rappers such as FREEZ and BRANDON ALLDAY at a show I was throwing. Since STREET LEGAL did me that favor, I've considered him my friend and I think that he is a good kid. Reminds me a little of myself.

SPY

A promoter/rapper that moved to Minnesota from Texas with his brother. SPY's a real dude, we got a lot in common. He brought GRINDTIME north battles to Minnesota.

HECATOMB

CARNAGE's crew. DESDAMONA, MAC SPILLZ, CAPACITY and a few others.

TUESDAY NIGHT OPEN MIC AT THE BLUE NILE

I got lucky. I never had to hit up open mics. Since I brought a high school fan base with me into the real world after graduation and got plugged straight into the network of groups that were building our scene, I got to skip that step. Most emcees and artists are not that lucky. Most emcees go to cyphers and open mics to practice their skills before they take the next step into doing shows. The most common routine at an open mic is to show up, sign your name on a list, and when your name is called, get a turn to rap on the mic. Even though it's mostly for an audience of other artists and their friends, it's good practice and the first step to getting your name out. There has been hundreds of open mic nights at all different places throughout the metro area but the most official in our history has been Tuesday nights at the Blue Nile. Hosted by DESDAMONA and KEVIN WASHINGTON, it has happened every Tuesday for ten years strong. Though I don't have a personal connection with it, many many artists in our community do.

PLAIN OLE BILL/JORDAN DAILY

Jordan Daily is most commonly known in our community as SLUG's little brother (haha). But for a good amount of time during the last decade, he was a lot more than that. Jordan ran FIFTH ELEMENT for many years and, in my personal opinion, did a great job. A good DJ from Seattle, KING OTTO, also worked at the store.

I called in a lot of favors with Jordan, most notably selling tickets to our underground parties through him. The parties were held at warehouses where you had to get a ticket to find the location. They weren't 100% legal if you know what I'm saying (haha). FIFTH ELEMENT was one of the two secret spots to get tickets.

I felt we had a good relationship, though I bet I was always stressing him out trying to get paid out for our sales as much as possible (haha). Jordan's side kick at the store was a young dude from New Brighton (a northern suburb) named Bill. Bill DJ'd under the name PLAIN OLE BILL. PLAIN OLE BILL was taught by older DJs to hone his skills before coming out in public so I don't have any memories of him coming up or being weak. When PLAIN OLE BILL hit the city he was already good enough to fill headline spots. The first time I saw him spin, DJ TREY booked him to fill a prime spot at one of our underground parties and he held it down solid.

PLAIN OLE BILL went on to DJ for MUSAB, he was a co-founder of the successful club night GET CRYPHY, and then went on to DJ for P.O.S., which might have brought P.O.S.'s stage performance to another level.

JUST LIVE

JUST LIVE was a Christian rap group that built a nice following and even crossed-over to other audiences.

MAHDI "DJ NEX" BRYANT

An old school DJ from the crew SCHOOL OF THOUGHT, MAHDI DJ'd into his 40's. I've heard he was a teacher and helped put on many pivotal members of our community, from STAGE ONE, GLO, and SESS, all they way to the LONG DOE CAMP. The only time I ever spoke to MAHDI was the last time I saw him at a club downtown. We had a short interaction that started with, "Hey, what's up?" I replied, "Dude, I been seeing you for years but I don't think we've ever spoke." He responded, "I know I was thinking the same thing." We shook hands and introduced ourselves very pleasantly. Sadly, MAHDI passed away in August of 2011. From what I have been told by mutual friends, he was very loved and respected as a legend.

I am setting myself up for failure here because I most likely forgot somebody and somebody I forgot is going to take it too serious and be upset. Know that I am human, I did my best, and I didn't include anyone who I didn't meet or wasn't around before 2007.

CHAPTER 22 PART 1: BETWEEN PIMPS, POETS, AND THE PRESS

"I'm outside." I hung up the phone, grabbed my backpack, locked the door, and stomped out the crib. The voice on the other end of the phone was my childhood friend and first rap partner Itoro. As teens we had dreams of being big rappers, we played our first shows together, and Itoro was actually the founding member of KANSER. Less than a year after I graduated high school and really got on the underground grind, Itoro faded out of KANSER and a couple years later faded out of rapping. He still dabbled in it but had gotten a grip of school done learning how to edit videos amongst other things.

"Is this your shit?" I asked referring to the dark blue SUV truck Itoro was driving. "Man, come on," Itoro replied smirking that I was impressed by his ride. We hadn't been real tight since he left KANSER but he always made it a point to check in with me at least twice a year, play chess, talk basketball, or whatever. I had known Itoro for a decade and a half but I didn't really know dude. I didn't know where he got the money to buy this truck and I didn't even wanna ask. "What's cracking wit you?" he said.

"Shit, rap music and trying to eat," I replied. "Ok, ok rap music and trying to eat. I feel that," he said. "What we wanna get into Itoro?" I asked. "Whatever man. But first I gotta go grab a bag a dro."

Now normally if one of my homies rolls up to my house, I hop in the ride, and they tell me they wanna go get drugs, that means they've made arrangements and we're gonna roll over to somebody's house who is expecting us and purchase whatever's good. So, that was my interpretation of what Itoro meant.

On the drive over North, I just assumed our destination was a place of residence. We were in mid-conversation bending corners over Northside when the next thing I knew, Itoro pulls into a parking lot of an abandoned corner store and yells, "Where the weed at!" out the drivers side window.

Within five seconds, three different dudes were at the car flashing dime bags at Itoro trying to undercut each other. I was cool but kinda surprised and on-guard a bit. Then, coming from my left side, a squad car rolled up. I nudged Itoro who was weighing his options. He looked up at the squad car and pretty confidently said, "They ain't gonna do shit." The police got on their bull horn and said, "Quit selling drugs on this corner," and then drove away.

Itoro bought a bag, stashed it by the gas cap, and we rolled out. "What's the matter Zach? You ain't never bought dro off the street before?" he asked. I quickly and honestly replied, "Fuck no!"

I never buy drugs off the street. Maybe when I was younger my homies would cop dime bags outside the city center downtown but not as an adult. Itoro laughed at me for a hot second then we rolled back over South, parked off Hennepin in Uptown, Itoro rolled a blunt, and we smoked. I've never been a big weed head so all my close homies love getting me chopped. Since I hadn't seen Itoro for a hot minute I was down to get blowed with him.

"Damn man, I'm kinda chopped. I always thought the herb cats sold on the streets was just some bullshit," I told him. "Most of it is, but I got my spots," he replied.

Itoro and I chopped it up about a few different things that day but what sticks out to me and what's relevant to the book is this conversation. "Zach, man I'm proud of you, Harry (UNICUS), and y'all niggas for how far y'all have taken KANSER and this Minneapolis hip hop shit. I be in spots where people bring y'all name up. I be trying ta tell motherfuckers I started that KANSER shit and bitches don't even believe me. I let 'em know I was a founder but I don't have anything to do with them knowing who y'all are or any popularity y'all have...you feel me?"

Since I was high I thought I could read where Itoro was taking it so I just replied, "Man, you just had your own path dog. I ain't still mad at you for leaving the group. That shit was 10 years ago."

"Na, that's not what I'm saying. All the shit you guys have done I didn't wanna do with my life. I like rap, I like writing raps, and I liked to battle back in high school and all...man, what I'm saying is...I like to rap, but I don't love hip hop, you feel me? Back in the day if we would have got a record deal, I would have done shows and worked hard but I wasn't trying to grind it out and I didn't give a fuck about building a hip hop scene here. But I'm proud a y'all niggas for what y'all did, you feel me?"

With that statement, "I like to rap, but I don't love hip hop", Itoro explained to me a good many things that I almost felt foolish it took me that long to figure out. In a similar conversation I had a couple years later with a local rapper named CLEVA, who was also a pretty hood cat and who had also got me blunted up (but I swear, I barely smoke), CLEVA broke down to me beyond that old "Are you in it for the love or the money?" question. Cats like me were in it for the love, the party, giving people a place to have a good time, and all that. Even though I was to the point where I was feeding myself from it, my original intent was based in love. And, though he had always had a good time coming out to my shows and parties, the dream of getting paid off music was his driving force behind him rapping. It was so simple it was complex...and maybe not that deep of a thought but it sticks out in my mind.

For years (and I mean years) I have been standing outside of rap shows with my box of CDs and backpack full of t-shirts selling my shit. I've never got to the point where it flies out the box but I've had my good days and I am to the point where I don't have to hustle anymore. I don't walk up to kids like I used to and say, "Yo, you like hip hop? You should cop my shit...$10."

My favorite sales pitch back in the day was stepping to a couple and telling the dude I had a great idea. He should buy his girlfriend my CD. That shit worked a lot, but I'm too old to hustle like that anymore. God willing, I've gotten to a place where I can just post up with my box and enough people know who I am. They just walk up to me and buy something. Back around 2002-2004 when you might catch me still in people's grills throwing out a sales pitch, I started to notice I was always being outsold by P.O.S.

For a while he was selling his first group's CD, CENOSPECIES, but now he was selling burnt CDs called *False Hopes*. He was selling them for $5 dollars cheaper than I was and moving about double the units. P.O.S. had a good hustle. People liked him and he made them laugh when he was trying to sell them CDs.

The *False Hopes* CDs weren't just him. They featured his new crew, DOOMTREE. Their music had that SLUG/ANTICON rap sound to it. But, as time passed, their production and originality became immense. Besides DESSA, who attended Southwest High School, all the DOOMTREE members went to Hopkins High School, a western suburb of Minneapolis. DOOMTREE later became the first, but not last, hip hop artists from the suburbs that I personally respected.

Back around the same time period, my little brother Eli was living and hustling out a broke down dope house on my mom's block. My brother had become addicted to cocaine ... but he seemed to have so much of it...it didn't matter. My little brother and I hadn't been close since we were kids; but, in the summer of 2002, I spent a couple weeks flopping at his house when I was between places to stay.

Eli had a close partner named TONY BONEZ. Eli was always hyping TONY up to me on the rap tip. TONY BONEZ is a thugged-out white dude who grew up right off of Bloomington and 26th on the Southside. He's pretty authentic (rap music, exaggerations considering). Not saying he's the hardest dude in the world, but he's at least witnessed most of the things he raps about. Street cred aside, TONY BONEZ and his main partner, BIG WIZ, are real likable dudes and built a pretty relevant Southside fan base. Then, their game was taken to the next level when they plugged up with Eastside St. Paul veteran DJ D-MILL. D-MILL had the plugs to get them into better clubs, better studios, better flyers, and organization. BONEZ and WIZ formed the LONGDOE camp consisting of a pretty good amount of inner city street rappers from the Twin Cities that were hustling to get heard. CLEVA, AQUAFRESH, MIKE THE MARTYR, SOLUTION, T-LA SHAWN, MOROCCO to name a few.

LONG DOE brings in national acts like DEVIN THE DUDE, TWISTA, OBIE TRICE, AG, and FREEWAY on a regular basis. They always have new CDs out and they even go down to Mexico on spring break and perform in tourist spots such as Mazatlan, Mexico.

In May of 2003, my little brother Eli was arrested for murder in the 1st degree. The feelings and emotions from Eli going to prison are hard to relate or describe but when I would pop up at LONGDOE/BONES & WIZ shows I felt like I was around people who understood. BONES & WIZ have a giant super Southsider following and most of them kids either knew my brother and would ask how he was doing or had friends or family members of their own locked up and could relate to what I was feeling. During most BONES & WIZ shows, one of them would shout out all the homies they had in prison at that time and I would hear my brothers name often which would make me feel better about things at least for a short minute.

DOOMTREE and LONGDOE both represent a new breed of rapper/rap kid that didn't exist when I was growing up. DOOMTREE are suburban kids who were equally raised on punk rock and hip hop from a mainstream or underground level. Their style or dress, speech, and culture seem to follow SLUG, and there are hundreds, if not thousands, of kids in the Twin Cities that are on the same vibe.

LONGDOE, to me, represent the new inner city rap kid, really mainstream influenced. But most rappers in their camp at least mess with the underground and they are all down to do shows and grind. TONY BONES & BIG WIZ have always pulled a good inner city crowd.

My camp and myself are blessed to be able to fit in the middle. Being inner city rappers, but a lot softer and maybe less threatening to the Uptown crowds, TRADITIONAL METHODS, KANSER, INTERLOCK, and myself have been privileged to do many shows with both DOOMTREE and LONGDOE. Being in the middle has also given me a panoramic view of scenes and the differences in how both are and how both are treated by the local press.

On what I remember to be a Wednesday or a Thursday in October of 2003, I went to a LONGDOE show at a spot called The Lab in downtown St. Paul. There was I would guess 160 people there; almost all inner city, lots of flashy necklaces, and whatever popular mainstream rap fashions at the time were being worn. It wasn't the scariest crowd in the world but it wasn't soft. If I had to take a stereotypical guess there were at least five people with guns in the building. If not on their person, stashed in their ride outside. BONEZ & WIZ were doing their thing. I watched the majority of the crowd sing along with the words to their songs and have a good time.

The next day, SHIZ and I attended a DOOMTREE show at the Dinkytowner. There were a good 80+ people in the spot, and same as LONGDOE the night before, P.O.S. and his camp were building followers. Stereotyping the crowd, it was mostly punk rock/Uptown hipster type heads that DOOMTREE's music reflected. Heavy rock samples, abstract emo raps, and non- traditional stage performances.

I thought both camps were doing their thing and in about the same stages of development. In the months and years that have followed, I've watched the local press blow up and support DOOMTREE and totally ignore LONGDOE.

Soon after the week I hit both shows, a feature story was written about P.O.S. in a local weekly publication, *City Pages*, where a picture of P.O.S. was put on the cover with the headline:

"How did a black punk rock kid conquer the white world of indie rap?"

This was the story that broke P.O.S. and that statement became true the day that article came out. The article was written by Peter Scholtes. Peter has been around trying to support local rap through the press since before my time. I appreciate Peter, he used his power to help P.O.S.

As I read article after article praise DOOMTREE for being the next big craze for our music scene, I watched their shows quadruple in attendance and P.O.S. get signed to RSE which enforced a seal of approval to ATMOSPHERE fans who were a perfect audience. DOOMTREE also has an indie rock crossover due to their sound and style that the local press fell in love with. That has led to events such as the yearly DOOMTREE BLOWOUT sell-out of the First Avenue main room. DOOMTREE members have already four times been on the cover of the *VitaMN*, the newly established Twin Cities publication (the new *City Pages*).

To this day, September 17th, 2011, LONGDOE has never had an article in any local publication and their shows have since struggled a bit in time without any help. I would like to put in quotes, "DOOMTREE is the shit to me." None of what I just wrote is taking any credit away from them nor is it trying to pin the TREE against LONGDOE. I am only stressing the fact that the majority of people who have covered our hip hop scene are not truly involved in it. They are soft, hipster, trendy indie rock kids who did not grow up in our city and only cover hip hop that they feel comfortable around and not threatened by.

I think it's not fair. I appreciate and believe in DOOMTREE as well as LONG DOE's music and I think they should have both been given an equal chance to get press. The press has a lot of power when it comes to music. In 2011 and beyond, I hope the local press goes in a good direction covering local rap.

My favorite local writers who have covered rap are Chris Riemenschneider, Pete Scholtes, Steve McPherson, and Kandis Knight. But by far the best coverage we ever had was when SLUG dabbled in journalism and had a weekly column called "Permanent on Surfaces" that ran in *The Pulse* magazine and covered local rap. SLUG was with us back then, knew everybody, and was at every show...... so he knew what the fuck was really going on.

DOOMTREE, being the first suburb rap group to find large popularity, along with their youth and new sound, spawned a lot of hatin' from other rappers. UNICUS and myself did not participate in the hating. But, I do feel guilt that I did not defend them as much as I should of when people were hatin' in my presence.

"And now you're in my ear talkin' shit about DOOMTREE" - BIG ZACH(NEW MC)

On an incredibly hot summer night in 2002 my roommates and I threw a giant party on 10th and University just outside Dinkytown. I would guess between all the floors of the house, the giant yard, and the parking lot we lived next to, there was almost 700 people there. It was the biggest party I'd ever thrown that wasn't in a warehouse.

In the middle of all the party commotion, my little Southside homie Arthur punched CECIL OTTER in the face. When I tried to get an explanation of why this happened, I came to find out they were freestyling with each other and Arthur picked a battle with CECIL, so CECIL started serving him.

Arthur, who was probably hella faded trying to explain himself to me said, "Suburb kids shouldn't be able to rap." I laughed and replied, "Arthur what do you think dudes in New York think about us rapping?" Arthur had broken OMAR rule #2 from chapter 4 which states: You cannot beat someone up just because they out-rapped you.

In my opinion every rapper from St. Paul or Minneapolis that has hated on DOOMTREE to me broke OMAR rule #1 which states: You cannot get out-rapped in your own neighborhood by an outsider. All of us inner city rappers let a girl from Southwest, a dude from LA, and a bunch of kids from Hopkins come into our city and out-rap us!!.... We should be fucking ashamed of ourselves (haha).

Observing the crowds that identified with LONG DOE and DOOMTREE made me realize that the B-boy hip hop I had identified with since I was 14 was dying. I looked myself in the mirror and I realized I was kind of an odd ball. I've had a certain set of experiences that has made me who I am. I'm a welfare baby white rap kid from South Minneapolis, I dress kinda like a B-boy hippy, my brother's in prison for murder, half of my close friends sell drugs, I'm a giant party thrower, and I talk with slang all the time.

I am who I am and I like myself, but I realized there wasn't a large demographic of kids like me that I could market my music to. Realizing this made me feel ten times more blessed that somehow I still had enough kids that supported my music that I could support myself. I credited this a lot to the fact I live in Minnesota and came to the realization then that we have one of the most supportive music/hip hop scenes anywhere on the planet and I am lucky as fuck to be from here.

Around this time, ATMOSPHERE released a song called "Say Shhh" describing what it's like living in Minnesota. In the song SLUG says this line,

"If no one in your crew walks around with a gun, say shhh" - SLUG

This song has become very popular, and to many Minnesotans, it has become an anthem. The first time I heard this song was at Gasthof's. The second time I heard it was at the Red Sea. Both times I heard it I was with friends who had guns on them. The second time at the Red Sea my friend Denny almost shot somebody, but TRUTH MAZE convinced him to put the gun away.

"Almost came close to killing one night at the Red Sea / but Truth Maze made him put it away / lives saved / souls to take we pray" - BIG ZACH (NEW MC)

CHAPTER 22 PART 2 : THREE TRUE STORIES

I read in a book by the Dalai Lama that jealousy is a number one instinct. You naturally feel jealousy like you naturally feel pain or hunger. But, to act envious, or in modern hip hop terms, to "hate" on someone just because your jealous of them is wrong and creates evil energy.

On New Years Eve 1999, a 20 year-old girl named Anna called me and asked me if I could buy the keg for her New Years Eve party since I had just turned 21. I said sure and invited a handful of my homies who were looking for a party that night. Anna had a big two-story house over by Lake Harriet. It filled up with a lot of her friends, most of whom were richer kids I had gone to high school with. I remember the party being bright with good energy, young happy people getting drunk early. A group of my homies came through including BIG WIZ and DILLON PARKER.

At one moment, they were sitting in a circle rolling a blunt and I was standing outside of the circle drinking a bottle of Boone's Farm. It was right at that moment I heard a reaction by some girls in the front of the house. I can't remember if they screamed or just got excited, but I looked over to see what they were reacting to. They were reacting because the actor Josh Hartnett had just come into the party. Even though we had graduated from the same high school in the same class, I don't think we had ever met. After graduation, he became an actor and starred in TV shows and movies. He was friends with Anna so he had come to the party to celebrate the new year like everybody else.

I am ashamed to admit, at that moment I felt an emotion I don't think I had ever felt before in my 21 year-old life. I felt jealousy that turned instantly into hate. My drunk dumbass then turned to BIG WIZ, DILLON PARKER, and the rest of the homies and said, "Yo! It's that actor dude...Yo! Let's rob this dude!" Everybody started laughing at me and BIG WIZ called me a clown. I said, "Watch, bet I rob this dude."

I don't know how much time went by, but I pumped myself up about it until I finally ran into the dude at the top of the stairs on the second floor. He walked by me, and like the moron that I was, I said, "Hey, ain't you that rich actor dude?" He looked at me and said something super normal like, "Hey Zach, I'm Josh. We went to high school together." That through me off a little bit. Then I slurred out something else like, "Yo, you need to drop down on cheese." (That translates into "Give me all the money in your pockets.")

From what I can remember, he just looked at me weird and walked down the stairs. I don't know how many of my homies were behind me or what they thought they saw, but they reacted like it was funny. When I woke up hung over the next morning, the first day of 1999, the first thing I thought was, "Holy shit, this girl I brought home has the nicest ass I have ever seen." Then, the second thought was, "Holy fuck, did I say something stupid to that actor dude...what the fuck did I do that for?"

That was the moment I realized I had a little hater in me. Later that night, I opened the doors to my weekly Sunday night show, HEADSPIN, and the first kid who showed up, who was not at the party with me the night before, said, "Damn Zach, I heard you robbed that actor Josh Hartnett!" I got a sinking feeling in my stomach that has never really gone away. Because of the little popularity I have and the fact that he is famous, that rumor spread like wildfire. This was even before Facebook existed.

A few months later, I went to a talent show at St. Paul Central high school to scope out some young rappers. I spotted Josh Hartnett there and he came over to me. I was like...fuck. He told me he was there to see his little sister who was in a rock band and asked me what I was doing there. That was the only conversation I ever remembering having with Josh Hartnett. But, because of my own hater-ness, people have believed I robbed him at a party for years. I can only hope that Josh Hartnett never heard those rumors. I bet you in a one-on-one fight ... Josh Hartnett would probably kick my ass.

Once upon a time, I believe a boy was born with a very beautiful soul. That boy was born albino and I think he grew to believe that race does not exist. That boy and I are the same age. He grew up wherever he grew up and I grew up in South Minneapolis. I met that boy when I was 21. He had become a rapper.

My first real memory of him rapping came at his first show at the show I hosted on Sunday nights, HEADSPIN. I recall the power kept going out during his set, stopping his performance. He seemed like he had a good routine and prepared but kept getting halted by the power failures. Even with the power failures, he held himself well. He sounded like he had been influenced by KRS ONE. He and I were both trying to become popular rappers. Being young, we both made mistakes and did dumb shit along our paths.

That boy grew up and slowly became a very popular rapper in my city and beyond. People from all over started to love his music and feel like it represented my city very well. Not sure if he was from my city like he claimed to be, I became jealous of him. And that jealousy became hate. I hated on him because I wanted the spot he had. God had given me my own spot and my own path that I should have been happy with, but I wasn't. So, I hated on him.

Luckily, my hate did not grow to consume me. One night when I was older, I was at a girl's house hanging out in her basement after three in the morning when one of the boy's songs started playing on her iPod rotation. As I listened and began to hate inside my head, my hate was overpowered by the strength of his music. I sat on the floor to get closer to the speakers so I could listen more closely. That is when the truth came to me. I was jealous that I didn't make this song. This boy was painting a picture of the Northside of Minneapolis better than I was able to paint a picture of South Minneapolis, where I grew up. The power of that boy's music and that acceptance cured me of the little bit of hater I had inside myself. I do not have that inside myself anymore.

Once upon a time, I believe a kid was born in the Southside of Chicago. He grew up and went through things that made him who he was. After he turned 18, he moved to St. Paul. That kid could rap pretty good, kinda sounded like he had been influenced by NAS and Q-TIP.

I first ran into this kid at the monthly battle I was hosting at the Loring Pasta Bar. I thought he had real bad energy the first time we bumped into each other and my instincts told me to stay away from him. But, trying to mentor more than I should have, I eventually tried to give him some tips that I watched him use successfully. Afterwards, that kid and I became friends. He had a lot of knowledge and taught me a few things as well. I grew to like him and forget about my first instincts.

The kid I had begun to like began to grow hate in his heart. And that hate grew strong. For his own reasons he aimed that hate at all the local rappers who offered him opportunities and that hate became stronger than any hate I had ever seen inside a person. I tried to offer my advice and opportunities I could provide to the kid to try to put out his hate, but I was unsuccessful. The kid then began to hate me as well and that hate became even stronger. So strong it overpowered the good inside the kid and he became something he wasn't. He became something like a demon.

On a spring day when I was 30 years old, I was walking from the bank to the bus stop in Seward neighborhood pretty close to where my sister lives. As the bus approached, my cell phone rang. It was my friend BRANDON ALLDAY. Just as the bus pulled up and opened its' doors, BRANDON talked me into helping him put up some posters so I made the decision to wave off the bus. As I walked back to the corner, I thought to myself, "There must be some reason I'm supposed to be on this corner."

I was on the Southeast corner of 25th Street and 27th Avenue in South Minneapolis when a silver four-door car driving south on 27th pulled up kitty corner from me. The car sat there for an extra second. I thought the driver waved at me but I couldn't be sure through the windshield. The car then turned diagonal and drove right at me. Figuring it could have been anyone from the Southside I knew just goofing off, I didn't move. The car accelerated, and right before impact, I saw through the windshield that it was that kid whose hate had consumed him.

Thinking very fast, I jumped up so I wouldn't be run over and I smashed into the windshield. The car collided with a small wooden fence I was standing in front of. If I would have stood still, my legs would have been crushed between the two.

The windshield spider webbed when I smashed into it and I flew somewhere between 15 and 20 feet backwards over the small fence and some bushes that were behind it. I rolled out of it on the grass and stood up right away. Looking left, I saw BRANDON had rolled up just as it had happened. BRANDON jumped out of his car with a pretty shocked look on his face. I limped toward him and stated, the obvious, that I had just been hit by a car. With hate in him, the kid, now a 27 year-old man, who had hit me with a car, jumped out of the car, pulled out a knife, and started yelling, "You wanna ruin my life?! You wanna ruin my life?!" I told him to put the knife down but he didn't. He came in closer to try and stab me. I ran. I ran across the street. I'm slightly ashamed to say that because it is the only time in my adult life that I ran from another man that wasn't the police.

Then, the kid who hit me with the car, opened the back seat and pulled out his 3 year-old son. The baby was crying from all the commotion and the kid approached me to fight him in the street with the baby in his arms. A police car then rolled up and two cops got out. Trying to make sense of what happened, one cop put me in a squad car while the other asked witnesses what happened. The kid was arrested and I was let go.

The kid attempted to kill me because of his jealousy over rap music. To add some humor to the story, I don't feel I'm a popular enough rapper to be that jealous over. Since the kid got out of jail, he has sent me apologies saying he had demons in him. Though I would like to never see that kid again, if he reads this I will say the apology was heard. And I hope he prospers in the rest of his life.

When I got home after I had been hit by the car, I believe I was in shock. I was alone and didn't know how I was supposed to feel or what I was supposed to do. I felt emotions I had never felt before and they were hard to understand. I sat there for over an hour not knowing what to do with myself. I looked at my phone but I didn't know who to reach out to. Then, my phone rang. It was the boy from the previous story. The one I had hated on when I was younger. He had heard what happened and he was the first person to call and see if I was alright.

We spoke briefly and he told me if I needed anything to call him back. Because of that phone call I would like to publicly apologize for words of hate that stepped outside the lines of the competition of rap that ever came out of my mouth about that boy.

His rapper name is BROTHER ALI. Salaam

CHAPTER 23 :
TOP 25 AND BEYOND

Every once in a while I used to check DUnation.com, the former home of the Minnesota hip hop gossip message board. About once every few months the post came up, "Who are the top emcees ever out of Minnesota?" Some people post up their favorites and others post up their friends. Dumb rappers would post themselves. The couple times I saw the question posted I had to hold myself back. I feel I know for a fact who are the best emcees ever in MN. Only because my dumb ass life has been caught up in this for so long, I'm probably the closest thing to an "idiot"...I mean "expert" on the subject.

There have probably been over a million people who lived in Minnesota at one point at some stage of their lives and tried to rap; which is all good. Everyone has the right to try any art; everyone's got a right to draw. But, for the best-ever list, you first have to throw your homies out the window if you got some friend that raps. Maybe when you and your fellas get drunk on the weekends he can spit a tight freestyle. Or maybe you know somebody that makes songs in their basement and they're pretty good; your uncle knows somebody that knows somebody and there trying to shop his demo. That's fine and good luck to whatever you're trying to do. But, in my opinion, M.C. stands for Mic Controller, Move the Crowd, Master of Ceremonies, Make 'em Clap, and all definitions that are defined by going out and getting heard.

Whether that means getting in cyphers at school, parties, or in the streets. Whether that means going to open mics. Whether that means getting in battles, entering tournaments, or just defending yourself when other emcees try and test your nuts. Or whether that means making music any way you have to and then getting it heard by anyone who will listen...you gotta make them listen.

Live shows, tours, local shows of all sizes, clubs, bars, parks, churches, wherever you play you gotta be a live emcee. Studio rappers might be able to write rhymes, whatever's good, but to be a live emcee you gotta get on the mic in front of people. It takes practice and lots of work.

I wrote down almost 90 emcees. All the ones worth mentioning I could think of. Then, scored them on these categories:

TIME IN THE SCENE: From when you got on locally 'til you either quit or moved. If you took major time off, I subtracted it. In all respect, if you were the hot shit in '88 but you were done by '91, I didn't get a chance to check it.

RECORDED MATERIAL: How much music you have put out on wax, tape, CD, and the internet.

SUCCESS: I graded this one on a curve. Some people were given more opportunity than others and some made good with what they had to work with. For example, if you dropped a tape in 1994 and you couldn't get shows anywhere because shows were hard to come by, I can't compare you with someone who came out in 2004 and their homie who was already successful put them on and brought them on tour.

HUSTLE: How hard you worked. Some came from the bottom up. Some people got big hook ups and it might look like they just got put on but they still had to bust ass.

STAGE: All aspects of your live show.

FREESTYLE: How good you are at coming off the head. Minnesota takes pride in our freestylers.

DOPENESS: This is purely my personal opinion. How dope I think you are.

BATTLE: How many battles you won, street, stage, songs and/or tournaments.

INFLUENCE: How much influence you had on MN hip hop; how many people you inspired.

HOSTING: I believe emceeing also embodies being able to host events and control the crowd.

TALENT: This one is God given, how you used your gifts and used them to emcee. For example, being able to sing, beatbox, scream, rap, dance, play instruments, shit, juggle...I don't know.

CONTENT: I stopped listening to rappers who rap about rapping over ten years ago. Though there are some emcees on this list that don't focus on subject matter, and I gave extra points to the ones who do.

TOP 25 EMCEES IN MINNESOTA HISTORY

AS OF SEPTEMBER 18, 2011

25: KNOWLEDGE MC

When I was a teenager he was the best freestyler I ever heard in my life.

24: ST PAUL SLIM

Should be in the top ten but, he did a term in the Marines that took him out the picture from like 1997-2002 which were important years. If you watch a SLIM performance you get a raw real perfect performance of what emceeing is.

23: EXTREME aka E Da 5'9 aka DISPUTE ONE

Born with one of the dopest voices ever. He's been a part of RHYMESAYERS, INTERLOCK, DIALOGUE ELEVATORS CREW, and D.R.S. He's been a teacher to many young rappers.

22: MU AH DIB

Endless talent. In all his groups, TWISTED LINGUISTICS, HEIRUSPECS, ACOUSTIC BEATDOWN, and the INTERLOCK ALL STARS, he plays the background more than anything else. He's the plug two that can outshine the whole project. He's toured the country three times over but is still underrated. Beyond his ability to rap his ass off, inside his soul he is a beautiful spiritual instrument. He has a singing voice that was descended to earth from God's own choir and he can beatbox to the rhythm of the universe's pulse.

21: GLORIOUS L aka GLO PESHI

His body language made him the funnest dude ever to watch perform. He has so much positive energy inside of him it just spills out into the world when he's on-stage. His voice and freestyle are as fresh as they come. He gave birth to the ABSTRACT PACK and gave birth to the HEADSHOTS crew which gave birth to the new scene.

20: BUDAH TYE

Good chance he's won the most battles in Minnesota out of anyone else in the last 20 years. He used to walk around with a championship heavyweight belt around his waist to let you know who he was.

19: CRESCENT MOON

With his success touring with ODD JOBS and KILL THE VULTURES, and touring the world as EYEDEA's and SLUG's hype man in ATMOSPHERE, I would have put him higher but I don't know if he's truly an emcee. I've always suspected he's something else. He has gone on to make folk music in a band called ROMA DI LUNA. He also won a few battles in his day.

18: UNICUS

9 multiplied by 2 equals 18. It's simple mathematics. Peaceful emcee and person. He is the least competitive person on the list. He just loves hip hop and loves to be on the mic. Probably close to a thousand shows under his belt.

17: GENE POOL

Real raw lyrics and delivery. Laid a lot of bricks for the scene back in the days with PHULL CIRCLE, RHYMESAYERS, and the DYNOSPECTRUM.

16: SHAWN SKIE

The best emcee ever to come out of Eastside St. Paul. Pure freestyler, pure battle rapper.

15: MUJA MESSIAH

He's my personal favorite rapper in the state. He's a B-boy and a D-boy. Very witty, clever writer, clever enough to keep the politics inside the punch lines and hustle the truth.

14: NOMI

Has toured the country twice over with ODD JOBS, now lives out in the bay area. Has a solo emcee project out called POWER STRUGGLE with producer DJ DETOX that is real mature and is worth checking out.

13: DESDAMONA

Just on the fact of being a white girl from Iowa who got on the scene at like age 24 before you could be a white girl rapping gives her mad points. She had to work the hardest of anyone on the list. If it wasn't for her, girls, especially white girls still would have a hard time getting on the mic around here.

12: FELIX

As the front man for the band HEIRUSPECS, he is great at controlling the energy of a crowd. Best rapper over a live band in the state. Very good at getting a crowd's attention if they've never seen him before. Always thought the only thing that he's missing is deeper topics. I think he's just starting to explore that now.

11: TOKI WRIGHT

He's got stage, content, style, and skills. Traveled the country doing back up vocals for BROTHER ALI. Spiritually, he is very special to us. He saved us from a split and kept the colors and backgrounds of our world diverse and conscious.

10: CARNAGE

He's a beast. Been around a long time and paid a lot of dues. On-stage he can be very unselfish with a true understanding of how to assist someone else he is on-stage with and make them look good. Great emcee, great host, great beatboxer.

9: NEW MC aka BIG ZACH aka ZACHARIAH

18 divided by 2 equals 9. It is simple mathematics.

8: BROTHER ALI

Once a couple saw me at a bar. I overheard the girl say, "Oh my God! Look that's Zach from KANSER!" The guy said, "Who?" She said, "You know...NEW MC, he's a local rapper." He replied, "I ain't never heard of him, maybe if it was BROTHER ALI or something I would give a fuck." True story.

7: SESS

It is not just romanticized that he was one of the illest because he passed away early. He was the illest. He had a giant influence on EYEDEA, ABILITIES, SLUG, NOMI, KANSER, the rest of the PACK, and others. Since he passed away early he has become a legend and I believe his energy has watched over all of us since.

6: MUSAB aka BEYOND

The most popular rapper in MN '96-97. His first solo was the first CD ever put out by RHYMESAYERS. Authentic and intelligent, he keeps evolving and later signed to HIEROGLYPHIC EMPORIUM. Now he lives in Las Vegas.

5: P.O.S.

At first I didn't even put him in the top 25 because he is not a great emcee in the traditional sense. He doesn't battle, he's not a good freestyler, and he is younger than anyone else on the list. But after a second look at it I realized what really mattered. P.O.S. hustled CD's on the streets and did shows until SLUG and RSE put him on, and then P.O.S. brought his whole crew with him. He stayed true and didn't forget anybody. DOOMTREE is the same crew of homies that P.O.S. was rapping with and making music with in high school and they created a type of rapping and music that might be more original than any of the rest of us. By the rules of the life force known as hip hop that puts him up to number five.

4: TRUTH MAZE

Fully embodies what emceeing is. He has an older flow, but his raps aren't his strong point as they are for most others on the list. He can step on-stage with no songs, no background music, no nothing, and still entertain the crowd. Held the beatbox crown for years. Best host in the city. He is the sole survivor of the hip hop scene that took place in the 80's, and for the most part died off. The energy of that scene lived on in TRUTH MAZE and he carried it with him to share and influence the rest of us and help give birth to so something new.

3: SLUG

The world knows him as a great songwriter and the dude who created emo rap. But I'll always remember him as the dope shit talking battle rapper from the HEADSHOTS crew with a fresh freestyle serving kids in a dark warehouse underground rap battle in 1995.

2: I SELF DEVINE

I have a memory of him on-stage doing a sold-out all-ages show downtown back in 2000. The sound went out during the peak of his hypest song and without a working mic he was still a monster on-stage. Very respected. Good host. Real evolved flow but built on an old school foundation. He is a teacher by nature and has been one to all of us, even when he was forced to use tough love.

1: EYEDEA

When I first met EYEDEA, he was my little dude. I told him to come to a party over Southside once when he was 15, where I introduced him to DILLON PARKER. I told DILLON that this 15 year-old kid could rap better than I could and DILLON snapped out. DILLON was mad thinking I was on some under-confident shit (haha), but I knew this kid was special.

I believe hundreds of years ago during a dark time in American and Jamaican history, Devils enslaved Gods and carried them in boats over the Atlantic Ocean. The Gods brought with them a strong energy or life force that later mixed with some diverse artistic sprinkles of New York. That was the birth of hip hop.

Hip hop is a living thing. Not like a person, a tree, or even a soul is a living thing, but it is an energy that has life. I am here to fulfill one of my life's purposes as a griot and pass down stories of a piece of hip hop that took its own form in a metropolitan area towards the top of the Mississippi river known as Minneapolis/St. Paul. It is our own energy that I have been a part of, and this energy will forever be a part of me. This energy does not have a name, but at the end of the 90's, it was represented by some of the events that are recorded in this book (such as Headspin Sundays and SOUNDSET Wednesday's).

A similar but slightly older, slightly more powerful, piece of hip hop had its own form around the same time in the metro area of Los Angeles, California on the coast of the Pacific Ocean. This life force does not have a name either, but was represented by the Good Life open mics, Project Blowed, and I'm sure many other things.

I was not there to witness the birth, growth, or existence of The Good Life or Project Blowed, but it's energy did reach out and have a small influence on the energy we were building in Minnesota. From what I have heard and seen second hand through music and documentaries, I believe that these two life forces were the purest and strongest forms of hip hop that existed on earth in the 1990's.

For those who participated in or were a part of either energy, it was the essence of our lives and gave us something to be a part of that was bigger than ourselves. The many styles that developed inside either of these energies were different, but both stayed pure and strong.

In the year of 1999, a contest took place in Cincinnati Ohio called Scribble Jam. This contest was the purest and most competitive contest to ever take place in the advanced art of emceeing. It was hosted and watched over by a neutral party who had true understanding of what the energy was, KEVIN BEACHAM. Several emcee warriors from different places took place in this event but in the end it came down to a final two. A powerful warrior that represented the Good Life and Project Blowed named P.E.A.C.E and a young sharp witty kid that represented Headspin Headshots and History named EYEDEA.

The skill level was so close that the two emcees had to battle twice with EYEDEA finally coming out the victor. When I caught wind of the outcome of the event, I contacted young EYEDEA to congratulate him on his victory. He tried his best to refuse the props I was giving him. I thought he was being humble but he kept repeating, "I beat him on a lie."

The line he was referring to went:

> *"I don't wanna say this / but you're not alarming me / Freestyle*
> *Fellowship bit their style from Bone Thugs and Harmony"* - *Eyedea*

EYEDEA stressed to me the fact that that was the line that won him Scribble Jam and defeated P.E.A.C.E. but that statement was not true. He told me P.E.A.C.E. bowed to him and hugged him after that battle, but said to him, "You know that's not true, right?"

The way magic moves through the universe of hip hop when EYEDEA returned home to us, he brought with him the energy of victory defeating the most powerful hip hop force there was in the Good Life and Project Blowed. This caused an increase in power to our own energy, and the Twin Cities hip hop scene became ten times what it had been. All of us reaped the benefits. From our energy, local artists immersed into national popularity such as ATMOSPHERE, THE MICRANOTS, BROTHER ALI, HEIRUS-PECS, P.O.S., and many many many more.

The outcome of the '99 Scribble Jam battle did not hold down the movement that was happening on the southern part of the West Coast. Their artists also became stronger in popularity including FREESTYLE FELLOWSHIP, JURASSIC 5, ABSTRACT RUDE, SCARUB, PIGEON JOHN, 2MEX and many many many more.

> *"Like the '99 Scribble Jam / P.E.A.C.E should of won /*
> *but it's good / y'all know the outcome"* - *ABSTRACT RUDE*

It was EYEDEA that put us all on and brought light to our existence.
That's why he is number one.

I'm known as a dude who has a grip of crazy stories. It must be because I fuck with so many different types of people, or maybe it's just in my karma. One of the last stories I leave in this book is a thank you.

On October 9th 2007, I was stapling up posters for an upcoming show in Uptown Minneapolis outside of The Wedge grocery store. The Wedge is the big "Organic Co-op" on the Southside. To stereotype the people who shop there, they are neo-hippies, self righteous and trendy (I hope it doesn't sound like I'm bashing them cuz I used to stop in there to buy burritos all the time).

Anyways, I had just finished putting up some posters when I started peddling my bike down the Lyndale Avenue sidewalk. About ten feet in front of me were two homeless looking bummy type white dudes. One was pushing an old bike with a basket and the other was walking next to him. I answered a call on my cell so I was talking more than biking, moving the peddles as slow as I could but still staying balanced. The two dudes in front of me moved to the left side of the sidewalk and signaled for me to pass them. Since I wasn't in a hurry, I didn't, but I heard them say something smart to me under their breath that I ignored.

I peddled about 15 feet down the sidewalk and then noticed a small stack of 20-dollar bills to the right of me on the grass that separated the sidewalk from the street. I think since I was in mid-conversation on the phone I said out loud, "Oh shit I just found a bunch of money!" I quickly grabbed it and threw it in my cargo pocket. As I looked up, I saw the two bummy looking cats staring at me puzzled. Then, as if I could see the cranks, knobs, and little hamster wheels turn inside their little brains, they looked at each other and then approached me. I was like, "Fuck, here we go."

Stuttering and unsure of themselves, the two men started speaking over each other. "Yo man, that's our money," they said. I told my homie on the phone I would call him back and replied that if it had fallen out of their pockets I would have seen it go from the left side of the sidewalk to the right side right in front of me.

Since that made sense, the two men started spitting out more elaborate stories saying they had dropped the money a half an hour ago and had been walking up and down Lyndale looking for it and they had sold scrap metal to the scrap yard. As their story kept getting more elaborate I thought to myself, "It's only money and these dudes look like they need it more than I do." So I said, "If you can tell me how much it was I'll give it to you." Their reply was quick and confident...$60. For a split of a second I thought it must be theirs cuz it roughly looked like $60. But when I pulled it out, it was four twenty's. "Eighty dollars," I said. "I'm out of here."

I started to bike away the way I came. I didn't feel either of the bums could whoop me, but the longer I argued with them the worse of a position I put myself in and it was only half about the money. I wasn't gonna let myself get robbed in broad daylight by a couple of bums, especially not in Uptown.

I was on my boy's BMX, and even swerving through people, there was no way they would be able to catch me with them being on foot. But the next thing I know, the weirdest shit in the world cracked off. These two dudes started yelling, "Somebody stop that guy! He robbed us!"

Immediately, three or four people coming out of the grocery store tried to grab me. I maneuvered quick like some sort of video game but by the time I bent the corner into the alley out of the Wedge parking lot, I could hear maybe six voices yelling, "Stop that guy, stop...thief!"

I shook the last lady who was a Wedge worker on her smoke break behind the building and had a clear path to freedom. I could still hear voices behind me but no one in front of me. I crossed the street and recognized about a quarter of the way down the block there was one guy putting something in his trunk. I saw him but didn't think he would intervene. He looked up, heard the lady behind me yell stop that guy probably thinking I stole her purse, and then tackled me off my bike...breaking my nose.

This whole event took place in maybe sixty seconds tops and started out with me thinking, "Oh shit it's my lucky day! I just found a bunch of money!" By the way I reacted to the dude who broke my nose he could tell right away I wasn't a thief or running from anything I had done wrong. The two bums caught up behind me and were like, "Oh man, we didn't want all this to happen. We just thought you should split that money with us."

As I bled out my face, the police and ambulance showed up but none of the people who were chasing me through the parking lot seemed to be around anymore. They told me I needed to go to the hospital (which I already knew) but, since I didn't have medical insurance, I knew if I put a foot in the ambulance it would've cost me $1000. So the dude who actually tackled me off my bike drove me to the hospital.

To make the rest of the story short, I was told my nose was crazy fucked up and I needed to have surgery with only a small window of time. They said I needed it the following weekend. Before then, the swelling would get in the way and not too long after that the healing process would get in the way. They booked me for the following Friday, but when I told them I didn't have medical insurance there was somewhat of a huge record scratch...without medical insurance I was fucked.

By the end of the next day, my partners SHIZ and UNICUS, along with 10K BREAKS, had put together a benefit the following Tuesday which raised over $3,000. Half the groups in the city preformed for free and people came out the woodwork to donate money.

Everything that's ever happened to me in life, good or bad, I've always been able to make sense of why it happened. This bike "accident" wasn't that easy to rationalize. I couldn't tell you where I went wrong or what I was supposed to do different. It was a pretty odd event.

However, when the benefit show/Twin Cities hip hop scene raised enough money for my surgery in one day, I was pretty moved. Less of a lesson, maybe more of a statement, I have for the most part given my life to the advancement of my city's hip hop scene, and in this story, they really gave back. On top of that, when DJ OMARI OMARI, who is the biggest salsa dance DJ in Minnesota, showed up and put a hundred in my pocket, I also realized it went outside of hip hop. I appreciate the donations more than I could put into words.

Since the dude that broke my nose had homeowner's insurance and the accident happened in his back alley, I ended up getting a settlement of 11,000 dollars after it was all said and done. With that money, I paid off every bill I had (along with some of my homeboys bills), flew KANSER down to Atlanta to do a song with PROF opening up for ASHER ROTH, and went to NEW ORLEANS. Eh, it was a good time. Guess it all worked out.

In late December of 2007, I sat in a basement of a St. Paul bar called the Turf Club eating pizza with NOMI, local beat maker BENZILLA, and all the band members of HEIRUSPECS. It was a birthday show celebrating HEIRUSPECS being around for ten years strong. It was also between sound check and the first of two sold-out shows, so the day hadn't even gotten started yet.

I had just turned 30 about a month before and I looked around the room at men, adult hip hop musicians and emcees I had known since we were kids. When I was 20 years old I could only visualize two outcomes of our hip hop careers. Either we would have blown up big or rapping would be long behind us. I didn't foresee that I would be selling the most CDs/making the most money in my life off music at age 30.

Between shows, I had a real good conversation with FELIX. He wasn't the teen-age weirdo hater kid who formed INTERLOCK ten years earlier. He was a pretty well rounded adult and was a better emcee now than he ever had been. Even though I still had to hustle and stand outside the show with my box of CDs, I couldn't see FELIX doing that anymore. I couldn't see him in a B-boy "crew". I couldn't see him trying to battle anybody or even talk shit about anyone anymore. He was the lead rapper in HEIRUSPECS, debatably the most successful rapper ever out of St. Paul, and I was proud to be rapping along side of him at his show.

I looked at NOMI at the show as well and saw somethin' similar. This wasn't one of the young kids from ODD JOBS/CMI who was a HEADSHOTS' superfan. This was another grown man who had followed his dreams and pursued hip hop as hard as he could. I was proud to consider him an old friend.

CHAPTER 24 :
PROF AND DUENDAY

PROF AND STOPHOUSE

In early 2007, I was 29. I must have been broke because I was brainstorming how to make some money. I had tried to bring back battles in the same form RSE held the Golden Mic Contest back in '98, holding a battle between myself and ILLICIT at the Dinkytowner. We made a flyer billing BIG ZACH (New MC) vs ILLICIT, "A Battle for the Ego". We had a crowd of maybe 60 people show up and made a little money but ILLICIT didn't take it serious enough to make it truly entertaining (I won).

Trying to figure out who I could battle that would draw interest, I contacted EYEDEA. But, by 2007 he thought battle rapping was dumb. So, I had the idea to post on DUNATION.com that I was proclaiming myself the best battle rapper in Minnesota. I posted that I booked a date at the Dinkytowner three weeks out. If anyone wanted to respond to my challenge they would have three weeks to prepare. Then, in more detail, I wrote that I didn't want to battle a no-name. I wanted a challenge.

I wanted someone like BROTHER ALI, TOKI WRIGHT, or a DOOMTREE member to accept my challenge. Knowing none of them would but by presenting the fact that I wasn't scared of anyone would add more hype to my claim and maybe draw out a semi-popular local rapper to accept. I worded it as humble as I could so I wouldn't sound like an arrogant asshole. When I went to hit post I took a second to re-think what I was about to do.

I had always hated on hip hop message boards and prided myself that I never ever in my life would put up a post. I would be opening myself up to a lot of shit talking if people took this wrong and once I hit post I would probably have to battle anyone that accepted. Fuck it...I posted it anyway.

By the next day, my post was the hottest topic on DUNATION. A 22 year-old rapper from Southside named PROF had accepted my challenge. PROF was from Powderhorn neighborhood and was seven grades behind me at South. I knew PROF a little. He rapped with a dude named RAHZWELL whose cousin was Shawn Neis (Chapter 17).

PROF was an up-and-coming local rapper with a small but growing fan base. A perfect fit for the event I was trying to make happen. I got ahold of PROF and went over to his house where I explained to him my idea. It wasn't a fake professional wrestling event or anything but we should be prepared. It has to go at least eight rounds I told him or people would feel like they didn't get their money's worth. I told him nothing was off limits and that we would split the door no matter who won or lost. Most importantly, we had to make it entertaining.

My guy DILLON PARKER called me a couple days later excited saying, "Zach, I've been instigating the battle between PROF and you over DUNATION. I'm gonna have your post up to 200 comments, watch." DILLON's real smart that way. He was on the message board talking shit about me and PROF just to hype it up and use the message board as a tool to promote the event.

For the majority of my free time during the next week, I sat in my room and practiced freestyling. I over-prepared with comebacks for everything I thought PROF would hit me with. I went into the battle fully-prepared, assuming that PROF was up every night training as hard or harder than I was...which was not the case at all.

RAHZWELL later told me that the night before the battle, the Gampo Brothers (PROF & RAHZ) were out drinking and RAHZWELL casually asked PROF over a beer, "You getting ready to battle BIG ZACH tomorrow?" PROF responded without much thought, "Yo, whatever...KANSER's old...I'm about to shit on Zach." RAHZ told me he tried to give PROF a speech that he should take the battle more serious but PROF was just like whatever.

So, 200+ excited people overcrowded the Dinkytowner the next night to watch the battle. PROF and I had enough mutual friends that at least half the crowd was people that were connected to our social circles. That made the energy in the room fun.

I'm standing on-stage too afraid to un-focus, completely prepared, warmed up, and ready to freestyle with 15 rounds worth of punch lines and rebuttals against PROF half-way memorized to fall back on.

Not to my knowledge, PROF was standing across from me without one premeditated line and only a little bit of battle tournament experience. With all that said, he was completely confident he was gonna shit all over me. SHIZ played host and referee and DJ MASHOUT dropped the first beat.

I went first as part of my game plan and hit PROF with a couple warm up lines that got good reactions from the crowd. Then, Prof kicked a sloppy freestyle and rhymed the word shit with dick a couple times. PROF coming so lazy in the first round almost threw me off but I hit him with a couple more blows in the second round. One of my lines must have sparked PROF because he hit me with the best line of the battle in the second round.

*"In five years KANSER's gonna be living under a bridge /
trying to teach Unicus' kids how to use a syringe"* - PROF

The 200 person room let out a slow "oooh" which was obviously louder than any laughs I had gotten on PROF so far. It didn't shake me but, in my head, I knew, if he followed strong, it would put him ahead. But, he didn't follow strong. His face almost looked confused after the crowd hit. He then stuttered and weakly freestyled through the end of the second round rhyming the word shit with dick again. That's when my 29 year-old experience kicked in and I realized that PROF thought the crowd boo'd him.

He thought the crowd thought his line about Unicus' kids was too mean while I knew the crowd thought it was the hardest line so far in the battle. I knew he was shook and I knew I had him then. I proceeded to chop the shit out of PROF for eight more hilarious rounds while he played a good sport standing there getting laughed at. I kept all my jokes light-hearted so PROF's friends thought it was funny. PROF was such a good sport about it I didn't want SHIZ to announce me as the winner. I just hit PROF with one final line and ran off-stage, then, ran out the door of the Dinkytowner, up the stairs, and around the block. It was a personal victory lap and it felt good.

When I returned from the opposite direction, 60+ people were standing outside the Dinkytowner giving me handshakes and compliments. The Yoda Jedi master of all that is hip hop, TRUTHMAZE, was even out there and he gave the biggest compliment he ever gave me. Even at 40+ years old, TRUTHMAZE has a teenage like sparkle in his eye when it comes to fun hip hop shit.

As people filed out up the stairway of the Dinkytowner, I collected the money from the door and paid all the openers very generously. I brought PROF in the kitchen of the Dinkytowner and we split $534 which, divided in half, was $267 apiece. Not that much in the big scheme of things, but considering my rent at the time was $250, it was like making my rent in eight minutes in a way of looking at it. I gave PROF a short speech that I had lost enough battles that I knew it would sting a little bit when he woke up to-morrow and for the next couple days but it was nothing and it was just entertainment.

In the next year or so, two other rappers, ANALYRICAL and SHELLTOE, challenged me to battle them at the Dinkytowner. I crushed SHELLTOE pretty bad but he might have been the best battle rapper in the state at the time and had made a pretty good buzz around town for himself so, just like with PROF, after the battle we walked with almost $300 each.

ANALYRICAL gave me a little run for my money before I just outlasted him. Sadly, the crowd was smaller so the rapper (ANALYRICAL) that did the best against me made the least money. Added to my career of local tournaments, I won the year anniversary battle at the Loring Pasta Bar (Vesh vs Aquil Chapter), the Midwest Show-down at First Ave for $1500 (most of which went to my little brother's lawyer fees and he still got 20 years in prison). I also won the Twin Cities Celebration of Hip Hop MC Battle twice in '04 and '05, and took 2nd in '03. I won the Twin Cities Scribble Jam regional in '04 and took 2nd in '05. Along with the some tournaments I entered and won out-of-state, I would guess I have the 2nd best battle rapper career ever in the state of Minnesota behind EYEDEA of course. But now, at 33 years of age, I am retired.

I watch some of these GRINDTIME battles on YouTube nowadays (2011) and some of those dudes are incredible! They're younger, faster, fresher, and have just taken battle rapping to a level I can no longer compete with. Plus, the rules have changed. These GRINDTIME kids aren't freestyling or rapping over beats so the game is different. GRINDTIME north has included me and I have judged three times for them. At 33, I wanna rap about happy things and write songs that tell stories about my life. I don't have the time or energy to keep up.

Soon after the PROF battle, PROF and I became better friends by going down to Bracket Park and playing basketball. PROF told me after the battle that it had stung a bit and he felt like he lost his swag a little. We shot hoops for a while and talked about rap.

PROF & RAHZWELL then had a meeting with DILLON PARKER and I. They asked if they could become members of INTERLOCK. We played three good packed local shows together, and like the case of the original INTERLOCK, I got to make some new friends, go to some new parties, and make-out with PROF's female roommate. But soon after, DILLON, UNICUS, and I decided it was time that KANSER/MORE THAN LIGHTS, DILLON, and the other members of INTERLOCK went in different directions and we put the INTERLOCK crew to rest.

Luckily, DILLON and PROF clicked real well and started a new company called STOPHOUSE MUSIC GROUP. What DILLON, PROF, and STOPHOUSE have since been able to achieve, DILLON wanted to do with me but it couldn't work for many reasons. DILLON and PROF want to be rich and famous off rap for as close as you can come for the right reasons. I, on the other hand, have a spiritual connection to emceeing that is so deep it defines me...or maybe I was just born to be a broke rapper...but it's who I am. DILLON PARKER is one of the best friends I have ever known and most likely I will still owe him money on the day I die. He put together my first solo album, *White Jesus*, which I still believe is my best work. I wouldn't have been able to make it without the direction of DILLON.

PROF is one of the most talented and driven rappers I have ever met. His stage presence is second to none in Minnesota and I am one of his biggest supporters. PROF gives me credit for helping put him on the scene. Some of that credit I'll take but really it was PROF & RAHZWELL's former DJ Ashanti (DJ SCARZ) that convinced me to pay attention to PROF. I knew Ashanti from around the way. Ashanti asked me as a favor to host a couple PROF & RAHZWELL shows so I was one of the first cats from the local scene to notice PROF was dope.

I introduced DILLON PARKER to 84 CAPRICE who later became the main beatmaker for STOPHOUSE. Then, through me, DILLON PARKER met ANT, who later invested and put on STOPHOUSE.

PROF also found himself a perfect match in DJ FUNDO, who in my opinion, is now (2011) by far the best DJ in Minnesota. His skills on the cuts are average but his instinctive ability to back an emcee and to party rock any type of crowd are the best I have ever seen or worked with. FUNDO is also a Gampo/out-of-control party animal perfect for PROF. These dudes are nuts, and sometimes, in small doses, are hella fun to be around. Once at party at PROF's house I saw PROF get so drunk he wanted to know what it felt like to have a ice cube shoved up his butt so he got on all fours, pulled his pants down, and convinced a girl to shove a ice cube up his butt!! Then PROF started screaming, "It's cold!!" It was hilarious ... and super weird... but still hilarious.

Jumping ahead on September 9th, 2011, PROF pre-sold-out the First Ave main room for the release party of *King Gampo*. PROF is the 5th local rap act to sell out the main room and only the 3rd to pre-sell it out. The other four, ATMOSPHERE, BROTHER ALI, P.O.S. and DOOMTREE, all got the cover of one of the local papers, either *The City Pages* or *Vita.MN*. PROF hadn't got any big local press in over three years prior to his release party being sold-out.

DILLON PARKER, PROF, and the rest of STOPHOUSE have the drive, focus, and talent to make big things happen. I am excited to see how things turn out.

Fun Fact: On June 4th, 1999, the front page of The Minnesota Daily, the University of Minnesota newspaper, read, "Racial Allegations Put Spin on Shut-Down of Hip Hop Show." On May 27th, 2009, ten years to the week after Headspin Sundays were shut down at Bon Appétit, the cover of The Minnesota Daily read, " The Dinkytowner Café and Bar set to close at end of the week: Many fear closing the bar and venue will be a great detriment to the local hip hop scene." The Dinkytowner was right across the street from Bon Appétit.

ALICIA STEELE AND DJ GABE GARCIA

After MESH and DJ ELUSIVE drifted away from KANSER to start families and follow their own paths, UNICUS and I pushed on. DJ FUNDO, DJ ANTON, and DJ LAST WORD filled in for us for a few hundred shows. That kept us afloat until we eventually found two new additions to twist up our flavor, a female singer named ALICIA STEELE and DJ GABE GARCIA. They are two of the coolest people I have ever met and I'm glad the universe brought them into my life. I hope that we can push on and make more music together.

DUENDAY AND MY DRUG PROBLEM

I, Zach Combs aka BIG ZACH aka NEW MC, have a drug problem. It might not appear that I have a problem to any of my friends because I have always steered clear of what I call "dark side drugs" like heroin, crack, coke, meth, etc. It might not appear I have a drug problem because I barely ever smoke weed and barely drink liquor. But, I love to trip. When I was 16, I tried shrooms for the first time, and combined with my giant imagination, I went on a journey to places I had never been before (physically I just walked around Riverside neighborhood to the Franklin bridge).

As I've gotten older, I've grown to believe that shrooms open windows within our minds that are infinite. I've used them like natural medicine, helping me to heal and deal with all the abuse and dysfunction that had gone on in my family growing up...other times I was just getting high.

I've also done some experimenting with acid, microdots, mescaline, and ganja butter...well I don't know if I should call it "experimenting". Once you've done it so many times it's really not experimenting anymore...it's just tripping for fun. I have also been known to pop an ecstasy pill from time to time....now to me, ecstasy is a psychedelic but kinda flirts with the darkside a little.

If it's a bad habit or not, I'm not wise enough to know. I do know that God's energy works its way into my life through whatever channel it chooses so I would like to tell a story about how God guided my path through my drug problem.

On New Year's Eve 2009-2010, my roommate SHIZ and I decided to stay close to home for the night. We walked to the Cabooze, a bar/big concert venue only four blocks from our house, to party.

WOOKIEFOOT, the biggest festival group in Minnesota, was having their annual NYE celebration and SHIZ and I thought it would be safe to go hang around some hippies. SHIZ and I only knew a few people there. ALICIA STEELE, who had recently joined KANSER, was performing with one of the opening groups ROSTER MCCABE (Alicia's younger brother Alex is the lead singer for ROSTER MCCABE). We had a good time watching ALICIA play with ROSTER.

I popped a couple X pills at the Cabooze in celebration of the new year and even talked SHIZ, who hadn't taken one in over two years, into popping one with me. Rolling through a good night, SHIZ and I ran two blocks down to the Triple Rock where another local band we're friends with was playing a NYE show, BLACK BLONDIE. There I ran into MUJA MESSIAH and got a little carried away giving him a 15-20 minute speech on why I thought he was a better basketball player than I was (we played at the same open gym that week). MUJA could tell I was high and kinda got a kick out of it so he listened to my whole rant.

Continuing to roll, SHIZ and I ran through the cold back to the Cabooze where I ran into some young girls I knew from Duluth, Minnesota. Laura, Taylor, and a few of their friends had driven down to the Twin Cities for NYE. Laura and Taylor were both cute little 19 year-old girls who always seemed to be down for whatever and have a knack for popping up in my life at extremely fun moments. I asked how they were doing and, rolling themselves, they replied they were having fun but some older dudes had been creeping on them. I told them I would be around if they needed me and I stepped back up on a risen part of the club to watch the end of WOOKIEFOOT's set.

With SHIZ directly 12 feet in front of me ordering a drink at the bar, I watched the little pack of girls dance and try to enjoy themselves in a club packed full of 1,000 drunk bar hippies. Then, as only to intensify my ecstasy peak, a dude about my age creeped up on the girls from the rear. When his approach wasn't accepted, he squeezed one of the girl's butts.

Now since I've partied my life away, this couldn't have been the first time I was out with female friends and one of them got their butt squeezed, but I must not pay good enough attention because this was the first and only time in my memory I can recall this happening right in front of me. I quickly slid between them, looked dude in the face, and said, "Dude...dude, you gotta move around...you gotta go." I wouldn't say I was very angry. It was more like the drugs and my big brother feeling of watching over the girls, combined with my delusional overconfidence that SHIZ and I could beat the shit out of every hippie kid in this club since we were in our own neighborhood, set off a panic button in my brain. I didn't want WOOKIEFOOT to see me get into a fight at their show. That would probably hurt our chances to get booked at some festivals.

"What, is that your girl or something?" the dude responded. With a drug enhanced vision in my head of how fast SHIZ and I would have this dude in a puddle of his own blood if he didn't leave, I said, "No, she's my cousin...and you gotta move around now." Dude tried to apologize or some shit but I just needed him to leave and he did. Over the loud music I don't think the girls or SHIZ were aware of the interaction but inside myself I was so pumped up I told SHIZ we had to dip.

It was freezing when we stepped outside. I don't know if it was really as cold as it felt or if the ecstasy was fucking with my body temperature, but the next four blocks were scary long. After what felt like forever, I got to my back door and sat down in my kitchen with relaxing relief. I chilled, breathed out, inhaled, and got myself together. I thought to myself, that was an okay New Years. As SHIZ went to bed, I sat in my kitchen riding out my high, enjoying sitting by myself in my dirty kitchen way more than I should, and figuring my night had come to a close. Then a knock came to the back door.

I opened it and it was MORE THAN LIGHTS' former bass player, Chris Hunnicutt. Chris is a super confident dude who talks to people like they're trying to catch up with him. With this style of interaction he walked right by me through the kitchen into my bathroom to take a piss saying, "Come on, Zachariah, we're going downtown to the Marriott Hotel." With barely a thought or a question I said, "Fuck it, I'm down." I grabbed a bottle of Champagne that was in my fridge and left the house.

When we walked out to the street to Chris' car, there was a second car we were following. It was Laura, Taylor, and two of their friends. Before I could jump into Chris' car, Laura jumped out and asked if I was sober enough to drive. I wasn't but I did the math in my head. 30 years old, X'd out, and driving in my own city was probably a safer bet then a 19 year-old girl X'd out from Duluth trying to follow her GPS through downtown Minneapolis on NYE.

I got into the driver's seat, adjusted my mirrors, and focused. It was one of those moments where you think to yourself, "I could be making a big mistake." Laura asked me if I knew how to get to the Marriott downtown. I said yes and started driving as Chris followed. I was driving pretty good before my dumb ass started driving down the bus lanes downtown. All the girls in the car started screaming and I realized that I was following the way the bus takes me downtown by instinct and had gotten into the bus-only streets that curve around the Metrodome and the Light Rail tracks. As the girls screamed and I tried to find a turn, two cop cars actually crossed our path and must have either not noticed or had bigger fish to fry that night.

Finally I got us onto 7th Street headed north and realized how high I must still be, teeny-bop pop radio songs blaring in the car sounded great. The car felt like a dance club X'd out with four girls and pop radio blasting. As we drove down 7th Street approaching the Marriott, we were quickly surrounded by the circus of downtown NYE. Even in the cold, there were people everywhere in the streets and on the sidewalks. All types of drunk people stumbling, wearing crazy hats, and girls who came out in nice dresses now looking super sloppy.

We found a place to park and walked about a block to the Marriott. People were everywhere screaming "Happy New Year" just being jolly. Normally, the Marriott City Center is a fancy place and you wouldn't see 100 people hanging out in the lobby by the elevators after 2am. But, it seemed like anything goes on NYE. As we hit the elevator button, it was the first time I thought to ask, "Where are we going?" One of the girls told me they had a friend who had a room on the 18th floor. We all got onto the elevator but the buttons only went up to the 3rd floor. Within the three seconds we debated what to do, a 19 year-old couple stepped into the elevator and the girl said, "Big Zach!"

I recognized her as a girl who comes to shows that I had probably met once or twice. Then I looked up at the dude who I didn't recognize. I noticed his pupils were dilated. Then, I looked back down at the girl and noticed her pupils were too. I said, "You guys are on X, huh?" They both said yeah and told us they had come from a DJ party at The Loft. Figuring the more the merrier, I said, "We're all on X too...you should just roll with us." So, they let the elevator doors close behind them and we went up to the 3rd floor. When the doors opened, we found ourselves at the after-party to the HEATBOX New Years show. It was wild! There was music, police that didn't seem to give a fuck, and people everywhere drinking Champagne straight outta bottles.

I got a text from KANSER's new DJ, DJ GABE GARCIA. He was downtown so I told him to come and meet us. The night just seemed to keep getting funnier and eventually we found ourselves on the 18th floor in somebody's hotel room. The young dude who had jumped in the elevator with us started talking crazy trying to tell me that ANDRE 3000 from OUTKAST isn't the greatest rapper of all time even though I clearly know he is. I was like, "get this kid outta here...talking crazy and shit." Our argument continued into the hallway until we were asked nicely to leave.

Laura, Taylor, Chris, DJ GABE GARCIA, the two kids from the elevator, whose names were Kelsey and Matt, and I now were in the hallway of the 18th floor of the Marriott Hotel at 4am on ecstasy with nothing to do till Matt offered for us to come to his place. I asked where he lived. He told us the East Bank. We all looked at each other trying to decide what to do and then Matt said, "I got weed at my crib." That was all the motivation we needed so we were on our way.

Less than 20 minutes later, we all flooded into Matt's crib. It was your typical broke down college party house where we found six of Matt's roommates and/or friends hanging around smoking a vaporizer in the living room. I was 10+ years older than everyone there and would have felt a little awkward if I wasn't rolling and if four out of eight of the kids didn't recognize me as the dude from KANSER. As everyone introduced themselves to each other, a couple of the college kids asked if they could take a picture with me and overwhelmed me with compliments on my music.

Being "BIG ZACH" has brought me to some weird places. I'm 30+ years old and for the 189th time in my life, I had walked into a college party and got treated like the captain of the football team. Part of me felt like explaining to these kids that I wasn't that cool and I was just the old dude here to mooch their weed. But, like many other times in my "broke rapper" life, I decided to just go with it. Matt briefly introduced me to his friend whose name was Matt also (easy to remember). They said they were a rap group and told me I had hosted a show they played the previous summer. "Oh fuck, these kids are rappers," I thought to myself. The last thing I wanted to deal with at 4am on New Years was listening to some rappers. As they tried to connect their iPod and play me some of their music, I thought to myself, "Oh man, I got baited over here by some rappers and now they're gonna force me to listen to music. Well, fuck it. If this is how this night is going to end we're at least going to have some fun with it."

"Yo yo! Are you guys trying to play me your tracks right now...is that what you're trying to do right now .... turn it off I don't wanna hear that shit!" I announced as everyone got quiet. I paused for half a second to allow the energy in the room to go in the direction of uncomfortable hoping everyone in the room would think I was being a big asshole and blatantly refused to listen to these young kids' music. Then, I followed it with, "If you guys want to impress me, then pull up the beats and perform your best two songs for me right now in the living room. I want a New Years concert right here right now."

It was fun and everyone in the room started to laugh or get excited. The two Matts spent the next three minutes looking through their beats trying to decide which songs to do. Then, they tried to start a song twice but kept forgetting their lyrics. By their 3rd attempt, I said, "Come on dudes, I ain't got all day...one more chance." They both took a breath, calmed themselves down, and started. A real cool relaxing beat came through the stereo and MATT CARTER and MATT THORNTON, aka the rap group DU-ENDAY, performed a song called "Rain Drops".

There was over ten people in the room, but for the most part, DUENDAY was performing for me. They were young kids into underground hip hop and truly just wanted me to take the time to listen to their music like they must have listened to mine. They kept glancing at me with hopeful looks in their eyes. It was one of the most honest moments I ever experienced and I found their song to be beautiful. Neither of the two Matt's jumped out to me as great developed emcees, but their voices complimented each other and their simple style of rapping went perfect with the beat. They rapped honest lyrics that described what it was like being their age growing up on the Southside and going to college. I was loving every second of it...then I realized I was on drugs.

I wondered if this song really sucked and I was just so high that it sounded good in the moment. I glanced over at DJ GABE GARCIA looking for confirmation, GABE nodded his head that the song was dope. The room clapped when DUENDAY finished their first song before they started their second. Their second song was a little more up beat with a few nice lines. When their second song ended, I asked DUENDAY if they could perform those two songs at KANSER's next release party that was coming up in about two months. Within weeks, I asked DUENDAY if they would give me a chance to try to manage them. I made sure not to sell them a dream. I gave them a realistic outlook of what I could do for them and over the next year I got them as many shows as I could, helped them skip mistakes that UNICUS and I made when we were younger, and tried to teach them as much as I know. I truly love and believe in DUENDAY's music.

As I type this I would say they are my favorite rap group in 2011. In exchange for the little I was able to do for them, DUENDAY, Kelsey, and their friends let me hang out all year. On New Years Eve '09-10, these young kids definitely thought I was a celebrity... two months later they all knew I was just the old dude passed out on their couch. I love to party, and at 32, a lot of my friends are starting to settle down and raise families. These kids are in their rage phase and I, hands down, had the funniest year of my life partying with them. That's big.

Minutes after DUENDAY finished their second song, the party moved upstairs in Matt's house. Before I made my way to the second floor with everyone else, two college girls asked me to come into the bathroom with them. They shut the door, shut off the lights, and started dancing around covered in different colored glow sticks. Next thing you know, I was making-out with one girl, then the other, and then a few really cool things happened that I will leave up to the readers imagination...but, before more really cooler things happened, I got over stimulated.

The combination of a great New Years Eve, a sexual encounter with two super cute girls, the different color glow sticks that made up the only light in the bathroom, and a lot of ecstasy pills made me too excited and I just started babbling...babbling about nothing. From what I can remember, I started telling these girls about how much I liked the movie *The Curious Case of Benjamin Button* and they just stared at me with question marks on their faces...probably wondering why I just didn't shut up and get to work.

After maybe 15 minutes of babbling, both girls left the bathroom and went to bed. I walked upstairs in a delusional blur actually believing I had had a threesome in the bathroom downstairs. I let my imagination get a head of itself and called P.O.S. I left him a voicemail at 5:30am telling him I had a threesome with two young girls in a college house like it was a scene from Girls Gone Wild. I think at that moment I was so happy high on X my brain was flooded with what just really happened, what could have happened, and reality... I was all over the place. I walked upstairs to find Kelsey, Gabe, Chris, Laura, Taylor, and both Matt's listening to music in MATT CARTER's room. I was walking on cloud nine, unaware of the most epic fail that had just happened in the story book of my insignificant little life.

It wasn't until days later that I realized how hard I had blown it and that only a small percentage of men ever get to have two women at once (for the record, it wouldn't have been my first time with two ladies...but it would have been the most epic). I looked myself in the mirror and said, "You were too high to handle an epic threesome on New Years Eve 2009-2010... Zach, you have a drug problem."

"Good people attract good people / and good people make each other great." - In2wishin MC of DUENDAY

CHAPTER 25 :
WAY DIFFERENT WORLDS

It took me just over five years to finish this book and the chapter, Between the Pimps, Poets, and the Press, was the most difficult. I struggled to figure out how to put what I wanted to say into words that would not sound like I was dissing DOOMTREE. I have extreme love for P.O.S. and the TREE and I believe they love and respect me as well. DOOMTREE music and the culture that surrounds it is the best example I can use for how Twin Cities hip hop has changed from the culture I found and fell in love with 20 years ago. I for one do not try to fight the future, I try to embrace change. If things had stayed the same things would be boring. I think I loved hip hop the most in '98-'99 when I was hosting HEADSPIN Sundays (Chapter 8). But my whole look on music, hip hop, and life has changed so much since, I don't think I would still be rapping if we were still doing the same things we were back then. That era had its time, it happened and it's over.

DOOMTREE members used to come to HEADSPIN when they were in high school so they were part of that era with us. Then they were inspired to create something new. DOOMTREE is more intelligent than I am (haha). I envy how much press they get and how they seem to be able to move like a machine. I can throw a good show, I can throw a great party, I can bomb posters up, hand out flyers, I can finish a record, and I can show up on time to a gig and put on a good performance. But in comparison to DOOMTREE and RSE I have always felt like a drug dealer slanging CD's on the corner outside of their three-story office buildings.

The thing I have that DOOMTREE doesn't is the opposite thing I have over the CONCEPT crew from the 90's. It's what gives me credibility to write this book and it is the reason I wrote it. I believe there's ten others who have it, eleven of us total: FELIPE, SLUG, MUJA MESSIAH, MUSAB, UNICUS, ST. PAUL SLIM, I SELF DEVINE, TRUTH MAZE, CARNAGE, STAGE ONE and BIG ZACH (NEW MC). In 2011, we are the only emcees who have been played, interviewed, or performed live on The Current 89.3 FM radio station who also existed in the days of OMAR and CONCEPT.

The Current from Minnesota Public Radio is, in 2011, the biggest outlet for local music in the Twin Cities. It is the most powerful alternative radio station that our metro area has. Not only do they keep local rap on the playlist but they also have the "Local Show" on Sunday afternoons where they play prerecorded interviews and in-studio performances by local artists including rap artists. They also have "Redefinition Radio" hosted by KEVIN BEACHAM, an hour of underground old school and local rap on Saturday nights.

OMAR was the monster head-chopping battle rapper who stalked the streets of the Cities eating rappers alive in the early 90's (I wrote about OMAR in chapters 2, 3 and 4). OMAR was somewhat of a religious leader in the Minnesota movement of the Nation of Gods and Earths. I am no expert on their religion, but several people I know who follow or have followed the religion have told me OMAR was their "enlightener", which I believe means he introduced them to the religion. Like I said in chapter 3, I personally believe that some of the Five Percenters are the spiritual guardians of the culture and I believe some who were taught by OMAR have always watched over me.

CONCEPT was basically a rap gang of young Five Percenter black males that could be found in all different parts of the metro. If you claimed to be an emcee between 1994-1999 you definitely had to prove it to these dudes in one form or another. Many members of CONCEPT sold drugs, were in gangs, or ran the streets in some fashion (I talk about battling one of them in chapter 4).

One personal connection I have with The Current is a great relationship with KEVIN BEACHAM. He is one of the realest dudes I have ever met in music. KEVIN has done me so many favors through REDEFINITION RADIO from announcing my shows to giving birthday shout outs to friends I grew up with who are locked down in regional prisons close enough to pick up The Current. I also had a great experience when KANSER and MORE THAN LIGHTS was a featured guest on the LOCAL SHOW in 2008.

My personal experience with OMAR (slightly documented in chapters 3 and 4) started when he got on-stage and dissed me after I performed at a college in St. Paul when I was 17. I was scared of OMAR and didn't go back on-stage to retaliate. I stayed and watched the rest of the show but felt like a bitch the whole time. It's hard to describe what it felt like to claim to be a rapper and to be dissed by a much better rapper in what was the hip hop culture in 1995. One thing I can tell you is it would have felt worse to get destroyed by OMAR in front of people. About eight months after OMAR dissed me, I put on my first concert at Matthews Park in South Minneapolis. OMAR showed up at the end, took the mic, and ran through half of the then members of the KANSER TROOP; FATCAT, MESH and THE BROWN CHILD. OMAR was a grown man and he took the time out of his day to come to a park where a bunch of high school kids were throwing a very unprofessional rap show and destroy us. OMAR let us know we weren't shit but a bunch of little kids trying to rap, not real emcees yet. The list of rappers from that era OMAR ran through is long. I can tell you it includes TRUTH MAZE, FELIPE BUDAH TYE, KEL-C, and members of the ABSTRACT PACK. OMAR also tore up SLUG super bad in front of First Ave. In front of SLUG's girlfriend, OMAR told SLUG, "I'll rape your girl like a Velociraptor."

The Current has been super supportive of DOOMTREE. When DESSA released her solo album, *A Badly Broken Code*, in January of 2010, The Current was strongly behind it along with almost every other local music media outlet. The Current played DESSA in heavy rotation leading up to the release show and plugged the show constantly. Soon after, DESSA started to host and throw an annual CADENCE SERIES OF HIP HOP at an incredible super fancy upscale theater that overlooks the Mississippi River in downtown Minneapolis called the Guthrie. DESSA booked me to open for P.O.S. at one of her Guthrie nights and it was probably the most upscale show I ever did. DESSA is strongly driven, very talented, and one of the most witty and intelligent people I have ever met. I try to avoid conversations with her at all costs because I am way too intimidated to hold long conversations with women who are obviously that much smarter than I am (haha).

DESSA is very articulate and speaks very proper. I have heard her do commercials on The Current where, to my ear, it sounds like the furthest thing from a "rapper" speaking. DESSA also teaches college courses on writing raps at McNally Smith College of Music in downtown St. Paul.

For me it has been like growing up in entirely different worlds. When I was 16 and 17 the kids I rapped with from the Southside (B.C., MONK, FATCAT, MINDSIGHT, MESH) would catch the bus downtown or to the mall and look for freestyle cyphers to get into. We would look for members of CONCEPT and hope that we wouldn't bump into OMAR (haha). That, along with tagging my name on shit, was what the Twin Cities hip hop scene was to me back then.

Now at 33, in 2011, when I think of Twin Cities hip hop I think of getting in my car and turning on The Current and hearing a beautiful song by DESSA. I would guess it is even more extreme for TRUTH MAZE, STAGE ONE, I SELF, and SLUG who are way older than I am. They have existed in more worlds.

If I learned anything from P.O.S. it is to have belief in yourself. He once told me that his mom saw him making music on his guitar when he was real young and told him if he liked writing songs that he should do that for a living. I believe that planted a seed of belief in his mind which has grown to affect reality. In my personal opinion, I think P.O.S. believes in himself enough that he can bend the matrix more than the average person.

Before DESSA started rapping she was a spoken word poet. I think I first knew her as P.O.S.'s girlfriend when they dated for a short time. I believe that P.O.S. convinced her that she could rap if she put the time and energy into it. I think DESSA was already in her 20's before she made her first rap song. Now in 2011 it's debatable that she makes the best music that has ever been made by a rapper from Minnesota.

I believe the human mind exists in the brain the same as the soul exists in the body. I believe the human brain is a piece of meat that is inside the skull, but the mind is something extremely more powerful. Every thought you have is like a little impulse that shoots out into the world and affects your reality. When the human mind focuses, it can accomplish anything. Sometimes to accomplish something you need other people. You need to be tools for each other. Our minds are all plugged into each other like a spiritual matrix. I believe all the characters in this book, along with many many many fans, supporters, and other beautiful people built and created moments and music together.

Right before finishing this book I received a phone call from prison. Sad but true I have so many friends and family members in prison. I accepted the call. It was OMAR. He had heard about my book from members of RAW VILLA and asked if he could hear about his parts. I had never spoke to OMAR before even though he made a big impact on me. He asked about me, so I told him I was in this new group MORE THAN LIGHTS and that we played lots of music festivals. He said he played the guitar now, wrote songs, was into all types of music, and that he really liked the Dave Matthews Band. I thought to myself, "Holy shit, I used to be terrified of OMAR on the streets. Now we're on the phone talking about the Dave Matthews Band."

Sadly OMAR told me he is prison for 20 more years. What's missing from this book since OMAR went to prison is that OMAR and EYEDEA would have eventually ran into each other. It probably would have happened at the Golden Mic battles in chapter 9. If he ever gets to read this book this is my shout out to him.

CHAPTER 26 :
EYEDEA & THE BROWN CHILD

In the summer of 1995, my rap partner Itoro showed up at my grandma's house with three neighborhood kids from the West Bank; Anton, Simpson, who later went by MONK, and Quincy Blue, who later went by the BROWN CHILD (he eventually shortened it to B.C.). The four teenage kids told me that they had formed a rap crew called CANCER (later spelled KANSER). They never really asked me to join the group; they more-or-less just told me I was a member.

With a makeshift studio ANT helped me put together at my grandmother's house, we spent the next half a year trying to figure out how to write and record rap songs. Quincy, the youngest at only 14 years old, had a lot of good energy and potential. I taught him how to count bars and recorded and produced his first songs. I was pretty tight with all the KANSER members throughout my senior year in high school, through small shows, parties, and other high school adventures. Right before graduation, KANSER split into pieces and B.C. became a part of the VERBAL ASSASSINS. For over a year, KANSER and the VERBAL ASSASSINS threw shows together. Both groups also opened at some of the first RHYMESAYERS shows.

In May of 1998, KANSER released our second 4-track tape, *Network*, at Bon Appétit. B.C., who was now a junior at South High School, had small beef with EYEDEA who was a sophomore at Highland High School in St. Paul at the time. They were beefin' for an important reason; both felt they were the best high school rapper in the state.

B.C. was at the Bon that night with some of his friends. EYEDEA, who had come by himself, approached me before KANSER went on-stage. He told me he wanted to battle B.C. but was nervous that he would get jumped by him and his friends. Knowing that I had grown up in the neighborhood next to Quincy, EYEDEA asked if I could protect him. I agreed and went over to speak to B.C. about it. B.C. agreed to battle EYEDEA but made no promises that violence wouldn't occur if EYEDEA said something out-of-pocket.

When the KANSER set was over, I gave the battle prime introduction. "I don't know who the best high school rapper is, but I know it's between these two right here," I said. I then gave them both introductions before they stepped on-stage. After that, in front of about a hundred members of their peers, they got it over with.

As life moved on, I faded out with Quincy and other kids I had grown up rappin' with. We would speak from time to time but they were just on some different shit than I was. Quincy later joined a group called THE STREET KINGS and made a good attempt to make mainstream rap music. They got to open for big acts such as T.I. at The Myth night club in Maplewood and had created an alright buzz for themselves before the group fell into some legal troubles.

In October of 2010, EYEDEA passed away from a drug overdose. Eight months later in June 2011, Quincy "B.C." Blue was found murdered in St. Paul. EYEDEA had much more of an impact on Minnesota hip hop, but both B.C. and EYEDEA played about equal roles in my life.

EYEDEA passed away 14 years and one week after one of his mentors, SESS, passed away. I'll go as far as to say that I didn't know EYEDEA, the famous 2010 rapper, very well; he was an acquaintance. But, 13 years earlier, I met him when he was a teenage breakdancer who lived off of West 7th in St. Paul. He was a smart kid with a real witty sense of humor and I considered him my friend. I was four years older than EYEDEA but we had the same birthday (Nov 9th). And, in 1998, EYEDEA, Mario from the BATTLE-CATS, and myself had a combined birthday party at HEADSPIN. Ever since then I tried to always remember to call EYEDEA and Mario on our birthdays.

The night before EYEDEA passed away I was lucky enough to run into him at the 7th Street Entry. He walked by me and said, "Happy Birthday." I thought he was being a goofball since our birthday was still a few weeks out. Then he said, "I'm gonna be gone on our birthday so I wanted to tell you now." Of course, he meant he would be on tour. But, spiritually, I took something deeper from it.

Less than 40 hours later Mario called me and told me EYEDEA had passed away.

I've had many close friends in my life pass away and I am familiar with the effect it has on the family and social circle of the deceased. But when EYEDEA passed away it was like a black hole appeared in the universe of the Twin Cities. I was at the laundry mat, restaurants, and cafés overhearing people I didn't know talking about the death of EYEDEA. His death was covered in local papers and local TV news. I saw P.O.S. and TOKI WRIGHT have extremely emotional moments on-stage expressing their feelings over EYEDEA's death.

Later I stood in a sold-out crowd at First Ave watching a DJ from Colorado I'm into named PRETTY LIGHTS. I was surrounded by friends from a different scene who were unaffected by EYEDEA's death when PRETTY LIGHTS stopped the music and spoke to the crowd acknowledging EYEDEA and chopped up an EYEDEA vocal sample into a beat. I felt alone holding emotions inside myself as my friend was honored. I couldn't share them with anyone around me.

I didn't attend EYEDEA's funeral or his memorial show at First Ave, but a few days after his death, I crept up to 5th Element around 3am where fans and friends had placed flowers on the sidewalk under a TV screen that faced the street from behind the store's window. As the screen played one of EYEDEA's videos on repeat, I knelt down and prayed. A clear memory popped into my head of a time EYEDEA had told me that DJ MASHOUT once saw him on the street and challenged him to a battle with no audience. I giggled to myself picturing the two of them downtown just freestyle battling to each other with nobody else around. MASHOUT was just the type of character to do that.

After maybe ten minutes I got up and started walking south down Hennepin Ave. I did it at 3am because for my own reasons I didn't want anyone to see me I guess. A block away from 5th Element, I ran into DJ MASHOUT at the gas station. Life's funny like that.

"Heaven isn't some place we go to when we die /
it's that split-second in life when you actually feel alive"
- Eyedea

"But when my soul steps from this frame /
I will be reincarnated as rain"
- Eyedea